W9-AEO-091

STRUGGLE FOR ASIA

# STRUGGLE FOR ASIA

by

Sir FRANCIS LOW

FREDERICK A. PRAEGER
NEW YORK

BOOKS THAT MATTER

Published in the United States of America in 1955 by Frederick A. Praeger, Inc., Publishers, 150 East 52nd Street, New York 22, N.Y.



Library of Congress Catalog Card Number: 55-11624

Printed in Great Britain

## FOREWORD

THIS BOOK IS not meant for experts on individual Asian countries. It is intended to supply a background on Asian affairs for the average citizen, the man or woman who has neither the time nor the inclination to pursue intensive research, but who reads the daily papers and is frequently puzzled by developments which occur in Asia—developments that have often a very important bearing on the affairs of the West.

It is not the purpose of the book to praise or blame the workings of the Asian mind, but to explain them to Western readers as undeniable facts which must be taken into account in world affairs. Many people in the West will violently disagree with the attitude of some Asian countries towards world problems, especially Communism; all I can say is that a knowledge of modern Asia's background should enable the Western critic to understand, even if he does not sympathize with, the Asian point of view. Understanding, in turn, may bring a better appreciation of how to help Asia's new democracies to resist a form of government which is as repugnant to their nationalism as it is to the West. Only by a thorough comprehension of Asian susceptibilities can the West make its most effective contribution to the attainment of that co-operation between East and West which is vital to the future of humanity as a whole.

I have to acknowledge with gratitude the help I have received from the Foreign Office, the Commonwealth Relations Office and the Royal Institute of International Affairs, all of which have furnished factual information. My grateful thanks are also due to my wife, who has assisted in various ways to complete the task.

FRANCIS LOW

# CONTENTS

# LIST OF MAPS

*Chapter One*

# THE EAST AWAKENS

ASIA'S POLITICAL RENASCENCE is one of the most portentous world developments of the twentieth century. Just over a hundred years ago the peoples of Asia had either resolutely sealed themselves off from all contact with the West or were incapable of defending themselves against Western governments which backed the demands of adventurous European and American traders. The great continent slumbered, immersed either in its own culture and civilization or in its own internal quarrels. Well might Matthew Arnold write:

> The East bow'd low before the blast
> In patient, deep disdain.
> She let the legions thunder past,
> And plunged in thought again.

When in 1853 the American Commodore Perry sailed into Uraga harbour in Japan with a mandate from his government to secure, if possible, the opening of trade relations with the United States, the local inhabitants fled in panic from the foreign "barbarians". A year later when Commodore Perry, with the help of ten ships and two thousand men, was able to arrange the opening of the ports of Shimoda and Hakodate to American trading interests, he piously wrote: "Thus ends my visit to Japan, for which praise God". (One wonders how those words would have sounded in American ears on the day of Pearl Harbour.)

But long before this and for half a century afterwards European powers steadily acquired possessions in Asia. Between 1847 and 1868 Russia annexed Chinese territory which carried the Tsar's empire to the China Sea, and after a hard struggle established Russian dominion over the independent principalities in central Asia, east

Caucasus and Turkestan. All these regions and peoples are now within the iron grip of Russian Communism. Meanwhile other European nations had not been idle. With the opening of the Cape route the Portuguese, Dutch, Spaniards, French, and British had pushed their way eastwards by sea and had taken over control of Asian territory stretching from Arabia to the Philippines. The dawn of the twentieth century saw Western administration established over vast regions and populations, with China shackled by a series of treaties forced upon her by the leading Western powers, including the United States of America. Only Japan, awakened from her rigid isolationism by Commodore Perry, showed signs of that tremendous challenge to the West of which she became the spearhead.

Yet it had not always been so. To go back to prehistoric times, central Asia or Iran may well prove to have been the area where man evolved. South-west Asia is now regarded as the most likely scene of the earliest cultural development, and certainly the earliest civilization, in the history of mankind. All the great religions of the world —Christianity, Hinduism, Buddhism and Islam, to say nothing of Judaism, Zoroastrianism and Taoism—originated in Asia. When Europe went into the decline of the Middle Ages it narrowly escaped complete conquest by waves of Asian invaders. The Huns under Attila reached the neighbourhood of Chalons-sur-Marne before being stopped in the fifth century. Much later the Turks, in the fourteenth and fifteenth centuries, established themselves in the Balkans, and only the death of Muhammad the Conqueror in 1481 prevented an assault on Italy.

But the most dangerous of all Asian threats to Europe came from the Mongols under Jenghis Khan and his successors in the thirteenth century. Out of the vast steppes between China and Siberia swept one of the finest armies the world has ever seen, a mass of magnificently trained horsemen whose success as a fighting machine was due not so much to quantity as to quality. The Mongols, aided by strategy and speed far ahead of those of contemporary Western armies, smashed their way through heavier and better-armed troops whom they scattered like chaff before the wind. Had it not been for the death of their Khan after their conquest of Poland, Silesia and Hungary, and their withdrawal to elect a successor, the Mongols might have brought the whole of Europe under their sway. As it was, they left the West licking its wounds and wondering what had hit it.

The vivid impress left on Western minds by the Mongol irruption finds expression in the writings of Marco Polo. Mr. Maurice Collis[1] in his book on Marco Polo's travels in the thirteenth century mentions that when he reached Balk, the former capital of Bactria—now part of Afghanistan and the most easterly of the Greek states founded by Alexander the Great—Marco Polo, "in spite of his admiration for Kublai Khan and the exploits of the Mongols, took pride in the thought that a European conqueror had once penetrated so far into the East". Mr. Collis goes on:

> "We have to remember that no other European had been able to accomplish so much; even the great Roman Empire had stopped at the Euphrates. Nowadays, the feats of Alexander hardly move us, because we have seen all Asia fall under our power. But in the thirteenth century particularly after the Mongol invasions and the sack of part of Europe by these orientals, Alexander's reputation was at a dizzy height. Although there had been a pause in the invasions and the Mongols seemed to be settling down, the danger remained that they might attack again. How wonderful, therefore, to think that once a European had succeeded, not only in marching victoriously as far as Balk, but in planting a kingdom there, an outpost of Europe against the dwellers of the steppe."[1]

This excursion into ancient history is made with a purpose. It recalls that at one time Asia came near to dominating Europe militarily. It helps to explain something which has surprised and puzzled many Western observers who noted the early successes of the Japanese against Western troops in the second World War, the stalemate brought about in Korea by the intervention of Chinese "volunteers" against the highly modernized United Nations forces in 1950, Viet-minh victories over the French in Indo-China in 1954 and the astounding tenacity of the (mostly Chinese) terrorists in Malaya. Nor should we leave out of account the magnificent performance of the former Indian Army in two world wars, although part of that glory was shared by its British officers. We are faced

[1] *Marco Polo*, by Maurice Collis (Faber and Faber).

with the undoubted fact that the Asian soldier, be he Mongoloid or Caucasian, and provided he is properly trained and equipped, is capable under his own officers of holding his own with the best troops of the West. That, in the context of world affairs today, is a solemn thought.

It is a particularly solemn thought when we reflect on Asia's immense possibilities. Asia is by far the world's largest and most populous continent. It occupies about a third of the total land surface of the globe. It is larger than the two American continents combined; it is half as big again as Africa and four times the size of Europe. Asia's population exceeds that of the rest of the world by over 200 millions; in 1940 it was estimated at 1,196 millions compared with 974 millions for the remainder of the earth. Included in the continent are two countries, India and Japan, whose population is increasing faster than that of any other part of the world except South America. (This raises problems for both Asia and the West which will be discussed later.) Its peoples are a mixture, mainly Caucasian in the West, Mongoloid in the East and Malay on the southern fringes; they vary in colour from almost white to brown and yellow. Its chief religions are Buddhism, Hinduism and Islam; Christianity has made very little impact on Asia as a whole and the recent growth of nationalism and Communism are not propitious for its spread. Asia's millions are mostly engaged in agriculture, but industrialism is rising, particularly in Japan, which led the way, in Asian Russia, India and China. The continent's importance as a producer of rubber and tin needs no emphasis, but of late its oilfields, especially those in Arabia, have under Western exploitation assumed world-wide significance.

Culturally Asia may be said to have stagnated in the last few centuries as much as it did politically, but in historical times the cultures of China, India and Japan were all in their own way remarkable. When we talk of the cultural debt which Europe owes to Greece and Rome, we must remember that China, the world's oldest existing State with authentic history dating back to the twelfth century B.C., has a cultural tradition infinitely older than that of the West. Again to quote Mr. Maurice Collis,[1] Hang-chow, the capital

[1] *Marco Polo*, by Maurice Collis (Faber and Faber).

of the Sung dynasty Chinese empire situated south-west of modern Shanghai, was in the thirteenth century "the greatest intellectual and artistic centre in the world, greater than any which had ever existed anywhere, including classical Rome, and greater than any which has since come into existence, including Paris and London, because it could look back on a much larger and more solid evolution of intellect". True, the China of Mr. Mao Tse-tung is not the China of the Sung dynasty, but we cannot forget that Asia has a background of culture unparalleled in history. During the last few centuries Asia may have stagnated as did Europe in the Middle Ages, yet the significant fact for the West is that the world's biggest continent is today in the grip of a revolution. Who can say that this rebirth may not ultimately have results as momentous to humanity as the last century produced in Europe and America?

The revolution which has taken place in Asia, and is still in progress, is a complicated affair. Its roots lie deep in a revolt against Western domination. But that is only part of the story. Superimposed on Asia's nationalism is a struggle for economic and social regeneration caused by the impact of Western ways of life and ideas on masses of humanity which for centuries have patiently endured as their predestined lot the twin afflictions of poverty and want. They lived under the shadow of famine and pestilence, of maladministration and corruption. It would be fascinating to speculate on the course which the history of Asia would have followed if its peoples had not been rudely disturbed by the restless West; its evolution would certainly have been much slower. As it happened, the transfer of power from the feudal rulers to the middle classes and then to the masses, which in Europe took centuries to achieve, was telescoped over large parts of Asia into a remarkably short period.

That is why nationalism in Asia is so frequently mixed up with Communism, and why Asians themselves sometimes have great difficulty in distinguishing between the two. As an Indian journalist is reported to have said to an American colleague: "You tell me that Dr. Ho Chi-minh is a Communist. But if he is fighting against the French in Indo-China for the freedom of his country he must be a nationalist!" Ever since the stirrings of Asian nationalism against

Western domination began the Communists have been quick to exploit this feeling. "Down with imperialism and colonialism"—embodying one of Lenin's maxims—has long been one of the chief rallying cries of Asian Communists directed from Moscow; it is a cry which finds a ready echo in the heart of every Asian nationalist sincerely devoted to the cause of his country's freedom from outside control. Little wonder, therefore, that the average Asian does not today see clearly and unequivocally the menace to human liberty which the Western world knows to exist in Communism.

Mr. Jawaharlal Nehru, the Prime Minister of India, put the matter succinctly in his opening address to the Eleventh Conference of the Institute of Pacific Relations in October 1950. "When Indonesia was struggling for its freedom," he said, "it seemed a monstrous thing to ask any country to support Dutch imperialism there. . . . No argument in any country of Asia is going to have weight if it goes counter to the nationalist spirit of the country, Communism or no Communism. That has to be understood." In other words, when Asian countries were struggling to free themselves from Western dominion, Public Enemy No. 1 was not Communism; it was "Western imperialism". That feeling persists today even after Western imperialism has practically ceased to exist. Happily there are distinct signs among the nations of South-East Asia that the threat of Communist "imperialism" to their newly acquired democratic way of life is beginning to be realized.

Other reasons exist for Asia's recent complacence about Communism. For centuries the tradition of government in the East has been autocratic, and in a country like China, for example, individual freedom to men and women of the toiling peasant masses means very little. What they are mainly concerned about is food, shelter and personal security. Any indigenous system of government which promises and provides these things is to be welcomed. Fine resounding phrases about the liberty of man, the virtues of parliamentary democracy and complete freedom of franchise pass high over the head of the average peasant, obsessed as he is with the essentials of existence. In China, at any rate, parliamentary democracy as the West understands it was never given a chance.

But to return to the rise of Asian nationalism. It can be said with truth that before Europe interfered in the affairs of Asia during the past century there was very little of what we today might call an Asian feeling, that is, a feeling by Asian countries of being part of an international community. In the words of a Japanese writer:[1] "Asiatic countries have been brought into an 'international community' in the European sense more or less forcibly by outside pressure. It was as a reaction to this pressure brought to bear on Asiatic countries by the European world as a whole that elementary nationalistic feelings first began to take shape in all these countries. ... Nationalism in this first, pre-modern, state developed in the form of the ideology of 'expelling the barbarians' ".

The lack of an Asian feeling in earlier times is clearly evident from reference to history. It cannot be said that when emissaries from the England of Queen Elizabeth I appeared at the Court of the Emperor Akhbar in India there was much community of feeling between the Moguls and their Chinese neighbours of the type which Christianity engendered in Europe. On the contrary, in China and Japan the attitude of the rulers was one of supreme contempt for any kind of foreigner. From outside "barbarians" they expected nothing but homage. The Chinese Emperor Ch'ien Lung, in declining to accept an ambassador from Britain in the reign of George III, pontifically replied: "Our dynasty's majestic virtue has penetrated into every country under Heaven and kings of all nations have offered their costly tribute by land and sea". That type of attitude was not exactly calculated to promote the community spirit either in Asia or anywhere else. It was only when the China of Sun Yat-sen a century later was trying to free itself from the "unequal treaties" imposed by European powers that there spread throughout Asian countries a feeling of comradeship in revolt.

It began with Japan's dramatic victory over the Russians in the Russo-Japanese war of 1904–5. Japan's contribution to the rise of nationalism in Asia and the growth of an all-Asia feeling was remarkable, if peculiar. Alone among the larger countries of Asia Japan eluded the grip of the West. After the restoration of the emperor's authority in 1871 the ruling class in Japan never lost its

[1] *Nationalism in Post-War Japan*, by Masao Maruyama (Japan Institute of Pacific Relations).

power; instead it consolidated that power on a basis which made Japan in effect the world's first modern totalitarian state. With that amazing adaptability which is their distinguishing feature, the Japanese quickly realized that the strength of the West rested on industry, and that the only way to compete with the West was to develop industry along Western lines. "Machinery and technique we shall take from them," said a well-known Japanese leader of the restoration period, "but moral virtues we have among us."

Therein lay the secret of Japan's astonishing rise to world power. The ruling classes, by carefully eliminating all "dangerous thoughts" inimical to the régime, inspired and directed the aggressive nationalism which brought Japan through many triumphs to disaster in 1945. Yet forty years earlier Japan's victory over Russia—the first victory of an Asian over a European nation for centuries—sent a thrill of pride throughout the continent. It stirred up a flicker of nationalism, of revolt against the West, from one end of Asia to the other. The Japanese became the spearhead of Asia's political renascence. Unfortunately they conceived themselves not merely the spearhead but the leader, director and sole authority on the subject. In vain did Sun Yat-sen, the founder of modern China, reiterate in Japan and elsewhere his belief that the independence movement in Asia would succeed only if all Asian peoples stood together. The Japanese ruling classes believed themselves to be the divinely inspired instrument of Asian regeneration; they regarded with typical Eastern contempt all other efforts in that direction.

Thus was born the "Greater East Asia Co-Prosperity Sphere", proclaimed in 1938 as Japan's infallible remedy for Asia's ills. There is no doubt that Japan's ultimate aim was to extend her power over the whole continent, or at any rate the greater part of it. That is clearly evident from the policy enunciated by the Tokio cabinet after the outbreak of the second World War, which provided Japan's rulers with a unique opportunity of realizing their expansionist ambitions. The Greater East Asia Co-Prosperity Sphere was to apply to China (which Japan was then trying to subjugate) Manchukuo, French Indo-China, Siam, Malaya, Borneo, the Dutch East Indies, Burma and possibly India, although it was conceded that India might fall to German or Russian control.

One would have thought that to the countries included in the Japanese scheme the prospect of jumping from the Western frying pan into the Japanese fire would offer little attraction, but it was the astute way in which Tokio set about its business which won their support—at least in the beginning. U Nu, the Prime Minister of Burma,[1] frankly records that when Japan entered the second World War her reputation throughout Asia was poor owing to her aggression against Nationalist China, yet the Burmese nationalists in effect exclaimed: "Here is our leader against Western rule". Simultaneously with the attack on Pearl Harbour there was loosed from Tokio a flood of propaganda announcing Japan's policy of "Asia for the Asians" and the end of white domination.

As country after country fell to the Japanese as far east as Burma the conquerors duly set up indigenous governments, but these had little real power so long as the Japanese army commanders were in effective control. In fact disillusionment reached such a stage in Burma that Burmese nationalists under Aung San rebelled against their overlords and offered their co-operation to the British authorities during the campaign which led to the ejection of the Japanese by British and Indian troops of the Fourteenth Army. It was only when the Japanese saw defeat staring them in the face in the Pacific that, as a dying kick at their enemies, they handed over power wherever they could to the peoples they had claimed to liberate.

In this way Japan made her biggest practical contribution to the freedom of Western-controlled Asian countries. The inhabitants of these countries could not forget that under Japanese domination they had achieved at least the trappings of independence; they had tasted responsibility, and in most cases as a result of the Japanese surrender thay had acquired arms on a considerable scale. That is why, despite the sufferings caused in South-East Asia by the Japanese, despite the brutalities of their troops, there is surprisingly little hostility to Japan throughout the region today except in China and the Philippines. The general attitude of the intelligentsia is that whatever Japan's motives may have been she did at least strike a blow for Asian freedom, and that as far as war guilt is concerned she was more sinned against than sinning.

[1] *Burma Under the Japanese*, by Thakin Nu (Macmillan and Co. Ltd.).

This point of view found expression in what seemed to the West the astonishing decision of Mr. Justice Pal, the Indian member of the International Military Tribunal for the Far East, who contended that Japan could not be accused of aggression since her belligerence was the inevitable reaction to Western imperialism! Much on the same lines was India's attitude towards the Japanese peace treaty of 1951 which she refused, greatly to America's annoyance, to sign. Mr. Jawaharlal Nehru's Government declined to be a party to the treaty because its terms did not concede to Japan "a place of honour, equality and contentment among the community of free nations"; these conditions, India maintained, were not fulfilled because of the continued United States occupation of the Ryukyu and Bonin islands. Strange though this attitude may appear in Western eyes, it does represent an Asian feeling, and in no way can that feeling be roused more quickly than by interference from the West.

Asia may be a vast continent comprising many diverse races, creeds and cultures, yet there is one issue on which its strangely assorted congeries of nationalities is in agreement: it resents any attempt by Europe or America to settle its problems by force or otherwise without Asian consent and co-operation. The old suspicion of the West dies hard. Burns's passionate declaration in "Does Haughty Gaul Invasion Threat?":

"For never but by British hands
Maun British wrangs be righted!"

finds an echo in Asia, which substitutes "Asian" for "British". And this sentiment is as strong in the Arab States, in Iran and in the Commonwealth group of nations of which India is the centre as it is in Communist China. Asia badly wants all kinds of Western help, but it must be given on Asia's terms; there must be no strings attached. The new Asia stands for equality: what it bitterly resents is any feeling of inferiority in its dealings with the West. Unless the West recognizes this fundamental fact, relations between East and West can never be harmonious.

*Chapter Two*

# ASIA'S "TORMENT OF THE MIND"

THE STRUGGLE WHICH is taking place in Asia today is a struggle for Asia's soul no less than for the continent's material welfare. "There is torment in our minds," said Mr. Jawaharlal Nehru in his address to the Eleventh Conference of the Institute of Pacific Relations, "and there are all kinds of questions before us which we seek to answer. . . . It (the torment) takes different shapes in different countries, of course, and it is a problem for us ultimately to understand and to solve, with the help of others, I hope, but the burden is ours. Others can help, as others can hinder, but they cannot solve it for us."

This torment of the Asian mind arises from the clamant need to provide a decent standard of living for the 1,200 million human beings who constitute Asia's population. It is no exaggeration to say that on the ability of Asia, with or without Western help, to solve this gigantic problem may well depend the destiny of mankind. Here, again, the impact of the West on Asian countries during the last hundred years is largely responsible for the nature of the social and economic crisis with which Asia is faced. When the Western Powers took over control of large parts of the East, when they set up trading stations in countries nominally independent, they eventually upset the balance of Asia's traditional social and economic system; they opened a doorway on a hitherto unknown world.

No one can deny that in many respects the Western colonizing powers did an immense amount of good. They created stable régimes in place of the former insecurity; they stimulated the production of primary commodities and minerals for which there was a world demand; they brought wealth in the shape of trade to the territories concerned; they built roads, railways and irrigation works, and they improved the standard of public health. But they disturbed the ancient social order and what Mr. Edwin Montagu, British Secretary of State for India during the first World War, called the "pathetic contentment" of the masses. As the result of Western exploitation—designed, it must be confessed, mainly for the benefit of the Western countries involved—money flowed into Eastern lands but it seldom benefited the people in greatest need of it. Thanks to Western trade and enterprise there grew up a small section of the community in each country that took full advantage of the influx of wealth, but for various reasons, including the rapid increase of population where work was available under conditions of internal peace, the standard of living of the peasantry, which constitutes the bulk of Asia's peoples, did not rise. In many cases it actually fell in relation to world standards.

The latest available official figures reveal a tragic state of affairs. According to the *Economic Survey of Asia and the Far East, 1947*, the income per head in terms of 1946 U.S. dollars amounted to 23 in China, 35 in Indonesia and 43 in India compared with 1,269 for the United States of America and 660 for Great Britain. Much of this disparity is, of course, due to the terrific pressure of the population on the land in East Asia, a circumstance for which the Western Powers cannot be blamed except in so far as their exploitation and protection contributed to it by the lessening of famine, pestilence and internecine wars. In Japan, for example, a country which never came under Western occupation until after the second World War, there are 3,300 people to every square mile of cultivated land, 1,900 in Java, 1,100 in China and 940 in India. In the United States before the last war the figure was something like 36 persons to the square mile—not the cultivated mile, it is true, but even if we double the figure the result is sufficiently staggering.

As Professor W. Macmahon Ball[1] points out, the colonial powers usually failed to distinguish between economic progress and social security, and while a poor man may be content to stay poor in a poor man's country he may not be content to stay poor in a rich man's country. In other words, the gross inequality between the standard of living of the Western trader and the Asian middle class

[1] *Nationalism and Communism in East Asia*, by W. Macmahon Ball (Melbourne University Press).

which benefited from his activities on the one hand, and the vast mass of indigenous population on the other, could not fail in time to create active discontent.

Just as the victory of Japan over Russia at the beginning of the century kindled the spark of nationalism in many Eastern lands, so the Russian revolution during the first World War attracted the keen attention of Eastern sociologists. In the early nineteen-twenties bearers of the new Communist gospel spread to all parts of Asia, and it cannot be denied that that in the period between the two World Wars the Eastern mind was tremendously struck by the much advertised planned progress achieved in Russia. It was no good pointing out to these enthusiasts that a democratic government could have done the same thing in a more humane manner; what the East noted was that the Russian proletarian leaders had overthrown their imperial and feudal masters and had pulled themselves and their country up, so to speak, by their own boot-straps. It was also of little avail to argue that the Communist reorganization of Russia involved the callous destruction of many of its inhabitants and great suffering for others, that cultivators were being forced into collectivized farms, and that for the ordinary citizen there was no freedom of thought or speech.

To the Easterner, hardship and authoritarian rule are not the evils they appear to the West. The rest of Asia, for instance, seemed to be singularly unmoved by the liquidation of about two million followers of General Chiang Kai-shek—officially described as "bandits and reactionaries"—by Mr. Mao Tse-tung's Government after the Communists had established themselves in power in China. To Eastern peoples struggling for political freedom the most impressive thing about Communism was that the Russian leaders appeared to have found an answer to mass poverty and misery, and that they had done so by abolishing both imperialism and capitalism, the two systems they associated with the Western Powers which had so long exercised authority over them.

To the Western mind this will seem a lamentably lop-sided view, which totally ignores the grimmer aspect of Communist rule. But as one who long resided in the East I can only give the facts as I saw them; I can only repeat the arguments which I heard so often.

Moreover, during the second World War the Western democracies themselves extolled the deeds of their ally, the Soviet State, and the magnificent performance of the Russian army in defence of its homeland was regarded in Asia as yet another proof of the virtues of the Soviet régime. The wonder is that, outside China, Communism has not achieved much greater headway among Eastern peoples than it has actually done.

This brings me to a feature of the struggle between nationalism and Communism in Asia which may seem strange to people in the West. From its earliest days the Marxist creed was directed by its disciples in Europe and America almost exclusively to industrial workers in the cities who constituted the proletariat on whom the Communist state was to be built. The men of the Kremlin looked for recruits among poorly paid wage earners in factories; so strongly did this idea persist that for many years Marshal Stalin had obviously no faith in Mr. Mao Tse-tung's movement among the peasants of north-west China. Indeed, it is one of the ironies of fate that the great hero of China today, the foreigner whose portrait is carried in every procession alongside that of Mr. Mao Tse-tung—Marshal Stalin—is one who not many years ago treated the Chinese Communists with something approaching contempt.

In Asia the most fruitful field for Communism is to be found in the rural areas. This is not really surprising when we consider the facts. Communism appeals to the "under-privileged", that class of people who consider that they are not getting from society the kind of treatment to which they think they are entitled. In Asia the people to whom this description best applies are the peasants who, as I have noted earlier, have struggled for centuries against famine and pestilence, maladministration and corruption, insecurity and the tyranny of rapacious landlords. They constitute in every case the vast bulk of the population, since there has not yet grown up in Asia the large landless proletariat to be found in the West.

In India, for example, the cotton textile worker never loses touch with the land; his main idea in working in a cotton mill is to supplement the family earnings, and at regular intervals most millworkers return to their family holdings in the *mofussil*. It was not the Bombay millhand who fell a victim to Communism a few years ago when the call to action was sounded. Far from it; he proved to be a staunch nationalist. The people who provide India's Central and State legislatures with the majority of their Communist members live in the rural areas of Hyderabad, South India and Bengal.

This rule applies generally to the whole of Asia; peasant support gave the Chinese Communists the strength which enabled them to seize control of the country. Today the position may have changed; the Peking Government is now reported to have more party members among city workers than it has in the districts, but that does not alter the basic cause of its success. Nor does it disprove the claim that if Communism in China lost its appeal to the peasants it would soon lose its dominance in the country. It is among the peasantry of Asia that the Communist appeal to the masses must be fought and overcome. To discover how the battle is going it is necessary to examine the growth of nationalism, Communism and social revolution in the main countries and groups of countries in Asia.

*Chapter Three*

## THE MIDDLE EAST

NOTHING ILLUSTRATES MORE vividly the rise of nationalism in Asia than a glance at the map. Since the beginning of the century there has spread across the face of the "changeless East" of Victorian days a rash of sovereign states, some of which started their careers as mandates under the League of Nations. The first World War saw the end of the old Turkish empire in what is now generally known as the Middle East, and in its place we have the Arab States—Saudi Arabia (which threw off the Turkish yoke in 1913), Syria, the Lebanon, Jordan and Iraq—together with the Jewish state of Israel. After the second World War came a second and much greater development of nationalities in the East and Far East. Six new independent nations sprang into being—India, Pakistan, Ceylon, Burma, Indonesia and the Philippines. Two others, Korea and Viet Nam, were nominally given their independence but their territory is at present a bone of contention between the two major power blocs. The remaining Associated States of Indo-China, Laos and Cambodia, had their independence guaranteed under the Geneva agreement of 1954. China, Persia and Afghanistan have all been released from any hint of Western control.

Only scattered fragments of Asia's vast bulk remain under Western administration; they include Malaya, with Singapore island; Sarawak, Brunei and North Borneo in the island of Borneo; and Hongkong—all British—together with three small Portuguese possessions in India—Goa, Daman and Diu—which are a constant irritant to the Indian people and the cause of much ill feeling between the Governments of India and Portugal. (The last of a series of petty French enclaves in India were handed back in 1954.) By far the most important of these territories is Malaya, one of the world's chief sources of rubber and tin, which would probably have been self-governing today had it not been for the mixed character of its population and the clash of different nationalities in its political make-up. It will thus be seen that to all intents and purposes Asia's battle for nationalism has been won. Where Western influence persists it does so either by agreement with those concerned or on the understanding that its ultimate aim, as in Malaya, is full self-government.

It is difficult to split Asia into political blocs in the same way as one can demarcate clear lines of division in the West. While all Asian nations, with the exception of Israel, can claim to be "Asia minded" when it comes to dealing with the West, some of them differ sharply in their relations with one another. India and Pakistan, for example, disagree violently over Kashmir; Delhi and Colombo quarrel because of the treatment of Indians in Ceylon, and Communist China regards her old enemy Japan as little better than an American colony.

Yet the continent does fall into several more or less well defined groups. Whatever their future attitude towards each other may be, Russia in Asia and China at present form a solid Communist mass. On the other side of the curtain, associated with the Western powers of the South-East Asia Collective Defence Treaty (popularly known as SEATO after its Western counterpart NATO) for defence against Communist aggression, either open or subversive, are the Philippines, Siam and Pakistan, three nations which have little in common except the pact signed at Manila towards the end of 1954.

The most outstanding group is that known as the Colombo Powers, comprising the major part of Britain's erstwhile Asian empire and the former Dutch possessions. They include India, Pakistan and Ceylon, which became member states of the Commonwealth on achieving independence; Burma, which is now outside the Commonwealth but is closely associated with it; and Indonesia, the successor state of the Netherlands East Indies, a somewhat weak brother whose internal affairs are still rather chaotic. Although Pakistan signed the SEATO pact, which the rest of the Colombo Powers dislike, nevertheless Pakistan continues to be a member of the group.

The Colombo Powers believe in the parliamentary form of

democracy which most of them inherited from the British; they are strongly opposed to Communism in their own countries and have no intention, if they can manage it, of allowing a Communist administration to take the place of their present party governments. But this does not mean their acceptance of the American view of Communism as a curse which should be banished from the earth; they recognize the right of any country, Eastern or Western, to adopt Communism if it so desires, and they are prepared to live in harmony with it provided it does not attempt to impose its views on them by force. They still suffer from what I would call a hangover from Western occupation, and although imperialism and colonialism have departed they continue to regard these ogres with a lively horror which Communism does not inspire. To that extent they live in the past, though signs accumulate that they are catching up with the times.

Finally, we have the Middle East group of predominantly Muslim nations embracing Afghanistan, Persia, Turkey, the Arab States (which include Egypt), and Israel. In none of these states, except Persia, is nationalism threatened internally by Communism to any great extent, and I therefore propose to deal very briefly with them. Two things are of special significance in the Middle East today. The first is that, with the exception of Turkey which is definitely allied to the West, all Middle East countries share to a remarkable degree South-East Asia's antipathy to any kind of Western "imperialism", and are as touchy as the rest of the continent about political strings being attached to Western help.

The second is that there hangs over the whole region the shadow of Russia. In Victorian days the ogre was Russia of the Tsars; today it is Russia of the Communists, thereby demonstrating the truth of the old adage that while a country's form of government may change its national outlook remains unaltered. Tsarist Russia hungered for an outlet to the Mediterranean and the Persian Gulf. Communist Russia has never disguised its desire for control of the Dardanelles, while the mineral wealth of the Middle East recently revealed by Western exploitation must constitute to the hierarchy of the Kremlin an attraction vastly greater than access to the Persian Gulf did to St. Petersburg. If South-East Asia is one of the world's richest areas in rubber, tin and rice, the Middle East possesses enormous wealth in oil; its petroleum reserves are estimated at nearly 55 per cent of the world's total.

Up to the time of the second World War the British Empire, based on the sub-continent of India, the Suez Canal and Palestine, provided a powerful bulwark against possible Russian aggression in the Middle East. Today that power has almost completely disappeared. The countries in the front line of any Russian move towards historic objectives are Persia and Turkey. For some time after 1907 both Britain and Russia had, by agreement, their spheres of influence in Persia. This control ceased before the days of Reza Shah, the strong man of modern Persia, but it was revived during the second World War when Reza Shah's intrigues with the Nazis led to the occupation of the country by British and Russian forces. In 1943 the "Big Three" allied powers—the United States, Russia and Britain—guaranteed Persia's full independence and territorial integrity after the war. Russia's part in this agreement was completed, under strong American pressure, by the withdrawal of all Soviet troops in 1946.

Once again Persian nationalism, which has persisted for centuries despite great difficulties and periodic disruptions, asserted itself. It came into sharp conflict with Britain in 1951 over the long-standing agreement between the Persian Government and the Anglo-Iranian Oil Company to extract, refine and market the product of the Persian oilfields. The repeated political crises and mob disorders which marked the *opera bouffe* régime of Dr. Musaddiq, the champion of oil nationalization, ended in his overthrow in 1953 by General Zahedi, whom the Shah appointed as his successor but who had to use the army in order to assert his authority. The lesson for the West in the whole sorry episode is that in insisting on oil nationalization Dr. Musaddiq had Persian sentiment solidly behind him. Where he erred grievously was in refusing a reasonable offer and in using the Tudeh or Workers' Party, a Communist organization, to demonstrate on his behalf. The Tudeh Party came into existence after the last war. Following an attempt on the life of the Shah in 1949 it was dissolved, but Dr. Musaddiq's unscrupulous employment of Tudeh mobs kept it alive, and it was not until after

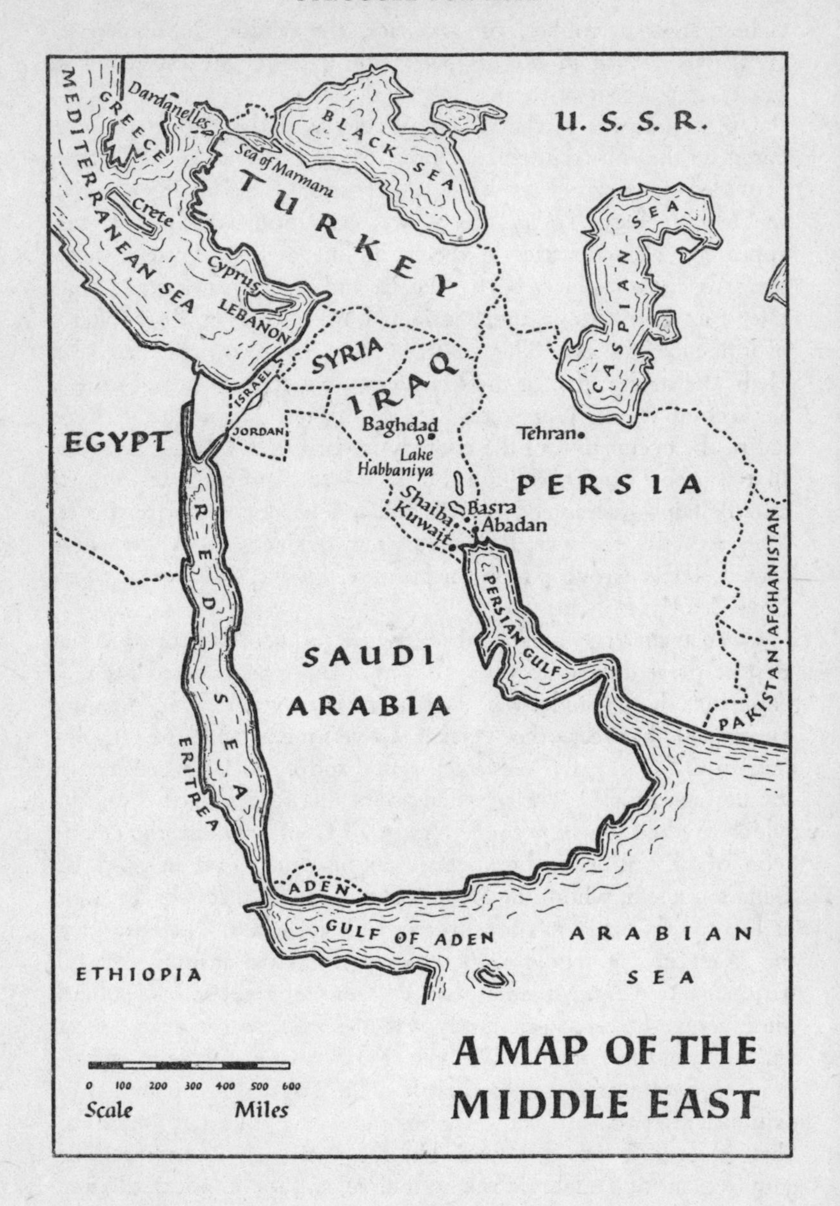
Dardanelles
GREECE
MEDITERRANEAN SEA
Crete
Cyprus
LEBANON
BLACK SEA
Sea of Marmara
TURKEY
U. S. S. R.
CASPIAN SEA
SYRIA
IRAQ
ISRAEL
JORDAN
EGYPT
Baghdad
Lake
Habbaniya
Tehran
PERSIA
Shaiba
Basra
Kuwait
Abadan
AFGHANISTAN
PERSIAN GULF
PAKISTAN
RED SEA
SAUDI
ARABIA
ERITREA
ADEN
GULF OF ADEN
ARABIAN
SEA
ETHIOPIA
0 100 200 300 400 500 600
Scale Miles
A MAP OF THE
MIDDLE EAST

his overthrow that firm action was taken against the party. Late in 1954 the Government of General Zahedi (succeeded in 1955 by Hussein Ala) announced the discovery of an extensive Tudeh Party organization inside the army and in the labour camp at Abadan; over 500 officers and technicians were arrested and a number executed. It was claimed on behalf of the army that these officers had joined the Tudeh Party during Dr. Musaddiq's régime, which had nearly destroyed discipline in the armed forces.

Persia enjoys a massive amount of American aid. After his accession to power, General Zahedi received from President Eisenhower the promise of $47 million as emergency aid in addition to the $23 million already granted for Point Four schemes, and the following year the total of emergency aid was raised to over $100 million in order to tide the country over the period until the resumption of oil exports began to bring in revenue. Britain provided a loan of £10 million. Persia needs all the foreign help she can get for the strengthening of her army and vigorous measures to raise the economic condition of the masses. The Tudeh Party, although driven underground, is still a force in the land, and will have to be reckoned with if living standards do not improve. American anxiety to prevent Communism gaining control in Persia can well be understood in view of the country's key position in the cold war. If Persia fell to the Communists, the whole of the vast oil resources of the Middle East along the Persian Gulf littoral would lie at Russia's back door.

Turkey at the western end of the Russian Middle East line is in a far more dangerous position than Persia. The Turks have the iron curtain on both their European and Asian frontiers—Bulgaria in Europe and Russia in Asia. They are under no illusions about Russia's ambitions, which were made painfully clear to them at the close of the last war. Moscow proposed a revision of the Montreux Convention governing possession of the straits between the Black Sea and the Aegean which would have given the Black Sea states, including Russia, Bulgaria and Rumania, a privileged status and—what was vastly more important—ensured joint defence of the straits by Russia and Turkey. Soviet pressure made itself felt in other ways—in Balkan affairs and in backing for the Georgian demand for a large tract of Turkish territory embracing the towns of Kars, Ardahan and Artvin. It is true that in 1953 Moscow officially renounced these and other unjustified demands, but the damage had already been done.

In self-protection Turkey accepted American military aid and economic help in 1949. Three years later she joined the North Atlantic Treaty Organization, rejecting Russia's protests by pointing out that she was entitled to take purely defensive measures and recalling that Moscow had in 1945 and 1946 given unofficial support to claims on Turkish territory. Coupled with its definite alliance with the West, the Turkish Government in 1953 took stern action against local Communists.

Up to 1954 Turkey's relations with the Arab States were not friendly. Most of these states owe their national existence to the allies of the first World War and, in particular, to the British, whose forces were mainly responsible for freeing them from Turkish domination. Syria and the Lebanon came under an unhappy French mandate which did not end until the second World War; the British mandate in Iraq ceased in 1932 and was replaced by a treaty which gave Britain the use of two air bases in the country, and the British Government entered into a special defence arrangement with the state of Transjordan, now known as Jordan.

In the years between the two wars and afterwards increasing wealth poured into Iraq, Saudi Arabia and the smaller shaikhdoms of the Persian Gulf as the result of Western development of the Middle East's oil resources. Yet this did little to lessen the Arab States' typical Asian suspicion of the West; they adopted the policy of playing off Soviet Russia against the Western powers until Moscow's ephemeral support of the Jews in Israel's war of independence profoundly disillusioned and disgusted them. Their anti-Communist feeling does not, however, prevent the Arab States from following Russia and other Asian nations into the "anti-colonial" lobby whenever issues of that type affecting the West are raised in the United Nations. Western help is welcomed so long as it is unencumbered; as one writer put it, dollars and understanding are regarded by the Arab nationalists as unrequited exports due to them by the West.[1]

[1] *Annual Register*, 1951 (Longmans, Green and Co.).

Within their own countries most Arab politicians have a wholesome dread of Communism. Their states are largely feudal in character; the people look to ruling families or "strong men" for leadership, and in all members of the group Communism is kept in check, often drastically so. Militarily the Arab States are weak, and the majority of them suffer—as Muslim nations seem liable to do—from highly unstable régimes. They are intensely jealous of one another; their main causes of difference spring from the conquest by Saudi Arabia of the Hejaz territory of King Hussain after the first World War. His two sons of the Hashimi dynasty were given the thrones of Jordan and Iraq, and for some time supporters of the dynasty toyed with the idea of creating a "Fertile Crescent" confederation which would include not only Iraq and Jordan but the smaller states of Syria and the Lebanon. Any idea of a union of this kind was fiercely opposed by Egypt, which considered itself the leader of the Arab States, and by Saudi Arabia, whose ruling house saw a powerful rival in a union of the "Fertile Crescent" type.

The only cementing factor among the Arab States is their common hatred of Israel, which established its borders in the teeth of armed Arab and Egyptian opposition when Britain gave up the Palestine mandate. They are linked politically by the Arab League, and for defence purposes by the Arab Security Pact, both of which bodies have as their chief objective united action in their dealings with the Jewish state. Egypt also used the League to secure as far as possible the support of the other Arab nations in her struggle with the British Government over the Suez Canal base.

The Arab States' attitude towards their fellow Muslim nation, Turkey, was coloured firstly by the ancient grudge which they bore against the Turks as their former overlords. Secondly, with Turkey and Persia interposed between them and Russia, they professed to see Turkey as a handmaid of the West while they remained virtuously aloof from such entanglements. A Middle East defence organization in which America, Britain and Turkey would play a leading part was scornfully rejected by the League, obsessed as it was with its own private quarrels.

Turkey's isolation from her Asian neighbours came to an end in 1954 with the signing of a treaty whereby Turkey and Pakistan agreed, among other things, to strengthen "peace and security". This development, obviously inspired by America because of United States military aid to both countries, was followed by staff talks between the two Muslim nations, which together possess armed forces totalling over half a million tough fighting men. So striking a move towards filling up the Middle East power vacuum created by Great Britain's departure aroused deep interest among the Arab States. Almost simultaneously two events helped to relieve East-West tension. The first was the Persian oil agreement; the second (and much more important from the Arab League point of view) was the settlement of the Suez Canal dispute. The Anglo-Egyptian agreement had one remarkable result; not only did it remove Egypt's main grievance against the West but it established a direct link between Egypt and Turkey by making the Egyptians—at Britain's request—a party to reactivation of the base in the event of aggression against Turkey as well as against the Arab States.

These developments coincided with increasingly friendly overtures between Turkey and Arab League countries. They were of special concern to Iraq which, as Turkey's nearest neighbour, appreciated the strength of a Turco-Pakistan alliance supported by America and the West. After a visit to Istambul, Senator Nuri es-Said, the Iraqi Premier, outlined the two factors guiding Iraq's foreign policy—her proximity to Turkey and Persia, and the Arab League decisions of 1949 and 1950. These decisions envisaged co-operation with the West provided there was a settlement of the Suez Canal issue and a solution of the differences with Israel. The first problem, he said, had been solved and only the second remained.

Nevertheless it was clear that the idea of a link-up with the Turco-Pakistan pact was very much in the minds of Baghdad's rulers. The first big step in this direction was the conclusion of a mutual defence treaty, open to others to join, between Turkey and Iraq early in 1955. Soon afterwards the British Government adhered to the treaty, and the way was clear for the handing over to the Iraq authorities of the air bases at Lake Habbaniya and Shaiba, given to the British under an earlier agreement. Their continued occupation would have been an offence to Iraqi nationalism after the transfer by Britain to Egypt of the Suez Canal base. From the point of view of the

West the solution was a most satisfactory one, since it definitely allied Iraq with the anti-Communist front. As in Persia, there exists in Iraq a good deal of public sensitiveness to any form of co-operation with the West which smacks of subjection to "imperialism". Arab xenophobia is actively fostered by the Communists, and it is not without significance that a recent ordinance promulgated by the Iraq Government contains strong measures to deal with Communism and similar activities, including deprivation of citizenship rights and detention for those who, as Communists are thereby "in the service of a foreign Communist state". Iraq suspended diplomatic relations with Russia early in 1955.

The trend is unmistakable. Turkey and Pakistan, the two anchors of the Middle East defence chain, are earnestly striving to get Persia, Syria, the Lebanon and Jordan to join Iraq as links in the centre despite bitter Egyptian opposition to a move which destroyed Egypt's commanding position in the Arab Security Pact. The Turco-Pakistan appeal may in time succeed in winning over at least some of the countries invited to participate. Many Arab states are now receiving arms from the West. If they can be persuaded that Israel has come to stay, the way would be clear for a comprehensive Middle East front against Communism. Despite their obsession with unwanted Israel, the Arab States are beginning to be impressed by the danger to which their newly found wealth in oil would be exposed in the event of a serious Communist threat to Persia or Turkey, a danger shared by Pakistan because of its proximity to Persia and the Persian Gulf. Their need for defence reliance on the West is admitted by themselves.

*Chapter Four*

## JAPAN'S AGGRESSIVE NATIONALISM

When we come to consider the rise of nationalism in Asia and the various forms which it took, the first question that naturally springs to mind is: why did Japan among Asian countries

> "So get the start of the majestic world,
> And bear the palm alone?"

Why did Japanese nationalism develop in a manner so different from that of Japan's great neighbour, China? Both were feudal empires; both were closed to foreign "barbarians" until the West forced its contact upon them in the nineteenth century; both were countries with a predominantly rural economy.

The answer lies not only in the differing character of the peoples and their rulers, but in their reactions to Western exploitation. The Chinese were from their earliest days a self-sufficient people, with their history as a civilized state going back to over a thousand years B.C. They occupied a great continental land mass watered by some of the world's mightiest rivers, and despite dynastic upheavals the great bulk of the peasantry pursued its tillage of the soil generation after generation in a seemingly endless chain. At a time when Chinese civilization was already old, a mixed group of immigrants from various parts of the mainland of Asia was struggling to establish itself on a string of islands skirting the coast. The immigrants had first to deal with the local inhabitants, the Ainus, whom they finally banished to the northern island of Hokkaido.

In many respects the early Japanese resembled the early immigrant settlers in England; they were a seafaring, fishing and agricultural people. From their Ainu predecessors they borrowed some of the ideas incorporated in their primitive religion, Shintoism, and from that religion there evolved some of the outstanding traits of the

Japanese national character—a passionate love of country, a belief in the divine origin of the ruling house and a determination to face death rather than dishonour. Living on islands off the coast of a great continent which could supply their wants, the Japanese were accustomed to take things from abroad and adapt them to their needs; they had nothing of the self-sufficiency of the Chinese. In addition they possessed what one writer has described as "the quick open mind of the child, with its eager admiration for the clever grown-up who can do so many things . . . quick to learn from other races".[1] It was this faculty, coupled with the political astuteness of her ruling class, which made Japan a world power almost before the urge towards nationalism in other Eastern countries had begun to take shape.

Japan, in effect, stepped from mediaevalism to modernity almost at one bound. Several factors, apart from the ones mentioned, contributed to this feat. For many centuries before the Meiji restoration of 1871, which marked the turning point in Japan's history, the country was ruled by one or other of a number of clans or noble families who exercised power in the name of the emperor. (A somewhat similar system prevailed in Nepal, where the ranas governed the country on behalf of the king.) From the twelfth century onwards the men who controlled Japan were called shoguns or generals, and the shogunate was still functioning when, some eighteen years after Commodore Perry's first historic visit, the feudal nobility decided after an internal struggle to restore the authority of the imperial house.

This had one remarkable result; for the Japanese feudal lords and people it was an easy step from the shogunate to the Western liberal idea of a monarch ruling on the advice of his ministers which, in their sudden burst of enthusiasm for Western methods, they desired to adopt. The difference between the change-over in China and that of Japan is well summed up in a recent Japanese study:[2]

> "In China the fact that the country was long exposed to the encroachment of Western imperialism, owing to the lack of adaptability on the part of the old ruling class, had the effect of

[1] *History of the World*. (Odhams Press, Ltd.) [2] *Nationalism in Post-War Japan*, by Masao Maruyama (Japan Institute of Pacific Relations).

imposing the task of basically revolutionizing the old socio-political structure upon the nationalist movement, which has been fighting against foreign imperialism. This probably explains the combination in varied forms of anti-imperialist movement and social revolution that formed an unbroken tradition of Chinese nationalism from the days of Sun Yat-sen through Chiang Kai-shek to Mao Tse-tung.

In contrast to this development in China, the men who destroyed the old régime and seized political control of a unified state in Japan were themselves representatives of feudal forces. Prompted by the need of countering the pressure from Western powers, they achieved the unification of the country under the authority of the Throne by rapidly liquidating the decentralized feudal forces, and carried through modernization 'from the top' by adopting the policy of creating 'a wealthy nation and a strong army'. Under these circumstances, the extent and form of modernization were naturally determined by the supreme objective of strengthening the ruling power as rapidly as possible."

Thus it was that Japan escaped the long struggle which other Asian nations had to endure either in establishing a completely new constitution in place of the old, as in China, or in gaining independence from foreign control, as in India and Indonesia. The men who really seized power in modern Japan, mostly from the old warrior class, broadened the basis of government just sufficiently to give it the outward appearance of Western parliamentary democracy, but they sternly discouraged the import of ideas which would have made the revolution as complete as it has been in, say, India and Pakistan. Instead, they concentrated on developing a highly nationalistic spirit with loyalty to the emperor and to the country as its twin supports. They had little difficulty in achieving their purpose, since the whole trend of Japanese tradition and sentiment helped to inculcate these ideas.

Simultaneously with the stimulation of national feeling, Japan's rulers adopted with amazing rapidity Western industrial skill and technique. Here again success was quickly won by centralizing power in the hands of a few big firms, the *Zaibatsu*, whose position in the world of commerce and industry became like that of the old feudal lords in shogunate days. Economic development, particularly industrialization, brought its inevitable concomitant, the growth of an urban working class which for a time threatened the country with a social revolution of the Western type owing to low wages and poor conditions of employment. But those at the head of affairs rode the storm successfully by encouraging expansionist ideas aimed at making the foreigner pay. The grievances of the peasantry, who exhibited anti-capitalist sentiment owing to low prices for their produce, were dealt with in similar fashion, the ringleaders being ruthlessly suppressed and the right wing elements heartily supported. Thus began Japan's long record of foreign adventure under her chauvinistic rulers which ended—temporarily at any rate—in the catastrophe of 1945.

At no time before Japan's defeat in the second World War could Communism within the country claim to be a nationalist movement. On the contrary, it was regarded as a poisonous creed by the fire-eating nationalists who ran the government, while the mass of the people disliked it because of its disrespect for the emperor and the fact that it was a subversive import from abroad. Yet Japan was included in the list of Eastern countries to which emissaries were sent from Moscow after the Communist régime established itself in Russia. At the First Congress of the Toilers of the Far East held in Moscow early in 1922 Zinoviev declared: "There is no issue without Japan; the Japanese proletariat holds in its hands the key to the solution of the Far Eastern question, and the presence at this Congress of the representatives of the Japanese workers is our only serious guarantee that we are at least starting on our way to a direct solution of the problem". Later in the year the Communist Party of Japan was secretly organized in Tokio with the help of the Comintern. It encountered many vicissitudes until its suppression and practical disappearance during the second World War.

In the period of relative political freedom which followed the first World War the Japanese Communist Party contrived to infiltrate into the growing Japanese labour movement and at one stage secured control of the Japan Labour Union Council. Up to this stage the ultra-nationalists who ran the administration made no systematic attempt to stamp out the party, merely contenting themselves with confiscating Communist literature and arresting persons whom they considered guilty of subversive activities. But in 1928, alarmed at the growing influence of the Communists, the government of Baron Tanaka suddenly undertook a nation-wide drive against them, in the course of which some fifteen hundred "dangerous elements" were arrested. Thereafter the party went underground, but it continued a running fight with the authorities in which it secured a certain amount of support in the form of protests against the despatch of Japanese troops for expansionist wars in Manchuria and China.

By this time Japan had become to all intents and purposes a police state, completely dominated by people whose gospel was a militant nationalism and who trampled underfoot most of the rights which the public had secured under the Meiji constitution. For Japan the period of the second World War began in 1937 with the "China Incident"—in reality a full scale war against Nationalist China—and became total with the attack on Pearl Harbour in 1941. In those days of stress and strain, when "un-Japanese" activities of any kind were savagely suppressed, organized Communism practically disappeared from the country.

It is one of the ironies of history that Communism did not raise its head again in Japan until the American occupation of 1945. Even after the surrender, the Japanese government which functioned under General MacArthur, the Supreme Commander for the Allied Powers, continued to enforce security measures against the Communists. But that restraint did not last long. About a month after his appointment General MacArthur announced sweeping reforms in accordance with the Allied Potsdam Declaration; all obstacles to the growth of "democratic tendencies" amongst the Japanese people were to be removed. The Japanese Government were ordered not merely to release all political prisoners but to suspend all laws which interfered with freedom of thought, speech, religion and assembly.

The Allied idea was, of course, to help to build up in Japan democratic forces hostile to the jingoism of her former rulers—forces which would work with the Allies on a liberal democratic basis. General MacArthur's declared aim was to take Japan along "the middle road to democracy", and in economics to achieve "a capitalist system based upon free private competitive enterprise."

In the numbed state of public feeling in Japan after defeat, the only party which was able to take immediate advantage of the Allied declaration was the Communist Party, which saw in it a golden opportunity to promote its creed. On release from gaol Communist leaders toured the country; they addressed meetings calling for the overthrow of the existing order and its replacement by a "people's government"; Communist literature poured from the printing presses. The party outlined a programme of action aimed at setting up a Communist state on lines familiar elsewhere. Nevertheless the Communists made little impression on the new broad-based electorate which voted in the first elections to the Diet under the Allied régime; they secured only three seats out of a total of 466. Inside the Diet their main demand was for further purging of undemocratic elements amongst the parties constituting the first post-war government, with incessant calls for the punishment of war criminals whom they broadly hinted were to be found inside the government fold.

Oddly enough, the Occupation gave them for the first time a really patriotic rallying cry; they described Japanese governments under General MacArthur as "servants of foreign imperialists" and on this issue they probably came nearer to the popular mind than on any other item in their programme. For a time they contemplated an alliance with the Socialists and would have used that party's strength in the Diet to further their own ends had the Socialists, like Barkis, been willin', but the Socialists were too "middle of the road" to relish such unruly bedfellows.

Moreover, the Communists were becoming increasingly involved in labour troubles which were bound to result in a clash with the authorities. So strong was their influence in the trade unions by 1947 that they attempted to organize a general strike to relieve distress caused by inflation. This proved abortive but, undismayed, they proceeded the following year to work for a general strike of government employees, a poorly paid section of the community. It was at this point that they incurred the direct wrath of General MacArthur. On his expressing the view that no person in the public services should resort to strike action, the government of Mr.

Ashida promulgated an anti-strike ordinance, thereby effectively drawing the Communists' teeth.

To add to their discomfiture the country began to feel the beneficent effects of American economic help, with the result that the trade union leaders started to move away from the Communists. Yet, strange to relate, the party scored its biggest parliamentary success in the general elections to the Diet in the early part of 1949, when it won 35 seats. This gain alarmed the right wing groups led by the new premier, Mr. Yoshida, who from then onwards watched for an opportunity to strike. He had not long to wait. Egged on by Moscow and by Cominform strictures, and encouraged by the number of Communist-indoctrinated Japanese prisoners of war returned to Japan by the Russians, the Communists became increasingly militant; they sponsored strikes, demonstrations, riots and finally violence in which U.S. troops were attacked. Nor were relations between the Allied Occupation forces and the Communists improved by the war which U.N.—mostly American—troops were fighting in Korea against North Korean and later Chinese Communist armies.

By this time the earlier impulse to democratize and disarm the Japanese was beginning in America to give way to a policy of building up Japan as a Far East buffer against Communist Russia and Communist China. Early in 1950 General MacArthur declared that the Japanese Communist Party had "cast off the mantle of pretended legitimacy and assumed instead the role of an avowed satellite of an international predatory force and a Japanese pawn of alien power policy, imperialistic purpose and subversive propaganda". A few months later the Supreme Commander ordered Mr. Yoshida's government to ban from public service all members of the Central Committee of the Japanese Communist Party. In a scathing denunciation of the party's policy General MacArthur accused its leaders of a whole series of actions "which would set the stage for the eventual overthrow of constitutional government in Japan by force".

The five-year-old *mariage de convenance* between the Communists and the rulers of occupied Japan had ended. With the Supreme Commander's words ringing in his ears, Mr. Yoshida took progressive steps to suppress Communist activities; all Communist newspapers and magazines were banned, warrants were issued for the arrest of Communist leaders, the Communist-dominated Federation of Labour Unions was dissolved and the Government proceeded to dismiss all civil servants with Communist sympathies. Other signs of the swing to the right were the return to public life of a large number of politicians, economists and writers who had been purged immediately after the Occupation, and the creation of a National Police Reserve of 75,000 men to deal with mob violence.

The signing of the peace treaty with Japan the following year brought a further accession of strength to the parties in power. With the disappearance of the Supreme Commander of the Allied Powers they became masters in their own house, subject, of course, to the security agreement with the U.S. which gave America the right to deploy its land, sea and air forces throughout Japanese territory "for the purpose of contributing to the maintenance of international peace and security in the Far East". The first signs of Japan's independence in foreign affairs caused some twinges of misgiving in Commonwealth countries, but they were definitely anti-Communist. Russia's policy in the Far East was denounced, and the Soviet Mission in Japan was drastically reduced.

Since then there has been a steady return to pre-war conditions in Japan, coupled with a revival of *Nihon Seishin*, the "Spirit of Imperial Japan". Many of the liberal reforms incorporated in the MacArthur-inspired constitution of 1946 have been whittled down. Almost immediately after the peace treaty came into effect in 1952 various "Occupation-initiated" laws were modified; these included measures for the prevention of subversive activities, labour regulations, changes in the control of the police and the release of war criminals. The net result of these "modifications", which aroused much opposition in the Diet and throughout the country from Socialists and other left wing bodies, including labour, was to place power in the hands of the Central authorities in a manner reminiscent of pre-war Japan.

A further step in the same direction was the revision of the anti-monopoly laws which meant that *Zaibatsu*, the Japanese equivalent of "big business", was restored to its former place in the country's economy. Opposition to the curtailment of labour rights encouraged the Communists, who had been driven underground, to instigate serious disturbances in Tokio on May Day of 1952, but by doing so they played into the hands of Government supporters. Right wing Socialists, who voted in the Diet against the Government's policy of restrictions on labour, were embarrassed by public disgust with the rioters.

All other changes in post-war policy were, however, overshadowed by rearmament. A clause in Japan's 1946 constitution renounced war as a sovereign right of the nation and prohibited the maintenance of an army, navy or air force. That clause was inserted at the instance of the United States, yet its virtual abrogation seven years later was due to American initiative. The position was clearly stated by Mr. John Nixon, the U.S. Vice-President, during his visit to Tokio in 1953. "If disarmament was right in 1946," he said, "why is it wrong in 1953? . . . Why does not the United States admit for once that it made a mistake? . . . I'm going to admit right here that the United States did make a mistake in 1946." The National Safety Force, which was held to conform to the constitution by existing purely for purposes of internal security, was in 1954 being transformed into a powerful National Defence Force with American aid under the Mutual Security Act. The expanded Maritime Safety Force contains the nucleus of a navy, and an American-supervised revival of armaments production is under way. Communist aggression in Korea and Indo-China and the victory of Communism in China provided the reasons for this remarkable change of front. General Chiang Kai-shek's complete collapse altered the whole complexion of Far East politics for the United States.

Yet it would be wrong to assume that the Japanese are wholeheartedly behind the American drive for rearmament. There are many conflicting cross-currents. A section of the intelligentsia, supported by Socialist and labour groups, is genuinely afraid that rearmament will lead to a repetition of the madness which involved Japan in the biggest disaster in her history.

The Socialists are divided into two parties or wings, their differences being mainly over foreign policy. Right wing Socialists, while willing to co-operate with the West, wish to end Japan's exclusive

realization of the fact that if the region was cut off from trade with Japan, that country's position outside the Communist orbit would become most precarious. Mr. Yoshida, when Prime Minister, on several occasions emphasized Japan's trade needs in this sphere. "China," he said, "is a natural market whether it is Communist or not"; and again, "Geography and economic laws will, I believe, prevail in the long run over ideological and artificial trade barriers".

Meanwhile tempting offers of trade with Japan are being made by both Russia and China, their object being to detach the country as far as possible from America. Japan is very anxious to secure fishery rights in Russian and Chinese waters; Japanese business men are becomingly increasingly attracted by the possibilities of trade with countries beyond the iron and bamboo curtains, and Mr. Chou En-lai's carefully calculated offer of a non-aggression pact to a group of members of the Diet visiting Peking in 1954 created a deep impression—as it was intended to do—in Tokio. Any return to normal diplomatic relations between Russia and Japan would, however, almost certainly involve consideration of Tokio's claims on Moscow, which include the return of the southern Kurile and other islands occupied by Russia since 1945 and the repatriation of Japanese war prisoners still held by the Soviet.

Some economic relief was in prospect towards the end of 1954 by Japan's admission to the Colombo Plan, the Commonwealth-sponsored development project for South-East Asia, and her reparations agreement with Burma, which opens the way to trade with that country. Japan's membership of the Colombo Plan should also lead to reparations settlements and trading facilities with Indonesia and the Philippines, two other war-ravaged neighbours which, with Burma, refused to sign the San Francisco peace treaty because of Japan's refusal to pay the heavy war damage compensation demanded by them. Mr. Yoshida's tour of America, Britain and other Western countries, undertaken in 1954 despite strong opposition from his political opponents, was likewise designed to secure not merely more aid from the United States, but increased trade with the West. His failure to realize the high hopes reposed in him was mainly responsible for his enforced resignation on his return, and his replacement by Mr. Ichiro Hatoyama, leader of the Democratic

Party, who formed a caretaker government until the elections of 1955. Mr. Hatoyama would have been Premier much earlier had he not been frowned on by General MacArthur; his ascent to power was yet another sign of the rising tide of Japanese nationalism, impatient of Mr. Yoshida's supposed subservience to Washington. The elections, which took place in February, confirmed Mr. Hatoyama in his position and, incidentally, the strength of the other conservative elements with which the Democratic Party may eventually unite.

Japan's underground Communists are turning more and more towards their Chinese brethren and away from Moscow. Peking is giving them every encouragement to do so by a policy of sweet reasonableness. By 1954 the pro-Chinese section had definitely won, and militant tactics were discarded in favour of cautious penetration of trade unions and advocacy of policies not far removed from those of the left wing Socialists. The Communists have, of course, to move carefully and to make use of fellow travellers and left wing Socialists to advocate nothing more drastic than trade with China, the stoppage of Japanese rearmament and the end of treaty relations with America. Their total membership is believed to be about 100,000, of whom half are active, but the actual work of the party is in the hands of a relatively small group.

Compared with Japan's trade unionists they are insignificant. The strength of the trade union movement is the outstanding factor in Japan's industrial life today; it includes several million workers and it has been conducting strikes for better conditions on a scale unheard of in pre-war days, when trade unions were illegal. Combined with the Socialists, the trade unions form a solid left wing element new to Japanese political life. The danger is that parliamentarianism in Japan may be discredited by scenes of the kind which occurred in the Diet in the middle of 1954, when screaming, fighting members had to be ejected by the police. Should parliamentary democracy fail, its place would almost certainly be taken, not by Communism, but by an authoritarian form of nationalism. Personalities still count for more than parties in Japan's political life.

*Chapter Five*

# THE TRAGEDY OF CHINA

ONE DAY DURING the second World War there came into my office in Bombay an American war correspondent who had just returned from Chungking. He had travelled to and from General Chiang Kai-shek's war-time capital "over the hump", as the air route linking Calcutta with Chungking across the mountains of Yunnan was known. It was by means of this singularly unpleasant air lift that the Western allies conveyed supplies to, and maintained contact with, Nationalist China during the war; journalists, especially American journalists, used it frequently. "Well, how goes the war in China?" I asked my American visitor after he had expressed himself freely and forcefully on the discomforts of the journey. His reply astonished me. "What that — — country wants," he exploded, "is fifty years of British rule."

I was astonished for two reasons; firstly, because the Generalissimo and his attractive wife were at that time the darlings of the White House, and secondly, every American from President Roosevelt downwards took an exceedingly poor view of British "colonialism", particularly as it applied to India. I soon gathered the reasons for the war correspondent's disgust. According to him, American aid to China in the shape of supplies and munitions, in the transport of which American lives were risked daily "over the hump", suffered gross misuse after reaching Chungking. They never got to the Nationalist soldier who was supposed to be fighting the Japanese invader. Either they were stored away by regional commanders in preparation for the private war after the war, or they found their way for cash payments to the Japanese through third parties operating in the large stretches of no man's land dotting the Chinese landscape. My informant rated the Nationalists' chances of survival in China after the war at fifty-fifty, but as events turned out he was hopelessly optimistic.

This story explains in part the reason for China's tragedy. China had a nationalist movement, the Kuomintang, which established itself over a large part of the country and led the fight against foreign "imperialism" not only from the West but from China's Eastern neighbour, Japan. But the movement perished miserably owing to the crassness of its leaders, who failed to live up to the principles of its founder.

The tale of Kuomintang corruption and nepotism needs no repetition; those who know him say that General Chiang Kai-shek himself is an upright man, but he exercised no control over his entourage and was apparently prepared to go on accepting—and depending upon—American help to such an extent that it was usual for the Communists to describe the Nationalist Government as anti-national in the sense that it was supported by a foreign power.

But what really proved decisive in the end was the Kuomintang leaders' loss of touch with the people who really mattered to them, the peasants and the small but important merchant class; they looked instead to the big landowners whose main idea was to preserve their privileges. Thus, when the real test came after the second World War, there was no public will to fight for the Kuomintang. The nationalist movement passed to the Communists who, ironically enough, are today almost as much dependent on another foreign power, Russia, as the Kuomintang was on the Americans. The difference is this: the Communists under Mr. Mao Tse-tung carried out their pledges of reform to the peasants, and for the present at any rate the new order has the backing of the masses. Whether that support will continue in view of Mr. Mao Tse-tung's reported intention to introduce collective farms at some future date is another matter, but as far as one can see ahead the Communist grip on China is secure.

In Japan the first stirrings of nationalism were centred by the ruling class in the person of the emperor. In China the situation was reversed. To begin with, the emperor was not Chinese at all; he was a Manchu, with the result that the embryo stages of Chinese nationalism were directed not against the foreigner but against the ruling house. Secondly, China is a vast country with a huge population compared to Japan, and at the time the West knocked heavily on China's door internal conditions were of the kind described by Mr. William L. Holland:[1]

> "The country was decentralized, and even at the end of the Manchu dynasty (1912) was largely without modern transportation and communication. There was a widespread small merchant class but no national market. The main functions of the imperial government were to collect the grain tax, repair irrigation works, put down rebellion, and conduct foreign relations. The monarchy was absolute, but its intervention in local life was necessarily limited by the vastness of the country and the nature of its economy. Provincialism and localism reigned supreme, and society was regulated mainly by the family and village elders, the gentry being the key political force."

It was not until the beginning of the present century that a Western-educated member of the Chinese intelligentsia from Canton called Sun Yat-sen enunciated a nationalist creed, but even then the emphasis was purely on internal reform. Early members of the revolutionary party swore to overthrow the Manchu dynasty, to establish a republic and to solve the agrarian question "on the basis of the equitable redistribution of the land". (Note the importance which the founders of Chinese nationalism gave to land reform.) Sun Yat-sen laid down three principles for which the party should work, namely, nationalism, democracy and "the people's livelihood".

These three principles, he insisted, must be achieved in three stages. The first was the suppression of political "bosses"—or "war-lords" as they came to be called—who had usurped authority in the provinces; the second was the education of the people, and the third was the establishment of popular self-government on Western lines. Although Sun Yat-sen believed in parliamentary democracy he was also familiar with Marxist ideas, a fact which explains some subsequent developments.

But Sun Yat-sen's was only one of many voices raised in the first decade of the twentieth century against the existing order in China; in a country of vast distances and poor communications his followers

[1] *Asian Nationalism and the West.* Edited by W. L. Holland for the Institute of Pacific Relations (The Macmillan Company, New York).

were really no more than a Cantonese party whose Western affiliations did not necessarily commend them to nationalists elsewhere. So, when the Manchu dynasty collapsed almost of its own inanition in 1912, its prestige completely destroyed by its failure to hold its own against the "foreign barbarians" from the West, there was no party organized on a really national basis to take its place.

Attempts to introduce the parliamentary system of government were little better than a mockery. A revolutionary general, Yuan Shih-kai, set up an administration which was but a pale shadow of imperial rule and in a few years the whole thing disintegrated. Central authority faded out, and war-lords, each claiming to be China's national leader, appeared in almost every province. Civil strife spread throughout the country. From this deplorable fiasco sprang two far-reaching and, for the West, unfortunate consequences. Western parliamentary institutions, which had never really been given a chance, were completely discredited, and the conviction grew that without military power reforms were impossible.

The first World War and the Russian revolution gave fresh stimulus to the intelligentsia and to the growing commercial classes who were disgusted with the gangsterdom prevailing in China. Japan's war-time demands, and the fact that she looked upon China as little better than a Japanese province, helped to arouse a really national consciousness, as also did the provisions of the Versailles Treaty handing over Germany's former special rights in Shantung to Japan. The various nationalist parties, including Sun Yat-sen's Kuomintang, began to draw closer together.

Meantime Marxist-indoctrinated agents from Moscow appeared on the scene; the new Soviet régime was anxious to get in touch with nationalist movements all over the East for the good reason that they provided a fruitful field for the propagation of Communist ideas. Russia had been quick to declare her intention of renouncing all tsarist government rights and extra-territorial privileges, including Russia's share of the Boxer indemnity, thereby creating in China a feeling as favourable to Moscow as it was unfavourable to the West.

The Chinese Communist party was founded in 1921 by a group of intellectuals which included Mr. Mao Tse-tung, a farmer's son, but for some years it exercised very little influence. Had the Western powers taken more interest in Sun Yat-sen's movement, had they responded to his appeals for help, the growth of nationalism in China might have followed a different course. As it was, Sun Yat-sen decided in 1923 to link up with the Communists for the purpose of achieving his nationalist objectives, declaring that he would no longer look to the Western powers. "Our faces", he said, "are turned towards Russia." The Chinese Communists, in view of their own lack of success, jumped at the chance of working with so striking a revolutionary figure.

Having turned his face towards Moscow, Sun Yat-sen reorganized the Kuomintang on thoroughly Communist lines with the help of Russian advisers like Borodin and Joffe. Russian officers trained the Kuomintang army. Western democratic methods were abandoned for rigid centralization of the Soviet type, and even when the Kuomintang government was established in Nanking it was made entirely responsible to the party, which in turn was controlled by its central executive committee. The whole paraphernalia of Communism, including security police and strict censorship, found its way into the Kuomintang machine. Nevertheless Sun Yat-sen never subscribed to the Communist creed; in fact he publicly stated that it was not suitable for China. All he wanted was its co-operation in the task of carrying out his programme of national unification and freedom from "unequal treaties".

The death of Sun Yat-sen in 1925 was a severe blow to the Kuomintang, and it was significant of the change which had come over the nationalist movement that the leadership went, not to a civilian, but to the commander of the party's fighting forces, General Chiang Kai-shek. Therein lay the seeds of the party's ruin, since whatever qualifications General Chiang Kai-shek may have possessed as a soldier, he lacked those qualities of statesmanship which the Kuomintang desperately needed. His early successes in the field were, however, remarkable. Setting out in 1926 from the south, he rapidly secured control of the provinces and cities of the lower Yangtse-kiang valley. By the time his National Government, established at Nanking, was fully in the saddle two years later,

General Chiang Kai-shek ruled more of China than any other administration since the fall of the Manchu dynasty.

Before this event an important development occurred; General Chiang Kai-shek broke with the Communists. Tension between the two wings of the combined parties, which increased as success crowned their military effort, reached such a pitch in 1927 that the Nationalist leader turned on his Communist allies with complete remorselessness. Accusing them of treachery, he executed or imprisoned large numbers and the remainder fled into the interior. General Chiang Kai-shek was now in undisputed command of the situation. During his march northwards he had strongly emphasized the nationalist character of his party; blatantly anti-foreign—and particularly anti-British—slogans aroused enthusiasm wherever the Kuomintang armies appeared. Britain was at this time the chief concessionaire in China through treaties obtained from the Manchu dynasty.

The year 1928 saw General Chiang Kai-shek with the ball at his feet. Now was his chance to put into force the third of Sun Yat-sen's principles, namely, reforms aimed at the economic security of the people—"the people's livelihood". True, his problems were immense, and in the teeth of tremendous difficulties an effort was made. Land reform laws were passed, but they were never carried out. Corruption and nepotism at party headquarters created a privileged class which soon wanted to maintain things as they were, with the result that the great mass of China's poverty stricken peasants was unaffected by the advent of the National Government. In short, the Chiang-Kai-shek régime became mainly a family concern—the "Soong dynasty" as it was dubbed—an oligarchy of vested interests instead of a democracy.

Far different was it with the Communists. Banished into the remote regions of Kiang-si province north of Canton, they launched a class war against the landlords in areas they controlled by confiscating their property and redistributing it to the poorer classes. As each district was reorganized in this fashion it was protected against Kuomintang authority by highly disciplined and skilfully led guerilla bands. The Communists retained a precarious hold on Kiang-si until increasing government pressure compelled them in

1934 to make one of the most remarkable treks in history—the "Long March" across the country to north-west China. Here they stayed with their headquarters at Yenan in Shensi province until they joined with the Kuomintang in the war against Japan, and finally emerged to sweep all before them in the civil war which followed.

Here also there rose to unchallenged leadership the massive figure of Mr. Mao Tse-tung. His triumph within the party did not mean a break with Russia, but it did signify the adaptation of Communism to Chinese conditions by methods most likely to appeal to the Chinese. The retreat from Kiang-si into another remote rural province and the success of Mr. Mao Tse-tung in the struggle for leadership were probably responsible for Marshal Stalin's long held view that the Chinese Communists were of no great consequence.

Meantime the Kuomintang was fighting a battle on two fronts. The early nineteen-thirties found it still waging war against the Communists while becoming more and more involved with Japan, which in 1931 invaded Manchuria, set up the puppet state of Manchukuo and began to treat China as a Japanese preserve. General Kai-shek devoted more of his energies to fighting the Communists than to resisting the Japanese, a policy which gave rise to growing indignation among his nationalist followers and particularly among the educated classes of the big cities. Force had to be used by the authorities to quell student demonstrations. But by the time the Japanese invaded China in 1937 Moscow had indicated its approval of a world-wide common front against the "fascist enemy", and for the second time the Kuomintang and the Communists joined hands in pursuit of a national policy.

Their co-operation continued until Japan's surrender to the Allies in 1945. But it left the Kuomintang in a far worse position than the Communists; driven by the Japanese out of the seaports and cities of the densely populated Yangtse valley to remote Chungking, the Kuomintang lost contact with the people. It came more and more to rely on the landlords of Schechwan province and on American aid. The Communists, on the other hand, seemed to thrive on the war against the Japanese; they extended their twin policy of "sovietizing" whatever territory fell to their power and of organizing the peasants in guerilla warfare.

Thus, when the war ended, the position of the two contestants for the control of China had radically altered. While the Kuomintang had atrophied, the Communists had expanded both their territory and their armed forces, the latter with munitions captured from the Japanese and with the covert help of Russia. Yet great things were expected of General Chiang Kai-shek on his return to Nanking; had he seized his opportunity he might have won the day. Unfortunately the Kuomintang was a spent force. It showed no vigorous leadership in any effort to redress economic grievances; instead it contributed to a rapidly worsening situation by uncontrolled inflation to keep its army in being. By 1947 even the American ambassador had to admit that the people were sick of the Nationalists. With characteristic astuteness Mr. Mao Tse-tung had meantime changed his tactics to meet new conditions. Less drastic schemes of land redistribution were adopted at an agrarian conference to please all but the bigger landlords.

When civil war again broke out in 1946 after the failure of General Marshall's mission to unite the rival parties, General Chiang Kai-shek was doomed from the start; the people had lost the will to support him. Even his last prop, that of nationalism, was undermined by his opponents. The Mao Tse-tung Communists proclaimed themselves to be the real Chinese nationalists by denouncing the Kuomintang as the hireling of a Western power. The military collapse of the Kuomintang was as swift as its rise to power twenty years earlier; as its fortunes waned, General Chiang Kai-shek stepped down from leadership while his successors tried to reach a compromise settlement with the Communists. When these attempts failed, as they were bound to do, he resumed charge of the remainder of the Nationalist armies in the south-east and eventually evacuated them to the island of Taiwan or Formosa, where he established his headquarters in Taipeh.

Conquest of Formosa was on Mr. Mao Tse-tung's programme for 1950, but the lack of a navy and air force, coupled with President Truman's order to the U.S. navy to neutralize the island because of Communist aggression in Korea, stopped all ideas of invasion. Peking, which became the capital of Communist China, obviously hoped that internal revolt would seal the fate of the Nationalists; in this it was disappointed. The Kuomintang Government, of which General Chiang Kai-shek had resumed the presidency, not only suppressed all efforts at revolt, but set about reforming itself, reorganizing its army and enforcing land measures which it had failed to implement on the mainland. Its offer to send troops to fight alongside the United Nations forces in Korea was refused, although at one difficult stage in the war many Americans looked longingly at General Chiang Kai-shek's idle divisions.

The present position is that General Chiang Kai-shek rules over Formosa as President of the Chinese "National Government" which, strange to relate, retains its seat on the General Assembly of the United Nations solely because of American insistence. Over the whole of the Chinese mainland the sway of the Communists is unchallenged; it has even been extended to remote Tibet, formerly under nominal Chinese suzerainty but now described officially as the "Tibet region of China". General Chiang Kai-shek hopes that at some future date, when the Chinese get sick of their Communist masters, he will stage a successful return to his native land; he claims to have a million men throughout the country ready to rise at his bidding. Of any such campaign there are no signs at present, nor as far as one can see.

This does not mean that the Chinese people as a whole are in love with Communism. They are in the hands of a group of resolute men —the "elite" necessary for every Communist coup—who are bent on imposing on them Communism as a state religion in place of outworn Confucianism. Following the example of Russia, Mr. Mao Tse-tung's motto is "Catch them young"; among the children the old Confucian idea of first loyalty to the head of the family is being replaced by first loyalty to the head of the state. The transformation is not without success. Mr. Frank Moraes,[1] editor of *The Times of India*, who visited China with the Indian cultural mission in 1952, records a British resident as saying: "If Mao's régime lasts another twenty years a generation will grow up which is completely Communist". Two years later the special correspondent of *The Times*[2] wrote: "indoctrination still captures the minds and enlists the

[1] *Report on Mao's China*, by Frank Moraes (The Macmillan Company, New York).
[2] *The Times*, October 6.

enthusiasm of youth. The girls especially seem responsive, and one might almost think Peking to be full of no one but earnest, pig-tailed adolescents".

The British resident's view is no doubt echoed by Mr. Mao Tse-tung, but in the meantime he has vast problems on his hands. Money must be squeezed out of a predominantly agricultural economy to pay for a vast corps of officials, a standing army of up to three million men, and the creation of heavy industries essential to re-armament and civilian requirements. In 1953 figures showed that food production was not up to standard and unemployment was increasing. A directive issued by the Central Committee of the Communist Party at the end of 1953 makes it clear that collectivization is considered the only solution, and that "a conflict among the rural areas" may be expected before the end is achieved. Realization of this fact and its possible dangerous consequences have since induced the Peking authorities to postpone collectivization. China's rapidly growing population constitutes the country's biggest internal problem.

Yet it would be wishful thinking for the West to imagine that the magnitude of the task facing China's Communist régime must necessarily bring about its downfall; Russia's experience, with all its strains and sufferings for the people, may be repeated in China. The coping stone of the vast monolithic structure governing the country was placed in position in September, 1954, when the newly elected All-China People's Congress adopted the new constitution in fifteen minutes. At its head is Chairman of the Central People's Government Council Mao Tse-tung. The next three key men are General Chu Teh, commander of the Chinese army, as vice-chairman; Mr. Liu Shao-chi, the party's leading theoretician, as chairman of the standing committee of the People's Congress, and Mr. Chou En-lai as prime minister and minister for foreign affairs. Supreme power rests in the hands of these four men who are, with the rest of the cumbrous government organization, in theory responsible to the People's Congress, which will meet once a year to rubber-stamp their decisions. The world faces the fact that in China Communism has triumphed, and at present shows no indication of relinquishing its hold.

*Chapter Six*

# DANGER IN INDONESIA

"I LEFT INDONESIA FEELING that the Government . . . still did not recognize that Indonesia was steadily plunging down into the kind of chaos which is no good to anybody but the Communists. . . . My general feeling about the future of Indonesia is one of gloom."

So said Sir Percival Griffiths,[1] a skilled observer, in an address to the East India Association (India, Pakistan and Burma) early in 1953. Unfortunately everything which has happened since then tends to confirm the speaker's pessimism. While the country awaits the long overdue general elections promised now in 1955—the first since the republic was founded—the Government depends on the support of the Communists to keep it in office, corruption is rampant, the services (civil and military) are riddled with intrigue, the economic situation is bad and law and order are unknown in parts of Java, Sumatra, the Celebes and the Moluccas. Unless the non-Communist parties are strengthened and regenerated by the general election, there is a distinct danger that in Indonesia, as in China, power will slip from the palsied hands of the nationalists into the grip of the Communists. One hopeful factor lies in the possibility that one of the bigger nationalist parties will secure sufficient support to enable it to rule independently of faction-ridden groups. The next few years will be acutely critical in the history of this multi-island state.

Indonesia and its sister island republic, the Philippines, constitute the south-eastern fringe of the Asian continent; they consist of an almost uninterrupted crescent-shaped string of islands stretching from the Pacific to the Indian Ocean. The Philippines are a relatively

[1] *Asian Review*, April, 1953 (East and West Ltd.).

compact group lying almost due south of Japan. Indonesia, on the other hand, straggles for nearly 3,000 miles and comprises about 3,000 islands, the biggest being Sumatra, Java, the former Dutch Borneo, the Celebes and the Moluccas.

In Java the republic possesses one of the richest in natural resources and most densely populated islands in the world; it contains more than half the nation's eighty million inhabitants. Together with New Guinea, the Dutch part of which is claimed by Indonesia, the islands form a screen between the mainland of Asia and the island continent of Australia. Their political future is therefore of considerable importance to both Australia and New Zealand.

Formerly known as the Netherlands East Indies, the "spice islands" which now comprise Indonesia were subject at one time to Hindu and Buddhist influence, but in the sixteenth and seventeenth centuries they came under the Islamic creed to such an extent that today about 90 per cent of the population is Muslim. Religion has therefore played a definite part in the growth of Indonesian nationalism and it still colours the republic's political outlook. Indeed, ever since Holland acquired possession of the islands through her adventurous merchant seamen from the sixteenth century onwards, there has always been a hard core of Muslim nationalism; it startled the Dutch after the first World War by demanding complete independence. The Dutch authorities dealt as drastically with that request as they did with other freedom movements up to the time of the Japanese occupation in 1942. When we contemplate the instability which afflicts Indonesian political life today we have to admit that part of this sad story is due to the character of Dutch colonial rule. There are other causes, among them the scattered nature of the islands, yet the legacy of European domination cannot be ignored.

Here we can legitimately point to the difference between the Dutch and British systems of colonial administration. Whatever its shortcomings, the declared policy of British rule in India was the eventual achievement of self-government by the Indian people themselves. It was an Englishman who founded the Indian National Congress, the great movement into which Mahatma Gandhi breathed the life of mass support. A government-sponsored system of higher education in numerous secondary schools and universities gave India a relatively small but highly influential middle class and intelligentsia, so much so that the problem of the "educated unemployed" became a pressing one. Successive Acts of Parliament conferred on Indians steadily increasing powers in legislatures and governments, culminating before the second World War in a constitution which set up autonomy in the provinces and dyarchy at the Centre. As the result of unofficial pressure in the legislatures, India's fiscal policy towards the end of British rule was framed strictly in accordance with Indian interests.

Dutch rule in Indonesia had many excellent characteristics—it prevented a land problem by restricting holdings and it conserved the village as an institution—but it did not provide an incentive to self-government or the machinery to achieve it on anything like the same scale as did the British *raj* in India. Leaders like President Soekarno and Vice-President Hatta were never given a chance to build up a mass supported nationalist movement on the lines of the Indian National Congress. Their activities were suppressed in the early nineteen-thirties, and they themselves were kept in prison until the Japanese occupation of the islands in 1942. Higher education was confined to a tiny fraction of the population, a practice which certainly avoided educated unemployment but deprived the country of that literate middle class on which democracy can be built. Furthermore, the Dutch displayed a marked tendency to keep business and commercial enterprise in their own hands, thereby creating economic discontent.

The net result was that when the Indonesians declared their independence on the Japanese surrender they had neither the experience nor the educated backing which the Indian sub-continent possessed, and the men who came to power were singularly ignorant of economic affairs. They belonged to a small professional class which regarded capitalism with a jaundiced eye as one of the manifestations of Western imperialism. This belief lies at the root of much of Indonesia's troubles.

As in most other Eastern countries the Communists formed a party in Indonesia soon after the end of the first World War. It spent the early years of its existence trying to capture the nationalist movement from the much older Islamic party; in the course of the struggle both came in for drastic repression at the hands of the Dutch authorities, and when the Communists attempted a revolution in 1926 it proved completely abortive owing to dissensions among the Communists themselves. Since then the party has been irrevocably split into two groups, the more orthodox describing the other—led by Mr. Tan Malaka—as Trotskyists.

During the Japanese occupation the Communists were entirely eclipsed by non-Communist nationalist groups. Leaders like President Soekarno and Dr. Hatta were released and were given every encouragement by the Japanese to build up a secular nationalist movement in return for support for the Japanese war effort. Undoubtedly they did help the Japanese to recruit forced labour and an Indonesian militia, but the contact they established with their own people—contact denied them by the Dutch—did much more to stimulate a really nationalist feeling than sympathy with Japanese aims. In fact, by the time the Japanese were compelled to surrender, Soekarno and Hatta had organized a following which was as anti-Japanese as it was anti-Dutch. That is why, in the interval between the end of the war and the arrival of the first Allied troops, the two leaders on August 17th, 1945, proclaimed Indonesian independence, backed by the Japanese-trained militia armed with weapons either acquired voluntarily from the Japanese or seized from them.

When British troops eventually landed to take over from the Japanese they found, much to their astonishment, a rudimentary indigenous government in being. True, its authority did not extend beyond Java and certain parts of Sumatra, but it could not be ignored and the British, who did not want to become involved in a war of independence, counselled the Netherlands Government to take the infant republic seriously and to negotiate with its leaders. First Dutch reactions were to denounce President Soekarno and his followers as Japanese puppets, but when the hard facts of the situation dawned on The Hague authorities they agreed to negotiate.

On two occasions during the long, involved and at times stormy dealings between the Dutch and their former East Indies subjects Dutch troops took "police action" which had unforeseen results. An attempt by the Dutch garrison in 1947 to force the issue led

President Soekarno to appeal to the United Nations for a settlement, and on the call of India and—oddly enough—of Australia the matter was referred to the Security Council. It was during the handling of the affair by a Security Council committee that the Dutch took even more drastic steps at the end of 1948. After prolonged and futile negotiations about the constitution of the proposed "United State of Indonesia", Dutch troops occupied Java and Sumatra and imprisoned the president, prime minister and other members of the republican government despite a cease fire order from the Security Council on Christmas Eve. Almost simultaneously guerilla warfare broke out all over the islands.

These events aroused much resentment throughout Asia, and especially in India which, having just achieved independence, emerged as the champion of all other Asian peoples seeking to throw off Western control. Mr. Jawaharlal Nehru, the Indian Premier, took the unusual step early in 1949 of inviting nineteen Asian, African and Pacific countries to a conference in New Delhi to discuss the Indonesian problem. The only country to refuse the invitation was Turkey; Australia sent a delegate and China, New Zealand, Nepal and Siam provided observers. The conference took the view that the Dutch action was a "flagrant breach" of the United Nations Charter and recommended a series of measures culminating in the complete transfer of power for the whole of Indonesia by January, 1950.

Another effect of the Dutch move was to alienate the British and Americans; with the powerful support of the United States and Britain the Security Council contrived a settlement on the lines of the Delhi recommendations. On December 27, 1949, Holland signed a treaty renouncing her sovereignty over the whole of her East Indies possessions with the exception of Western New Guinea —the fate of which was reserved for future consideration—in exchange for an Act of Union and certain economic concessions. Dr. Soekarno was elected first President and Dr. Hatta first Prime Minister of the United States of Indonesia, comprising sixteen states, territories and autonomous units.

But the federation did not last long. Before the end of the year the then republic of Indonesia (Java, Sumatra and Madura) had persuaded by pressure or otherwise the other much smaller units to accept unification, and the new unitary Republic of Indonesia came into being in 1950. One reason for the republican urge towards a unitary state was to prevent the development of fissiparous tendencies on the part of some of the autonomous units; the year 1950 saw a number of such movements, including "Turk" Westerling's revolt at Bandoeng and break-away revolts in Macassar and the South Moluccas. Negotiations with the Dutch to secure possession of Western New Guinea, known to the Indonesians as West Irian, failed completely; that territory is still in Dutch hands and remains one of President Soekarno's standing grievances against his former masters.

In the early stages of Indonesian self-government the Communists played a somewhat peculiar role. The Indonesian Communist Party (*Partai Komunis Indonesia* or PKI for short) was revived soon after the declaration of independence in 1945 and was joined by Indonesian Communists who had been in Holland in close association with the Netherlands Communist Party. That party took the view, as did the Dutch Government, that the republic was a Japanese-inspired conception and that the proper course was to reunite Holland and Indonesia. Personal contact with the nationalists in Indonesia quickly led the Indonesian Communists, who were flown out at government expense from Holland, to change their views; some joined the Socialists but all agreed on the principle of negotiations with Holland for a separate state.

As negotiations dragged on, circumstances altered. In 1947 the Cominform announced its new policy of dividing the world into two *blocs* and called on all true Communists to attack the "aggressive capitalism" of America and the West; early the following year this revised gospel reached the Indonesian Communists through their representatives who attended the so-called "South-East Asian Youth Conference" in Calcutta. In true Communist fashion they turned a political somersault; all previous agreements with the Dutch were denounced, and the party swung round to the hostile attitude adopted earlier by Tan Malaka's Trotskyists, who in 1946 had attempted to overthrow President Soekarno in favour of their leader. Nevertheless the split between the two Communist groups was not healed. The new Communist line caused a division in the

Socialist camp which some Communists had joined, and a section of the Socialists came directly under Communist influence.

Stimulated by an emissary from Moscow the reorganized Communist Party (PKI) decided in 1948 to attempt a *coup d'état* with the guerillas at its command, but the revolt went off at half cock and was swiftly suppressed by the republican government. Its leaders, most of whom perished, failed to appreciate the strength of nationalist feeling among the masses—a feeling of loyalty to President Soekarno and to the republic which he had proclaimed. After the collapse of the rebels, who received no support from Tan Malaka's strongly nationalist Trotskyists, the Prime Minister, Dr. Hatta, repeatedly proclaimed that he did not seek to suppress Communism as a doctrine but would resist any attempt to impose it upon the country by force. There is no doubt that the vigorous way in which the republican government dealt with the Communist revolt greatly impressed the United States of America and was largely responsible for the pressure which Washington brought to bear on the Dutch to grant independence to Indonesia after the second "police action". Another result of the Communist Party's ill-starred rebellion was the formation of the Proletarian Party which believes in Communism but not necessarily in being tied to the Kremlin; its attitude is distinctly Titoist.

Let us now turn to the events which brought the Communist Party (PKI) from its eclipse in 1948 to its key position in the government of the country six years later. Until the first general elections under the Indonesian constitution take place—they have been postponed till 1955—the Indonesian parliament will continue to be a nominated body of 218 members representing about twenty parties and groups. Seats are distributed according to the relative strength of the parties. The largest of these is the Indonesian Muslim League, known as the Masjumi, with an estimated membership of ten millions and a representation of 38 seats in parliament. The Masjumi is a highly complex organization which aims at the establishment of a state based on the tenets of Islam in much the same way as Pakistan was founded by Mr. Jinnah and the Indian Muslim League.

Yet it is far from being a purely theocratic party; its programme includes many items of social welfare such as minimum wages, maximum hours, accident and old-age allowances, and protection for the workers in regard to security of employment, health and housing. It aims at full employment by means of industrialization and has a close interest in the peasantry. In foreign policy the Masjumi stands for complete neutrality as between the United States of America and Russia and non-involvement in any war, cold or hot, owing to Indonesia's tender age as a nation. Up to 1953 the Masjumi participated in practically every Indonesian government, but in that year it was forced into opposition by the extreme jealousy of its rival, the Indonesian National Party (*Partai Nasional Indonesia*, or PNI for short).

The National Party, with 37 deputies in parliament compared with the Masjumi's 38, is the lineal successor of the pre-war party of the same name founded and led by President Soekarno. Once the largest party in Indonesia, it now ranks as second in size; it is the party of the small middle class and in its secular outlook has many points of semblance to the Indian National Congress. It draws its strength from the influence which its civil servant members exercise over the illiterate peasantry. Ideologically, according to Mr. David Ingber,[1] it is left of centre, and though by no means Marxist it follows a Socialist line in home affairs, advocating higher output, state ownership of vital industries and agrarian reform. In foreign affairs the PNI holds much the same views as the Masjumi, with a distinct leaning towards India. Also like the Masjumi, it stands for the incorporation in the republic of Dutch New Guinea.

Of the many left wing groups the biggest is the Indonesian Socialist Party (*Partai Socialis Indonesia*, or PSI for short) with sixteen members in parliament. Like the British Labour Party it advocates the welfare state; its leader is Mr. Soetan Sjahrir, who played a prominent part in the independence movement. Associated with him at one time was another well-known revolutionary figure, Mr. Amir Sjarifuddin, whose more leftist followers broke away in 1948 and formed another group; Sjarifuddin himself was killed in the 1948 rebellion, but the party lives on. Apart from the Communist parties, which include the PKI and Mr. Tan Malaka's supporters, there is a whole series of smaller groups ranging from left wing Muslims to splinter Communists.

[1] *Eastern World*, January, 1954.

This plethora of parties has bedevilled parliamentary rule in Indonesia ever since the foundation of the republic; as in France, governments have toppled with painful regularity owing to the changing character of uneasy coalitions. Until 1953 the Communists had little influence in Parliament; as recently as 1951 they were under suspicion of promoting what the then Prime Minister described as a "foreign supported conspiratorial movement" to assassinate President Soekarno, Dr. Hatta and members of the government. Nevertheless the strength of the Indonesian Communist Party (PKI) continued to grow for two good reasons. Firstly, in accordance with the declared policy of the republic, no restrictions were placed on its peaceful propaganda activities in disturbed areas, a privilege which it exploited to the full. Secondly, its control of the All-Indonesia Federation of Labour (SOBSI) gave it the unique opportunity of spreading Communism among the working classes. In Sir Percival Griffiths' words: "The Communists are not going in for violence; they are carrying on slow, peaceful and highly intelligent infiltration amongst the labour forces of the great plantations in Java and to a lesser extent in Sumatra".

These conditions prevailed in 1952; since then the position of the Communists has become much stronger. The last government in which the two biggest political parties, the Masjumi and the Nationalists, co-operated was forced to resign in the middle of 1953 owing to a dispute over the resettlement of squatters in North Sumatra. After two months of manœuvring there was set up a government headed by Dr. Ali Sastroamidjojo of the National Party—the defection of whose members caused the earlier crisis—and composed of a strange assortment of small groups, including the Communist Party with its sixteen valuable seats. The Masjumi and the Socialist Party were excluded from office.

Why did the Nationalists adopt the extraordinary and, to them, highly dangerous course of allying themselves with the Communists? The primary reason was undoubtedly their desire to prepare for a victory over the Masjumi in the general elections scheduled to take place in 1955. Both the National Party and the Masjumi depend on the acquisition of mass support through government officials, the one through secular officials and the other through religious teachers. With the Masjumi in the political wilderness the Nationalists can strengthen and expand their influence by means of every conceivable government agency, and they are prepared to pay the price of Communist support to keep their rivals out. Naturally the Communists are making full use of their opportunities; they have a free hand in the propaganda field, which includes government departments, and hammer and sickle signs are appearing in the villages. An Indonesian embassy has been opened in Moscow. President Soekarno acquiesced in the exclusion of the Masjumi because, it is believed, he fears that the party's triumph would mean the end of Indonesia as a secular state.

But this is not the sole aspect of the rot which is paralysing Indonesia. In 1952 the then Defence Minister, the Sultan of Jogjakarta, introduced measures to reduce the cost of the army which amounts to something like 40 per cent of the state budget. There was much need for this step, since the army consists of about a quarter of a million men, mostly ex-guerillas. The Sultan proposed to replace them with a small, well trained, well equipped defence force. Dr. Wilopo's Nationalist and Masjumi coalition then in power supported the move, but the ex-guerillas had their friends and the army became involved in a series of demonstrations and counter-demonstrations, including a riot in Jakarta (the capital, formerly Batavia) in which the protagonists of modernization cowed the legislators by smashing their chairs and demanding parliament's replacement by an elected body; the incident is remembered as the "Seventeenth October Affair". In the end the defence minister resigned and the reforms scheme was dropped.

But worse was to follow. When the Nationalists and their Communist allies took over power in 1953 the defence portfolio went to Iwa Kusuma Sumantri, who had spent two years in prison as one of the leaders of the Tan Malaka Communist revolt in 1946. The story of Sumantri's activities since he assumed office is told in an article in the *Manchester Guardian*[1] from a special correspondent in Jakarta. He first got rid of the young and able Major-General Simatupang, the Armed Forces Chief of Staff, by abolishing the Chiefs of Staff Committee. After that he proceeded to make army

[1] *Manchester Guardian*, June 23, 1954.

promotions of a highly political character, and the danger is that he may honeycomb the armed forces of the republic with Communist sympathizers. The moral is plain: if the Communists have the support of the army, or a substantial part of it, in any future revolt their success would be assured.

In the sphere of internal security the situation is equally depressing. Four areas of the republic are subject to disturbances; the Atjeh district of North Sumatra, the South Celebes, West and Central Java and the Moluccas. One of the most seriously affected areas is West Java, where for years the *Dar-ul-Islam* (Islamic State) movement has held sway. Its leaders are a group of religious zealots who are trying to put into practice the concept of a state on strictly Muslim lines. They have set up their own government, civil service and army, and they control an area which they are constantly attempting to enlarge. Recently they were joined by a large number of bandits from East Java, with the result that over a considerable portion of the island the writ of the Jakarta Government does not run. Another badly disturbed region is the Molucca islands, where a "South Moluccas republic" is demanding independence. The Indonesian Government declared a state of war in some islands of the group early in 1955. Nor is the feeling of insecurity confined to regions where security does not exist. It is partly economic, and partly due to disillusionment after five years of self-rule. "At present everyone in Indonesia lives on borrowed money. There hardly is a lower official without big debts or a higher one who is not a partner in some deal, no-one who does not on pay day try to change his rupiahs into foreign currency".[1]

After the signing of Indonesia's treaty of independence in 1950 the new state benefited by a "special project" loan of $100 million from the United States Export-Import Bank, Marshall aid worth $61 million and a Dutch loan and credit of 280 million florins. Under the Economic Co-operation Administration Indonesia received economic and technical assistance, but when E.C.A. was replaced by the Mutual Security Agency in 1951 the government which signed the M.S.A. agreement had to resign. American friendship is wanted

[1] "Disillusion in Indonesia," by a Diplomatic Correspondent (*Eastern World*, January, 1954).

less than ever by the Sastroamidjojo Government, and any help which smells of strings is anathema. Bad management has reduced the country to financial straits; there is no reparations agreement with Japan and money acquired during the Korea war boom in war materials was squandered on ambitious projects.

All these dismal facts, coupled with the freedom enjoyed by the Communists to strengthen their hold on every facet of Indonesian life, carry their own tale. Yet there are many Indonesians—and they are to be found both inside and outside the National Party which is responsible for the present "unholy alliance"—who honestly believe indigenous Communists to be innocent lambs compared to those who would link them in any way with the West. That is Asia's blind spot. Meanwhile the Communists in Indonesia wait, with one eye on China and what is happening in Indo-China. Incidentally, both President Soekarno and his Prime Minister are worried about the two million Chinese among Indonesia's eighty million people. Past governments took steps to restrict Chinese immigration, and the present government took up with Peking the future status and political allegiance of this important foreign element. Early in 1955 an agreement, regarded by Indonesia as satisfactory, was reached between the two countries.

There is always the danger in Indonesia that either a right wing (as in Egypt) or a left wing (as in China) group may seize power. If, on the other hand, nothing interferes with the holding of the general elections, there may emerge a national party strong enough to put the country on its feet and give it the government it deserves. The close affinity hitherto shown between Indonesia and the Colombo Plan countries encourages that hope.

*Chapter Seven*

# PHILIPPINES MAKE HEADWAY

IT IS A RELIEF to turn from Indonesia to its northern island neighbour, the Philippines. Here the national government, under a vigorous president elected in 1953, is clearly making headway in its efforts to stabilize the national economy, to redress the grievances of the peasants and to restore internal order. The Philippine islands have suffered for the last half century from most of the ills that beset an eastern country under Western control. This is all the more surprising in view of the fact that wardenship was vested in the United States of America, the country which achieved its own freedom from colonial status and which has always criticized—often harshly—the colonialism and imperialism of other Western powers. It was an American[1] who said: "During the period of United States rule from 1900 to 1946 it is doubtful whether the living standards of the peasants and agricultural labourers registered any marked improvement over the miserable condition of nineteenth-century Spanish rule".

The Philippines, in short, went through the usual experiences of countries in a similar state—a marked expansion of trade which benefited the small new middle class but not the bulk of the peasantry, collaboration with the Japanese during the occupation, and a Communist-led revolt which is only now being controlled. There is a set pattern about these former Western possessions despite the different character of their colonial régimes.

Like Indonesia, the Philippine republic is an archipelago; it comprises over 7,000 islands with a population of about twenty millions. Discovered by Magellan in 1521, they were annexed by Spain in 1569 and were named after the Spanish king Philip II. For most of the three and a half centuries of Spanish occupation the Filipinos

[1] Mr. Daniel Thorner in *Foreign Policy Reports* (April, 1950).

were in revolt; the rebellion which was in progress shortly before the islands were taken over from Spain by the Americans has been described as the first full scale national rising against the West in East Asia in modern times. The insurgents of 1898 did, in fact, proclaim the country a provisional republic independent of Spain. In the circumstances they did not accept their change of masters peacefully. For three years after the Americans annexed the Philippines in 1899 the nationalists conducted a guerilla campaign which had to be forcibly suppressed.

Once this phase was over, however, the Americans—like the British in India, but with greater speed—took steps to associate the people of the Philippines with the administration of the country both in the legislatures and in the civil service. During the first World War autonomy was granted under the Jones Act to a legislature with a senate of 24 members and a house of representatives of 92, subject to the supervisory and controlling powers of the Governor-General. This system of tutelage continued until 1934 when, in response to the growing Filipino demand for freedom, the Tydings-McDuffie Act created a Philippines Commonwealth with a single chamber government headed by an elected president. Independence was not, however, complete; legislation affecting currency, trade and immigration required the assent of the President of the United States, whose High Commissioner supervised Philippines finances. Financial supervision was held to be necessary in view of the recurring monetary crises of the previous constitution. Full responsible government was promised after a decade, a pledge which was fulfilled in 1946 following the defeat of Japan.

These successive steps towards freedom owed much to a fiery Filipino patriot called Manuel Luis Quezon. A lieutenant in the insurgent forces which fought the Americans for three years, Mr. Quezon decided to co-operate with the new rulers. He had a hand in shaping both the Jones Act and the Tydings-McDuffie Act; he was elected President of the Philippines Commonwealth in 1935, and only his death while head of a government in exile in 1944 prevented him from being the first President of the Philippines Republic two years later.

From the earliest days of the American occupation the economy of the Philippines was tied very closely to that of the United States; in fact the link was tighter than that between France and Indo-China. The islands were brought within the American tariff system in 1909, and the resultant free trade between the two countries rendered the Philippines almost entirely dependent on the United States. The character of Philippines economy was inevitably shaped by United States tariff policy; as Professor MacMahon Ball[1] points out, there grew up a group of United States traders and investors who benefited by that policy and who had influence in Washington. In 1947, for example, the Philippines constitution was amended to give United States citizens and capital the same rights as those enjoyed by Filipinos until 1974. These rights recall the trading concessions which the Dutch secured from the Indonesian republic in the independence treaty of 1949.

The American way of life was certainly exported to the Philippines, but it did not get beyond a small upper crust, and Mr. Francis B. Sayre, who was appointed High Commissioner in 1939 to prepare the Philippines for independence, bluntly stated: "The bulk of the newly created income has gone to the government, to landlords and to urban areas and has served but little to ameliorate the living conditions among the all but feudal peasantry and tenantry . . . the gap between the mass of the population and the small governing class has broadened and social unrest has reached disturbing proportions.

The same conditions persisted after independence; inefficiency and corruption were widespread, the government seemed unable to manage its finances, and a Communist-led armed peasant revolt defied all efforts at suppression. As recently as 1953 a Western commentator[2] described the Philippines as being in the thick of the battle for survival. "Agrarian disorders and an infamous election revealed that the Islands are far from secure as a bastion of democracy."

It is necessary to stress these conditions because they help to explain the struggle between nationalism and Communism which

[1] *Nationalism and Communism in East Asia*, by Professor W. MacMahon Ball (Melbourne University Press).

[2] "Manuel Luis Quezon: An Appraisal," by Alan Edmond Kent (*Asian Review*, April, 1953).

followed the grant of independence. Communism found its expression in the Hukbalahap revolt which began in 1942 during the Japanese occupation; the word "Hukbalahap" is a contraction meaning "The People's Liberation Army". Its leaders, chief among whom was Luis Taruc, conducted guerilla warfare against the Japanese as did similar nationalist and Communist bodies in other Far Eastern occupied countries. On the return of the American forces to the Philippines the Hukbalahaps, who were strong in central and south-eastern Luzon, the most northerly of the islands, asked for recognition and for the retention of their arms. General MacArthur flatly refused their request.

For a time the Hukbalahap leaders took part in political life and Taruc was elected to the legislature, but when President Roxas, who had been a collaborator with the Japanese, declined to allow him to take his seat after the 1946 elections he reverted to open rebellion. His strength and that of his fellow leaders lay in the legitimate grievances of the peasantry, who may not have been Communists but were prepared, like peasants elsewhere, to follow those who stood for agrarian reform. Their spokesmen said they hoped that the return of the Americans would mean a new era of social and economic justice, but when General MacArthur restored the old order they lost faith in him and in the Americans. As a sign of their purpose the Hukbalahaps proclaimed their objective to be, among other things, the overthrow of the "American imperialists, feudal landlords and bourgeois compradors".

President Quirino tried in 1948 to win over the Hukbalahaps by promises of agrarian reform and an amnesty; Taruc accepted the amnesty but after receiving certain payments as a prospective member of the legislature he did not keep his bargain and returned to join his followers in the hills. In the following year the Hukbalahaps gained strength owing to the Communists' victory in China, the failure of President Quirino's land reforms policy and the general deterioration of the country's economic state caused by administrative inefficiency and corruption. By 1950 rebel activities became alarming; Hukbalahap raids reached the outskirts of Manila, the capital, and the fight against them had to be transferred from the police to the army.

At this stage the United States Government intervened. In view of the 2,000 million dollars in the form of assistance which Washington had paid to the Philippines since the end of the war, President Truman's Administration announced the appointment of an economic survey mission under Mr. D. W. Bell to consider the economic and financial problems of the country and to recommend remedial measures. The mission proposed a further grant of $250 million to help to implement a five year programme of economic development, including the improvement of agricultural methods, the redistribution of land and greater security for tenants, legislation to provide for a minimum wage and the right of workers to organize their own trade unions.

Thanks to the mission's plans, which were accepted by the Philippines Government, and the boom in raw materials caused by the Korean war, the economic situation improved. Simultaneously the new Defence Secretary, Mr. Ramon Magsaysay, introduced a new technique in dealing with the Hukbalahap rebellion which showed promising results. Strict orders were given to the troops not to antagonize the peasantry in the disturbed areas, and resettlement schemes were introduced to remedy their grievances. By the middle of 1952 Mr. Magsaysay was able to claim that the worst of the Hukbalahap revolt was over. The Government then turned their attention to Chinese merchants accused of supplying the Hukbalahaps with money and arms, and over three hundred of these alleged agents of the Chinese Communist Government were arrested.

On the strength of his policy in dealing with the Hukbalahaps Mr. Magsaysay was nominated by the Nationalist Party for the 1953 presidential election in opposition to President Quirino, the nominee of the Liberal Party. In the Philippines, as elsewhere in the Far East, personalities count for more than parties—there is very little difference in policy between the Philippine parties in any case—and Mr. Magsaysay won by a handsome majority. In his presidential address he said he intended to improve living conditions in neglected rural areas and those of labourers generally, to re-examine the land tenure system, and to ensure that development programmes helped to raise the standard of living. According to a commentator,[1] "It was

[1] *The Annual Register*, 1953 (Longmans, Green and Co.)

generally recognized that the elections had resulted in bringing to power a man who clearly intended to grapple resolutely with the great social and economic problems facing the country and whose record suggested that he had the ability and determination to succeed in this endeavour if anyone could."

The omens in 1954 were fairly good. By the middle of the year the Hukbalahap numbers had fallen considerably and Luis Taruc himself had surrendered to the authorities. His place was taken by a man called Jesus Lava, a well-known Filipino Communist, under whom the movement is still active. Other insurgents troubling the authorities are the Moros, who live in the small island of Jolo, south-west of Mindanao, and bandits who infest the province of Cavite, immediately south of Manila. But the complete disappearance of armed revolt will depend as much on remedial social measures as on successful police action; the key to the triumph of nationalism in the Philippines lies in social revolution. Much therefore depends on the way in which President Magsaysay's five-year plan of development and reform is implemented.

*Chapter Eight*

# BURMA'S TRIUMPH

THE EMERGENCE IN Burma of a nationalist government steadily increasing in strength is one of the miracles of South-East Asia. Separation from Britain was still not complete in 1947 when U Aung San, the youthful architect of Burma's independence, was murdered along with six of his fellow ministers. The régime of his religious-minded successor, U Nu, was beset for a period of years by the rebellions of Communists of various brands and of Communist sympathisers, by Karen nationalists and other groups like the Mons and the Arakanese who demanded autonomy, and by a section of the Chinese Kuomintang army which fled from China across the border of north-east Burma after the defeat of General Chiang Kai-shek. Only a few years ago the writ of the Rangoon Government barely extended outside the capital city, and the country looked like collapsing into a welter of fighting factions.

By 1954, however, the spokesman of a British trade mission to Burma was able to report that 90 per cent of the country was under the control of the Rangoon authorities, and that the Government might be expected to dispose of all rebels within a year. That may have been an optimistic forecast, since Burma's troubles are not yet over. Describing the parade of armed forces in Rangoon on January 4, 1954, to celebrate the sixth anniversary of Independence Day, a Burmese writer[1] said: "Presumably as soon as the parade dispersed, the troops were rushed to the Kengtung state up north where operations against the Chinese nationalist intruders have commenced again, or to the Tenassarim area where those Chinese troops have combined with Karen and Mon rebels against the government, or to the middle of Burma where the Communists are fighting their last-ditch battles. Presumably, the Seafires flew on

[1] "Stocktaking in Burma," by Maung Maung (*Eastern World*, February, 1954).

straight after saluting the President to combat assignments over rebel strongholds."

Yet the fact remains that Burman nationalism has triumphed over difficulties which at one time seemed insuperable. Despite Burma's decision in 1947 to leave the Commonwealth and to become "an independent sovereign republic to be known as the Union of Burma", she remains on terms of the closest friendship with Great Britain and the other Commonwealth countries of South-East Asia, her neighbours India, Pakistan and Ceylon. Indeed, those who met U Aung San during his visit to London are convinced that had the decision later taken to accommodate India as a republic within the Commonwealth then been mooted, U Aung San might have been able to persuade his followers to constitute Burma a Commonwealth member state.

It is fitting that the first Prime Minister of the Union of Burma should be a deeply religious man, since Burma's Buddhist monks, the *pongyis*, from the earliest days played a prominent part in the nationalist movement. Burma's history has always been stormy; the annexation of the country by Britain, which took place in three stages from 1826 to 1886, was directly due to the disorderly and lawless conditions then prevailing first in lower and then in upper Burma. Later Burma became a province of the Indian Empire, and those familiar with the Indian Legislative Assembly up to 1937 will remember the distinctive appearance and dress of the Burman members; they looked very different from the Indian members, variegated though the latter were. For the Burman is a Mongolian, the descendant of tribesmen who migrated from Western China and Tibet, whereas the Indian is of Aryan stock, with features indistinguishable from those of the Aryans of Europe.

The incorporation of Burma in the Indian Empire gave rise to conditions which led to a certain amount of ill feeling between the two countries and stimulated the growth of Burman nationalism. Always a happy easy-going people, the Burmans took little interest in commerce and industry; these strenuous occupations were looked after by the British, Indians and Chinese, with the result that the usual colonial pattern in East Asia manifested itself. The new-found wealth of the country from the exploitation of its natural resources, timber, oil and rice, became concentrated in foreign hands; while British business houses developed trade and industry, the hard-working Indian coolie, imported to do manual labour in the cities and ports, was followed by the South Indian *chettiars* or money-lenders, who established themselves as agricultural bankers. Before the last war there were over a million Indians in the country, and the *chettiars* owned about a quarter of the agricultural land in the thirteen principal rice growing districts. Not that the *chettiars* wanted to buy the land; they took it over, often much against their will, from impoverished peasants, particularly during the slump in the early nineteen-thirties.

Thus it happened that the first stirrings of Burman nationalism were directed against Indians. Buddhist monks, who began by promoting a revival of interest in the country's cultural and religious past as opposed to the utility type of education introduced by the British, which forced them into the background, were responsible for the founding after the first World War of the General Council of Buddhist Associations. The Council became the nucleus of a nationalist movement based on resentment against foreign domination of the country's political and economic life. Both *pongyis* and members of the Buddhist-flavoured Thakin Party, the nationalist group with which the present Prime Minister of Burma, formerly known as Thakin Nu, was connected, found supporters among the discontented peasants for policies with a strong Socialist bias. The *pongyi*-inspired rebellion of 1930 and the anti-Indian riots of 1938 were aimed primarily at Indian moneylenders, but were rooted in a desire to oust British rule and all forms of foreign control. A Communist party, formed as in other South-East Asia countries in the early nineteen-twenties, existed in Burma in pre-war days, but its thunder was largely stolen by the Marxist character of the Thakin Party's programme.

If the Burmans wanted to get rid of Indians in the economic sphere in their own country, they followed them with almost pathetic faith in the political field. The British plan of gradually introducing self-government in India applied to Burma, but when the British Government separated Burma from India under the 1937 Government of India Act, politically minded Burmans opposed the idea mainly from fear that separation would deprive them of the achievement along with India of full self-rule.

There was yet another fly in Burma's nationalist ointment. Of the country's population of roughly 17 millions a quarter are hill people with autonomous ambitions of their own. They include the Karens, who are scattered throughout central and southern Burma, the tribesmen of the Shan states in the north-east, the Chins and Kachins of the north, the Arakanese of the west, and the Mons of the Tenassarim peninsula in the far south. Although the Karens have spread far from their original habitat in the Karenni hills south of the Shan states, they have always maintained their separate identity, and Christian missionaries influenced them far more than their strongly pro-Buddhist compatriots. They were therefore generally more ready to co-operate with the British, especially in the armed forces. For this and other reasons ill feeling flared up during the Japanese occupation between Burmans and Karens, and developed in post-war years into a full-blooded civil war which is only now beginning to die down.

A great opportunity was missed by the British Government soon after the outbreak of war. Burman nationalists offered full co-operation in return for the promise of early dominion status; this offer was rejected. To my mind the rejection was a tragic mistake; had Britain made it clear to both India and Burma that their unqualified support in the struggle against Nazi aggression would lead to their recognition as self-governing members of the Commonwealth at the end of the war, Burma might still be in the Commonwealth and many unfortunate developments in India might have been avoided. To people like myself who lived in the East the trend of events was unmistakable; it was crystal clear that if the Commonwealth emerged victorious from the world upheaval nothing less then full freedom would satisfy countries like India, Burma and Ceylon. And so it proved. The pity of it is that they did not fight the war with that pledge to hearten and encourage them.

Burma's period of Japanese overlordship during the war was a bitter experience. When the Burman war offer was turned down the Thakin Party, like the Indian National Congress on an earlier occasion, declared for full independence, and its militant leader,

Aung San, escaped to Japan. He returned with the Japanese on the understanding that they would grant Burma full independence. This the Japanese nominally did in August, 1943, but presumably because Burma remained a front line area the Japanese military authorities never relaxed their grip. In no other "liberated" country except Malaya were relations between the Japanese and the local inhabitants worse. U Nu, who held ministerial rank in Dr. Ba Maw's puppet government, has told the full story of Burman humiliation in his book *Burma Under the Japanese*;[1] members of the so-called national government were treated with insolence and contempt.

Small wonder that there rapidly grew up, covertly encouraged by their leaders in the government, resistance groups like the Thakin Party which were combined under U Aung San in a body with the high-sounding title of the Anti-Fascist People's Freedom League. Once again the pattern of South-East Asian nationalism under the Japanese occupation was repeated; disgust with the spurious type of independence conferred by the "liberators" led to the organization of armed bands who found themselves in sympathy with the objects for which the Allies were fighting.

In Burma, therefore, we had the strange spectacle of U Aung San, who co-operated with the Japanese as the liberators of his country from the British, turning round to co-operate with the British as the liberators of his country from the Japanese! He was able to do this because Burma, unlike Malaya and other South-East Asian countries except the Philippines, was freed from the Japanese by invading Allied forces. From March, 1945, the support of U Aung San and his AFPFL was accepted by General (afterwards Field Marshal) Sir William Slim's famous Fourteenth Army, comprising British and Indian troops, which inflicted on the Japanese a decisive defeat.

With the restoration of civil government in Burma it soon became evident that the old conditions could not return. A British Government statement belatedly promised the country full dominion status and set up an Executive Council under a British Governor temporarily to carry on the administration pending arrangements for the new constitution. The political pace was, however, set not by politicians of the old school who again appeared on the scene, but by

[1] *Burma Under the Japanese*, by U. Nu (Macmillan).

young leaders of the U Aung San type drawn from the AFPFL. Behind the League stood the armed guerillas of U Aung San's Burmese Patriotic Force, which was originally raised by the Japanese and subsequently turned against them.

The AFPFL refused to join the Executive Council except on terms which would give the party an absolute majority; the British Government wisely bowed to the inevitable and at the end of 1946 the Council was reconstituted on a pre-war basis with the AFPFL and its associates in control. On the invitation of the British Prime Minister, Mr. Attlee, a Burman delegation headed by U Aung San visited London early the following year; an agreement was reached recognizing the Executive Council as an Interim Government on the dominion model and providing that Burma's future should be decided by a constituent assembly to be elected in April, 1947. Two members of the delegation, U Saw and Thakin Ba Sein, refused to sign the agreement on the grounds that it was Burma's right to declare herself independent. They left the Government and joined the Communists, who formed the chief opposition to the AFPFL along with another extreme left wing party led by the former collaborator, Dr. Ba Maw.

The AFPFL scored a decisive majority in the constituent assembly elections, securing 173 out of 210 seats, whereas the Communists captured only seven seats. U Nu, who was U Aung San's deputy in the AFPFL, became president of the constituent assembly, which on June 16, 1947, decided that Burma should be an independent republic outside the Commonwealth. But before the transfer of power could be effected Burma's future was gravely imperilled by one of the most shocking acts of violence in the country's stormy history. A gang of armed men burst into the building where U Aung San was sitting in conference with his cabinet and killed him along with six of his colleagues.

U Nu was providentially absent when this ghastly massacre occurred; he was immediately appointed head of the administration by the Governor, Sir Hubert Rance. With the AFPFL solidly behind him, U Nu took swift police action; U Saw, Dr. Ba Maw, and Thakin Ba Sein were arrested on suspicion and after trial U Saw was executed with eight fellow conspirators, the ninth having turned informer. It was left to U Nu, the playwright, poet and man of religion, to inaugurate the republic, which came into being on January 4, 1948. The new constitution was, appropriately enough, based on the Irish model of 1937; it consists of an elected president and two chambers, a chamber of nationalities or senate with a majority of representatives of non-Burman units such as the Karens and hill states, and a chamber of deputies or lower house twice the size of the senate.

The new republic started its career with the best wishes of the British Government, from which it agreed to accept a military mission, but it speedily ran into serious trouble at home. Although it embarked on a programme of nationalization in pursuance of the AFPFL policy of nationalizing "the principal economic resources and industries of the country", the Government's measures were not sufficiently radical to satisfy the Communists, who demanded expropriation instead of the modest compensation paid to the original owners—compensation which the Indian Government protested against as inadequate in the case of the *chettiar* landlords.

The Communists themselves were split into two factions, the Burma Communist Party (White Flag) and the Communist Party (Burma) (Red Flag) but they both obeyed the Cominform command, spread from the South-East Asian Communist conference at Calcutta in 1948, to come into the open against non-Communist governments which had friendly relations with the West. White Flag Communists seized control of a large part of the country between Rangoon and Mandalay; the Red Flags operated much farther south in the Irrawaddy delta. These revolts led to a split in the AFPFL; the People's Volunteer Organization broke away from the Government in sympathy with the Communists. In an attempt to restore unity U Nu leaned still farther to the left, emphasizing the Marxist nature of his programme and the establishment of economic relations with Russia. But his concessions failed to mollify the PVO, which opposed any collaboration with Britain and demanded an alliance with the Communists; a section of its members openly rebelled although they did not join either of the Communist armies. The PVO defection led to mutinies in the army at two centres.

A further complication arose over the Karens, who demanded

autonomy. The republican constitution provided for a Karen state on the lines of the semi-autonomous Shan and Kachin states, but it was difficult to define a Karen state since the two million Karens were spread throughout the Irrawaddy delta and along the Tenassarim coast. Similar demands, backed in some cases by force, were made by the Mons in Tenassarim and the Muslims of Arakan on the East Pakistan border.

For a time in 1949 it looked as if the infant Burman state could not survive. A widespread Karen revolt, in which the Karen members of the armed forces joined, flared up and achieved startling initial success. The rebels seized Meiktila and Mandalay in the north, and a string of important towns in central and lower Burma stretching from Bassein to Toungoo. Their gains, however, proved too extensive for them to hold, and finally they concentrated in the Sittang valley and the neighbouring Karenni district with their headquarters at Toungoo, where they proclaimed a Karen state. Meanwhile the Communists, aided by one section of the PVO wearing white bands—those with yellow bands remained loyal—established themselves in the central Irrawaddy region between Prome and Magwe; they occupied the Yenangyaung oilfields where they levied toll on the Burma Oil Company.

Yet out of this seemingly hopeless confusion the Rangoon Government contrived during the next few years to evolve some kind of order. They were aided by two important factors. Firstly, the various rebel groups did not combine; on the contrary, left wing forces frequently fought among themselves. Secondly, the Shan and Kachin states on the whole remained quiet, Shan tribesmen refusing all invitations to join the Karen rebellion. The result was that the Government troops were able to tackle the revolts piecemeal. They first made a determined drive against the Karens in the Sittang valley. Hampered by shortage of supplies, the rebels were expelled from the towns, including Toungoo, and retreated into the more remote regions of the Salween and Karenni.

By the end of 1950 the Government had restored communications between Rangoon and Mandalay, although for several years road, rail and river transport was liable to interruption by marauding Karens. In an effort to pacify the Karens U Nu's cabinet in 1951 introduced legislation to establish a Karen state, but as the area contemplated was limited to the Salween and Karenni districts, in which the rebels were already exercising authority, it did not arouse much enthusiasm. In 1954 Karen rebels were still active in the Salween valley and around Tenassarim, and were receiving help from Chinese Nationalist troops infesting the border regions from the Shan states southwards. Government forces were, however, slowly but surely gaining the upper hand. The inauguration by the President, Dr. Ba U, of the new Karen state in the same year gave rise to hopes that Karen armed resistance would gradually subside as the Karens were given freedom within the new state to manage their own affairs, leaving defence, foreign policy, taxation and communications to the central Government.

In dealing with the left wing rebellion along the Irrawaddy the Government troops were greatly helped by a conflict which broke out between the Communists and their PVO allies. In consequence, the PVO "white bands" surrendered in large numbers and the Communists lost the towns of Magwe and Prome in rapid succession, together with the Yenangyaung oilfields. These losses gravely weakened the Communists. In some areas the Karen rebels in the locality made common cause with them, but by the end of 1953 the Rangoon authorities were able to declare the Burma Communist Party and its associates to be unlawful bodies, thereby leaving their suppression mainly in the hands of the police. Fortunately for the Burma Government, the Communist revolt took place in an area far remote from the Chinese frontier; no question of direct aid from the Chinese Communists could therefore arise.

The Burma Government's difficulties in dealing with internal rebellion were most unfairly increased by the presence on Burmese soil of Chinese Nationalist troops. These unwelcome visitors crossed the border from Yunnan in 1949 to escape from the victorious Communists. After an abortive attempt to return to Yunnan they settled down in the Shan states and elsewhere along the frontier where they became little better than bandits, engaging in smuggling, living on the countryside, terrorizing the hill people and, incidentally, creating friction between the Burman and Chinese Governments.

In response to Burma's complaint, the Political Committee of the U.N. General Assembly passed a resolution condemning the presence of Kuomintang troops in Burma, and at a conference in Bangkok between representatives of Siam, Nationalist China and the United States of America—the Burman representative withdrew owing to the Kuomintang attitude—agreement was reached on the evacuation of 2,000 men and their families. The Burma Government regarded the arrangement as unsatisfactory on the ground that the number to be repatriated represented only a small fraction of the forces involved. Nevertheless they assisted the evacuation by providing a corridor to the Siamese border, and by the end of 1953 the operation as planned was complete. Yet, according to the Rangoon authorities, it left some 10,000 Kuomintang troops still in the country, and these men continued during 1954 to constitute a threat to internal peace not only by supporting the Karen rebels along the eastern frontier but by banditry and other forms of lawlessness. From the Government's point of view the chief bright spot was that by 1954 90 per cent of the country was estimated to be under official control.

In the purely constitutional field the Government's position remained unshaken. The AFPFL in 1952 secured the support of 180 members in a chamber of 233 in the first general election after the achievement of independence. U Nu's Government is therefore in power for another few years with an ill-assorted opposition consisting of groups ranging from the Burma Workers and Peasants Party, an avowedly Marxist organization run on constitutional lines, to the right wing Burma Union League. The secret of the Government's success is the backing which the Socialists, who constitute the dominant factor in the AFPFL, enjoy among the peasantry, and the determination with which it is trying to create a welfare state. In its efforts the Government has freely accepted Western aid, including a joint Commonwealth loan from Great Britain, India, Pakistan, Australia and Ceylon, considerable economic assistance from America, and help for many important development projects under the Colombo Plan.

Replying to critics who complained that he was selling the country to the West, U Nu declared that his Government would accept aid from any quarter without political conditions, thereby throwing on the opposition the onus of securing assistance from Russia or Communist China on the terms offered by the democracies. On these grounds his Government in 1953 informed America that no further aid from that country would be accepted after the completion of the projects in hand because of Washington's alleged sympathy with the Chinese Nationalist Forces still trespassing in Burma. Despite its pre-occupation with civil disorders the Government is pushing ahead with land nationalization, the nationalization of industries and public services, state partnership plans in conjunction with British interests in oil and mining, the *pyidawtha* or village welfare programme and a mass education movement.

While maintaining diplomatic relations with Russia and Communist China, for which the Socialists profess great respect, the Burma Government supported United Nations action in Korea, and it is characteristic of U Nu's abounding optimism that there was organized in Rangoon in 1953 the first session of the Asian Socialists' Conference, which Mr. Attlee attended, and in 1954 the Sixth Great Buddhist Council or *Sanayana*, which will spend the next two years revising the Buddhist scriptures.

Burma's relations with Great Britain are excellent. With the Commonwealth countries of Asia—India, Pakistan and Ceylon—and with Indonesia U Nu's Government works in the closest co-operation in foreign affairs. U Nu attended the South-East Asia Prime Ministers' Conference in Colombo on the eve of the Geneva talks on Indo-China in 1954. There is no doubt that the contacts he then established with Mr. Nehru, the Indian Prime Minister, were responsible for the visit which Mr. Chou En-lai, the Chinese Foreign Minister, paid to Rangoon after his meeting with Mr. Nehru in Delhi on his way back to China in June of that year. Like India, Burma is friendly with Communist China but has no use for Communism at home. Also like India, Burma is worried about the possible expansionist character of Chinese Communism and the profoundly unsettling effect it would have should it approach Burma's frontiers by way of Indo-China or infiltrate across the borders of Yunnan.

If Burma can be assured on that score, and if she can enforce complete internal peace, leaving no cancerous growths to attract outside attention, then her future is bright. Her economy, tied up as it is largely with the Commonwealth, is essentially sound in view of her valuable resources in rice, oil and teak. Despite the fact that she has refused to sign a peace treaty with Japan until her reparations claims are settled, Japanese commercial ties are returning and already substantial trade agreements with Tokio have been signed. Burma's debt to Britain has been liquidated and negotiations are in progress for a settlement of her debt to India. In every way, both politically and economically, the strongly nationalist Union of Burma is surmounting its teething troubles.

*Chapter Nine*

# A CONTINENT DIVIDES

STRETCHING FOR SOME 2,500 miles from north to south, dividing the Far East from the Middle East, lie three new member states of the Commonwealth of Nations—India, Pakistan and Ceylon. Between them they account for well over 400 million people, or more than a fifth of the world's population. They are unique in the sense that, after Britain handed over power, they became the first Asian countries voluntarily to agree to stay within the Commonwealth. The resulting gain to democracy was tremendous. Along with Burma, a former province of the old Indian Empire, Indonesia and the Philippines, the three Commonwealth countries form a massive new Asian democratic bloc.

The splitting up in 1947 of the former British Empire of India into two separate states, India and Pakistan, was due to the upsurge of nationalist forces which had lain dormant for centuries. It is a truism that British occupation unified the sub-continent for the first time in history; not even in the legendary days of the Buddhist emperor Asoka or during the Islamic Mogul empire was the whole country under one ruler. South India eluded both Asoka and Akhbar. India's main population, the Hindus, are an Aryan race who spilled over the Khyber Pass from central Asia and displaced the original inhabitants who were either Dravidian or Mongolian. Centuries later the sub-continent was again invaded from the north by a series of Muslim conquerors, the last of whom, Baber of Samarkand, founded the Mogul empire. The British Indian Empire was built on the ruins of the Mogul state, but the Moguls left their mark in a Muslim population which was never absorbed by Hinduism and which eventually insisted on breaking away from the Hindus when the British left. That happened in spite of strenuous last minute British efforts to keep the country united, and it bequeathed large minorities to both countries.

Apart from the tragedy attending partition, the peaceful transfer of power from Britain to the two new dominions in 1947, and the great goodwill which accompanied the change-over, were due to two important factors. The first was the promise, dating back well over a century, that Britain would eventually hand over control of India to its own people—a pledge slowly, sometimes uncertainly, but in the end surely implemented by successive stages of increasing association of the Indian people with their own governance. The second was the dominating influence of Mahatma Gandhi's creed of non-violence on the Indian nationalist movement. Other contributing causes were India's freedom from enemy occupation during the second World War, which prevented the distribution of arms to organized groups, and the magnificent loyalty of the services, particularly the Indian army, which on many battlefields proved itself to be one of the world's finest fighting machines.

Trade led the English to India just as it took the Dutch to Indonesia, but it was never the wish or intention of the early British traders to assume territorial responsibility. As in other parts of the East the Portuguese were first on the scene. In the sixteenth century they set up along the west coast a number of settlements of which Goa, Daman and Diu remain, much to the annoyance of the Indian Government whose requests for their inclusion in the Union have so far met with no success in Lisbon. The efforts of merger enthusiasts to "invade" the Portuguese enclaves in 1954 led almost to an international crisis before they died down. But the French provided a much more serious problem for the East India Company, incorporated for trading purposes under a charter granted by Queen Elizabeth I in 1600; hostilities between the two countries in Europe were reflected in minor wars in India, in which Indian troops raised, trained and armed by European officers, were employed by both sides. Eventually the French were driven out, leaving behind them, like the Portuguese, a number of small settlements which had all been handed back to India by 1954.

These struggles for supremacy were a direct result of the decay of the Mogul empire and the collapse of government throughout the sub-continent following Hindu revolts against the Muslim dynasty. Much against the wish of its directors, the East India Company was forced, in order to protect its factories and trading interests, to take over the administration of vast regions until it became first the dominant and then the paramount power in India. As the Company's territorial interests grew, Parliament intervened in the interests of administrative efficiency, appointing a Governor-General in Calcutta and later compelling the Company to close down its commercial activities and to administer its holdings in trust for the Crown.

Yet the keynote in "John Company" days was the view expressed in 1818 by the then Governor-General, Lord Hastings, who looked forward to a time "not far remote . . . when England will, on sound principles of policy, wish to relinquish domination which she has gradually and unintentionally assumed over this country". Events occurred which postponed that date; they were the Indian army mutiny of 1857 and the consequent assumption of complete responsibility for the government of India by the Crown. The tragedies and horrors of the mutiny poisoned relations between Britons and Indians for decades, and in the heyday of Victorian imperialism India was regarded more as the "brightest jewel in the British Crown" than as a fit subject for self-government.

Indian nationalism and the desire of the people for western democratic institutions undoubtedly owed much to Lord Macaulay's famous Minute of 1835 laying down a system of education for the country in the English language and on purely English lines. Lord Macaulay himself glimpsed something of the possible consequences of his policy; in an oft-quoted passage in his speech in Parliament he said that if the day when the Indian people should demand English institutions should ever come "it will be the proudest day in English history". As English education spread, there grew up a small intelligentsia which sought an increasing voice in the country's affairs. "When we have drunk at the fountain of Milton and Burke", an eloquent Indian friend said to me on one occasion, "how can you expect us to be satisfied with anything less than liberty?"

Appropriately enough, it was an Englishman, Allan Octavian Hume, a retired civil servant, who presided over the birth of the modern Indian nationalist movement by founding in 1885 the Indian National Congress. The process of increasingly associating

Indians with the administration, announced in Queen Victoria's proclamation of 1858, began with the nomination of Indians to the councils of the Viceroy and provincial governors. In 1909, under the Minto-Morley reforms, provincial councils were enlarged to contain non-official majorities, although power remained in official hands. Ten years later came a big step forward, preceded by a declaration that the aim of the British Government was the "progressive realization of responsible government in India as an integral part of the Empire". The Montagu-Chelmsford reforms, as they were called, provided for a system of dyarchy in the provinces; provincial governments included Indian ministers responsible to legislatures elected on a limited franchise. Simultaneously the central legislature was given an elected majority, although power still vested in the Viceroy and the British and Indian members of his executive council.

In 1937, after a Royal Commission and a historic Round Table Conference in London, there was put into effect the first part of an elaborate constitution which conferred autonomy on the provinces and dyarchy at the centre, with a federal government designed to include representative of the Indian states. These states, or "Indian India" as they were called to distinguish them from "British India", were the relics of feudal days and the break-up of the Mogul empire when Indian nobles—Hindu, Muslim and Sikh—seized or held on to large tracts of territory. Over a long period the East India Company and the British Government entered into treaties or agreements whereby the rulers were left in charge of their states so long as they recognized the paramountcy of the British Crown. At the time the British handed over power in 1947 there were no fewer than 562 Indian states of all shapes and sizes, ranging from Hyderabad and Kashmir, with areas the size of Great Britain, to parcels of land which an Indian maharaja once described as "little bigger than a back yard". In area the Indian states covered nearly half the country and accounted for about a third of the population.

They were a strange mixture; in some a Hindu maharaja ruled over a predominantly Muslim population as in Kashmir, or a Muslim dynasty held sway over a Hindu majority as in Hyderabad. These were factors which gave rise to, and are still causing in the case of Kashmir, a great deal of trouble. Generally speaking, the states were much more backward politically than the provinces of British India. Most of the rulers exercised autocratic powers, and it was their fears of what might happen to their position which made them nervous about joining the Indian federation, to which they had agreed in principle, thereby delaying until too late the second or centre part of the 1937 constitution. The outbreak of the second World War stopped all progress, and there was thus lost the opportunity of creating a federal united India in which the provinces and states would have worked together. Whether that consummation would have preserved the unity of the country is one of the big "ifs" of history; one can only regret that it was never given a chance. When freedom did come it arrived amid such a blaze of communal passions that partition was inevitable.

The object of this bald recital of events is to show that, with all its faults and delays, the underlying aim of British policy in India was the realization of self-government by the Indian people, and the long—to Indians unconscionably long—period of training in parliamentary methods of government undoubtedly made for stability once the pangs of partition were over. India's progress towards independence was not, however, achieved without severe pressure from the forces of nationalism, leading at times to violence. For some years after its foundation in 1885 the Indian National Congress pursued a policy of ventilating its grievances by bringing them to the notice of the authorities in friendly fashion. But after the turn of the century it adopted a much stronger nationalist attitude and control passed from the moderates to men who demanded *swaraj* (self-government) at the earliest possible opportunity.

It was this cry for *swaraj* which perturbed the politically-minded Muslims. Indian Muslims constituted about a quarter of the total population of India; they were descendants of the Muhammadan invaders from the north or of converted Hindus. So long as the British—the "third party"—remained in power the Muslims were sure of adequate treatment as a minority; they received representation in government institutions in strict conformity with their population figures. Would they, the Muslims asked, receive the same treatment under a predominantly Hindu administration? If educational qualifications were to be the criterion for government appointments in a self-governing India the Muslims had further cause for disquiet. Whereas the Hindus took full advantage of the secular education system introduced by the British, the Muslims adhered far too long to their own schools and colleges which paid too much attention to religious instruction and too little to training for a business or official life. So long as appointments were made on a population basis the Muslims were safe, but should merit alone be the test the Muslims, in view of their educational backwardness, would—so their leaders argued—suffer.

With these thoughts in mind a group of Muslim leaders in 1906 founded the Muslim League, which took its stand on separate electorates for Muslims and the allocation to Muslims in the legislatures of weightage, that is, seats in excess of the population ratio. At one stage the Congress agreed to separate electorates, which were incorporated in the Montagu-Chelmsford reforms, but the idea was generally abhorrent to the majority community and the most the Congress in later times would concede was the reservation of seats in the legislatures. Even on that issue no agreement could be found, and the refusal of a unity conference in 1928 to grant the Muslims one-third representation in the central legislature had an important result; it led to the estrangement from the Congress of the Muslim leader and ardent "home ruler" Mr. Mahomed Ali Jinnah, whose rise in the Muslim firmament subsequently became meteoric. For a few years after Mahatma Gandhi assumed control of the Congress in 1919 there was a brief honeymoon between the Congress and the Muslim League, but when that ended they pursued permanently divergent paths.

Mahatma Gandhi's asceticism and his insistence on the rights of the common man made a tremendous appeal to the Hindu masses. So did his methods of conducting political agitation, which included *satyagraha* or "soul force", a form of non-violent passive resistance to authority. Between the two wars the nationalist movement led by the Congress gathered great strength, and civil disobedience movements organized by Mahatma Gandhi in pursuit of *swaraj* caused the government much embarrassment. While the Congress was predominantly Hindu, it did contain members of all castes and creeds, including Muslims, and could, in effect, be properly described as a truly nationalist party. This fact, coupled with the divisions which beset the Muslims during the inter-war years, undoubtedly contributed to the Congress leaders' refusal to take the Muslim demands as seriously as they should have done.

The crisis came in 1937. Under the constitution which took effect that year the Congress secured control of eight out of India's eleven provinces, and proceeded to form exclusively Congress ministries. On behalf of the Muslim League, which had not done too well in the elections despite the separate electorates awarded by the British Prime Minister, Mr. Ramsay MacDonald, in default of Hindu-Muslim agreement, Mr. Jinnah demanded League representation in the cabinets of Congress-majority provinces. The Congress refused. Appeals were made to the provincial governors, who were enjoined by the constitution to see that minorities were as far as possible represented in the government, but the governors quite rightly pointed out that while their instructions mentioned "minorities" they did not specify that the minority representatives should belong to a particular political party. The Congress satisfied the letter of the law by appointing minority representatives who were Congress party members.

Seldom have I seen a man in such a towering passion as Mr. Jinnah when this decision was announced. In an interview which I had with him in Bombay, he declared that the Muslims would be much worse off than they ever were in the days of British rule, since in eight provinces they were to be permanently debarred from having a voice in the seat of authority; those who were supposed to represent them would be mere Congress "stooges". With flashing eyes and in strident tones he declared he would never accept these conditions, which were "a negation of democracy" and would "reduce the Muslims to another depressed class". So far as the Hindus were concerned—Mr. Jinnah always referred to the Congress as a "Hindu" body—he was finished, and the Muslims must make their own arrangements to protect themselves, their religion and their culture.

Deeply perturbed by what I had heard, I hastened to urge the idea of coalition cabinets on a prominent Congress leader. From him I had an explosion of another kind. "How can you", he demanded, "as a representative of the British people, who believe in democracy and the rule of the majority, suggest that the majority party in India should give up its inalienable right?" To do as the Muslim League leader suggested (he continued) would give him the power of veto in every Congress-majority province and would render constitutional government impossible. The suggestion, in short, was monstrous. In vain I argued that, while I agreed with the Congress in principle, it might be expedient to treat the start of provincial autonomy as a national emergency, and to have coalition governments to allay Muslim fears just as Britain had a coalition government during the 1914–18 war. The Congress leaders had made up their minds and there was to be no going back. Much can, of course, be said for the Congress point of view. For a thousand years the Hindus had not been masters in their own country, and one could understand their burning desire to exercise the right which democracy had conferred upon them. What they could not foresee was the ultimate result of their policy.

The die was cast. Mr. Jinnah adopted the "two nation" theory, namely, that the Hindus and Muslims were separate nations and that a separate Muslim state was the only solution. Poets, we are told, are the unacknowledged legislators of the world. The word "Pakistan", which means "the land of the pure" (in religion), was coined by the Muslim poet Sir Mahomed Iqbal in an address which he gave to the Muslim League in 1930. In those days it was a poet's dream, but in 1940, at Mr. Jinnah's request, it became the official policy of the Muslim League. The ideal which it enshrined seized the imagination of the Muslim masses. Crowds flocked to the League standard in all parts of the country.

On the outbreak of the second World War the British Government made the same mistake in India as they did in Burma. There was great sympathy for the Allied cause, and had the Indian people been plainly told that in return for their help in a world struggle they would be entitled to full dominionhood of their own devising at the end of hostilities their history might have taken a different turn. The British Government's first statement that dominion status was the logical goal of the constitution then in force roused no enthusiasm in either Congress or Muslim circles. The Congress demanded immediate action towards freedom, and when that was refused its provincial ministries resigned, their powers being taken over by the provincial governors with the aid of advisers.

As the war situation worsened, the British Government stepped up its offers which culminated in 1942 in the mission of Sir Stafford Cripps, who brought proposals promising full self-government at the end of the war and the immediate association of leaders of all parties with the Central Government. For various reasons both the Congress and the League rejected the offer. The Congress considered that, with the threat of Japanese invasion hanging over India, only a completely responsible Indian government could give the necessary lead to the country, while Mahatma Gandhi in characteristic fashion declared that the British should "leave India to God; if that is too much, then leave her to anarchy". On the call of the Mahatma the Congress adopted the famous "Quit India" resolution authorizing a general civil disobedience movement in support of the Congress demand; a few hours later all the chief Congress leaders were arrested and put in prison, where they remained until the danger of Japanese invasion from Burma had receded.

Meanwhile the Muslim League under Mr. Jinnah's guidance became increasingly insistent on a separate Muslim state. The League celebrated the resignation of the Congress provincial ministries as a "Day of Deliverance". League Muslims would have nothing to do with civil disobedience; on the contrary they supported the war effort, as did most of the Indian people. Indeed the way in which the country and its enormous volunteer army helped the Allies despite the incarceration of its Congress nationalist leaders constitutes one of the most remarkable episodes of the second World War.

After the war fresh efforts were made by the Viceroy, Lord Wavell, to bring the Congress and League together on an agreed scheme for self-government, but without success. Elections to the central and provincial legislatures confirmed the hold which both the chief contesting parties had on the electors; the Congress captured practically all the general seats while the League scored sweeping successes in the Muslim constituencies. As a last resort the

British Government in 1946 sent out a Cabinet mission consisting of Lord Pethick-Lawrence, Secretary of State for India in the Labour Government, Sir Stafford Cripps and Mr. A. V. (now Lord) Alexander. The mission produced an elaborate but ingenious three-tiered scheme which provided for a confederation at the top and, in the middle, federations of provinces or parts of provinces opting for association in either Muslim or non-Muslim groups. Although clumsy in outline, the Cabinet Mission's plan did at least ensure the unity of India, including the Indian states, and for a time both sides regarded it with favour, the Muslim League because it conceded the principle of Pakistan and the Congress for the reason that it avoided partition. But difficulties over the details of the scheme and of the interim government which was to precede it proved insuperable.

Faced with complete deadlock and with rapidly rising communal tension—there had been bloody communal riots in Bengal, Bihar and the United Provinces, while in the Punjab the Muslims and Sikhs were at one another's throats—the British Government in February, 1947, issued a dramatic statement: it said it would transfer power not later than June, 1948, either to India as a whole "or in some areas to the existing provincial governments or in such other way as may seem most reasonable and in the best interests of the Indian people". It was left to Lord Louis (afterwards Earl) Mountbatten, who succeeded Lord Wavell as Viceroy early in 1947, to give effect to this policy. The reasons for the Labour Government's drastic decision were clear. Britain had emerged from a world holocaust in which her life had been at stake; she had promised freedom to India and she had no intention of becoming involved in either an Indian civil war or a futile war of repression.

Lord Mountbatten's plan of handing over power to India and Pakistan as new members of the Commonwealth provided a simple constitutional way out of a difficult situation; in view of the dangerous state of communal feeling he hastened the process of division which in the circumstances was accepted by the Congress leaders, much to their sorrow, as inevitable. Could the subsequent communal carnage and the mass migrations in the Punjab have been avoided if longer notice of partition had been given and arrangements made for the employment of adequate troops as a neutral police force in the disturbed areas? There can never be a clear answer to that question. British troops alone were insufficient in numbers for the task, and in any case their employment might have been misunderstood. Lord Mountbatten has been blamed for rushing partition on the sub-continent without proper preparation. Yet he and his purely Indian interim government were in possession of all the facts then available; they knew the resources—civil and military—at their disposal to deal with a situation which was swiftly approaching civil war. Presumably in the light of these known facts Lord Mountbatten made his decision, which was accepted by his Indian colleagues. At least one distinguished and independent-minded Indian statesman, Mr. C. Rajagopalachari, later Governor-General of India, said that if Lord Mountbatten had not transferred power when he did, there might have been no power to transfer.[1] From a man of Mr. Rajagopalachari's stature that was a most significant admission.

The British left one legacy which gave rise to trouble—the Indian states. Paramountcy lapsed with the transfer of power, and the states, like the provinces, were expected to accede either to India or to Pakistan. For most of them the decision was easy; the main snags arose over the future of Hyderabad and Kashmir. In one of his lighter moments H.H. the Aga Khan, spiritual head of the Ismaili Muslim community in the sub-continent, said the obvious solution would be for the Nizam of Hyderabad and the Maharaja of Kashmir to exchange *gadis* (thrones); in this way each state would get a ruler of the same religion as the vast majority of his people. Left to himself the Nizam of Hyderabad, most of whose subjects were Hindus, would probably have come to an amicable agreement with the Government of India, within whose territory his state lay, but a group of his fanatical Muslim supporters prevented him from doing so until their régime was overthrown by armed Indian intervention.

Kashmir, on the other hand, proved a strange exception to the general rule. Although its people were predominantly Muslim they had for many years received support from the Indian National Congress, and particularly from Mr. Jawaharlal Nehru, the Indian

[1] *Mission With Mountbatten*, by Alan Campbell-Johnson (Robert Hale).

Prime Minister, himself of Kashmir stock, in their efforts to secure democratic rights from the ruling Hindu Dogra dynasty. When in 1947 Muslim raiders from the North-West Frontier province of Pakistan invaded Kashmir—nominally in support of a section of their co-religionists who had been maltreated by the Kashmir Government—the Maharaja hurriedly acceded to India and handed over authority to Shaikh Abdullah, the Muslim leader of the popular movement who, as an old friend of Mr. Nehru, agreed to work with the Union of India. Pakistan's bitterness over what Mr. Jinnah described as a "fraudulent" accession continues to poison the relations between the two countries.

*Chapter Ten*

# INDIA: DEMOCRACY'S TESTING GROUND IN ASIA

WITH ITS 360 MILLION inhabitants and its large and expanding industrial resources, the Union of India today occupies a key position not only in Asia but in the world. Its emergence as a nation after the second World War, at a time when China was divided and Japan was under Allied occupation, led many of its people to hail India as the leader of Asia in the new age. Events in China since 1950 have somewhat altered their outlook. Intelligent Indians now envisage their country as a testing ground for democracy in Asia just as China can be regarded as a testing ground for Communism.

That is indeed a true picture; on the outcome of the struggle depends the future of a large part of the human race. The issue was put succinctly in a Washington State Department report published after Mr. John Foster Dulles's visit to the East in 1953. "If democracy succeeds in India", concluded the report, "all of South Asia is buttressed; if it fails the outlook in Asia will be very bleak indeed." Mr. Dulles himself summed up the position by saying: "There is occurring between these two countries (India and China) a competition as to whether ways of freedom or police state methods can achieve better social progress. This competition affects directly 800 million people in these two countries. In the long run the outcome will affect all of humanity, including ourselves".

The welfare battle in India is on: democracy *versus* Communism. A prominent Indian newspaper editor put the matter bluntly to me when he said: "If we can provide economic security plus freedom for the common man we shall win, but time is an important factor". Fortunately for India the administration of the country is not at the mercy of factions, as in some other newly liberated Eastern nations; the Indian National Congress Government under Mr.

Jawaharlal Nehru is in undisputed control. With Western aid, free from any kind of strings, it is tackling its truly formidable task with courage, but its efforts to raise the general standard of living in a land of mass poverty are handicapped by the rapid rise in the population. Four million new mouths are added to the number to be fed each year; in the last decade India's population increased by the astonishing figure of 42 millions, or nearly as much as the total population of Great Britain. It is difficult for welfare schemes to keep pace with, let alone improve the status of, this colossal growth.

Closely watching the Government's efforts is a small but well organized Communist party which draws its main support from a number of rural areas and which, by a freak of electoral fortune, constitutes the strongest group in opposition to the Congress in the Central Legislature. That party is bound to grow if the Government's plans to raise the economic condition of the masses do not produce adequate results.

For India the vital problem of nationalism was solved at the Commonwealth Prime Ministers' Conference held in London in 1949. India and Pakistan achieved dominionhood in 1947 on the understanding that they would each devise their own form of constitution and themselves decide whether or not they would remain members of the Commonwealth. For twenty years the Indian National Congress had been committed to the goal of a sovereign independent state outside the Commonwealth, and it was evident that nothing less than a sovereign independent republic would satisfy the national aspirations of the politically conscious public. But the goodwill attending the voluntary transfer of power —no one who witnessed it can ever forget the rapturous reception accorded to Lord and Lady Mountbatten on August 16, 1947, and succeeding days—stimulated a desire to retain what Mr. Nehru called "some sort of link" with the Commonwealth without restricting India's freedom in any way.

A formula giving effect to this ideal was evolved in London at the 1949 Commonwealth Premiers' Conference when it was agreed that a member state could be a sovereign independent republic with its own president and yet recognize the King or Queen as the Head of the Commonwealth, "a symbol of the free association of its independent members". Following that decision, which created a remarkable precedent in Commonwealth history, the Indian Constituent Assembly approved the result of its three years' labours in one of the most detailed constitutions ever devised, and in January of the following year the republic was inaugurated amidst great rejoicings with the election of Dr. Rajendra Prasad, a veteran Congress leader, as its first President. The triumph of Indian nationalism was completed by the integration of all the Indian states (with the exception of Kashmir) which were constituted as states of the Union, chief commissioners' provinces or merged with adjoining states. This welding of India into homogeneous unity was the crowning achievement of the late Sardar Vallabhbhai Patel, who for many years controlled the Congress party machine with an iron hand.

The only potential threat to India's new-found unity exists in the clamour for linguistic states. In British days the provinces—or states as they are now called—were formed on grounds of expediency which at least had the advantage of associating in a political entity various groups of people. Today's demand is for the creation of states which embrace all those who speak one of India's many languages, and the Central Government has already been forced to concede the claims of the Telugu-speaking inhabitants of Madras, who were united in the state of Andhra in 1953. But the dangers of linguistic states are much more obvious to the Congress party in power than they were in the days when the Congress in opposition encouraged these linguistic units. The Government of India's aim is to build up Indian nationals; it is not in the country's interest to create states whose people will cultivate an intense form of provincialism leading to fissiparous tendencies. Yet the issue is one which causes a deep cleavage in the Congress ranks, all the more harmful because the Communists strongly support the demand for linguistic states. According to Mr. M. R. Masani,[1] the Communist theory is that "each linguistic unit constitutes a separate nationality and that India is in fact a multi-lingual and a multi-national State. The Communists therefore demand not merely a readjustment of boundaries, but also that each State should be given the right of self-

[1] *The Communist Party of India*, by M. R. Masani (Derek Verschoyle).

determination and even of secession, as they claim is the case in the U.S.S.R.".

The ascendancy of the Congress Party was demonstrated in the first general elections held under the new constitution in 1951–52. These elections established a landmark in democratic history; they involved 176 million electors who polled 107 million votes to elect nearly 4,000 representatives in the lower house of the federal legislature and 22 state assemblies. That the elections passed off peacefully was a great tribute to all concerned, particularly as three-quarters of the electorate were illiterate. In the federal lower house—the Lok Sabha—and in all except four state assemblies the Congress won an overall majority, and in the four state assemblies where it did not achieve complete success it emerged as the strongest single party.

Apart from the expected Congress victory, the elections showed several significant trends. The first was the complete failure of right-wing Hindu communal parties like the Hindu Mahasabha to attract a popular following. To one of these groups belonged a man who shocked India—and indeed the whole world—by the assassination of Mahatma Gandhi in 1948. Mahatma Gandhi's efforts to conciliate the Muslims had always enraged Hindu extremists, who stood for an undivided sub-continent under Hindu domination. After partition, which the Hindu communalists hotly resented, the Mahatma's practical concern for good relations with Pakistan and with India's Muslim population drove a Hindu fanatic from Poona to shoot him in Delhi. India's horrified reaction to the crime undoubtedly helped to discredit parties which had little to offer the public except a theocratic state and the conquest of Pakistan.

The second feature of the elections was the eclipse of the Socialists, who expected to provide the chief opposition, and their replacement as the second strongest party in the legislatures by the Communists and their allies. The Communists captured 27 seats in the central legislature out of a total of 489, and 182 seats in the state assemblies. Although the Socialists polled twice as many votes as the Communists, their votes were so widely spread that they won only 12 seats at the centre and 126 in the states. Communist success was achieved by concentrating on a few states like Travancore-Cochin, Madras,

Hyderabad and West Bengal, where they were helped by Congress dissensions and inefficiency, by stark poverty and pressure on the land in rural areas, and by active organization over a period of years.

The emergence of the Communists as the second largest party in the elections—small though their total figures were—surprised most people in view of their chequered and uninspiring record. Moscow-trained agents tried after the first World War to spread the Communist gospel in India as they did in other Asian countries, but their impact was insignificant owing to the dominating influence on the masses of Mahatma Gandhi, and popular preoccupation with the struggle between the Congress and the Muslim League. In an attempt to give effect to the Communist International resolution of 1928 demanding action against British "imperialism" and the "unmasking" of "reformist" leaders of the Gandhi type, India's Communist pioneers became involved in a trial for conspiracy which resulted in their imprisonment. It was not until 1933, when most of them were released, that the Communist Party of India came into being. Its leaders scored their first success by capturing one of the big trade union organizations.

Up to 1935 the Communists kept themselves apart from both the Indian National Congress and the Congress Socialist Party, regarding them as "bourgeois" institutions, but in that year—following a broad hint from the Communist International—they proposed a united front with the Socialists "in furtherance of common objectives". This move formed part of Moscow's anti-fascist policy. The Socialists foolishly accepted, with the result that for the next five years they were subjected to infiltration which penetrated even the Congress itself, as well as peasant and student movements. Since the Communist Party was still under a legal ban, its members made blatant use of the Socialists' organization to build up their own, and not until 1940 did the Socialists decide to expel their unwelcome guests and to sever all relations with them.

On the outbreak of war in Europe the Indian Communists faithfully followed Moscow's lead by denouncing it as an "imperialist" struggle; their attempts to cripple the war effort quickly led to the arrest and detention of their principal organizers. It took them some time to realize that, with the Nazi attack on Russia, the fight had miraculously changed from an "imperialist" to a "people's" war, but once they did so they promised Lord Linlithgow's Government full co-operation. On that assurance the Communist leaders were released, and for the first time for at least a decade the Communist Party achieved legal status. Its policy became strongly pro-war and as strongly anti-Congress; Mahatma Gandhi was accused of "pro-fascist" sympathies, and by the end of hostilities the party had completely alienated itself from the mass of the Indian people. Yet during its years of freedom it had managed to establish itself in some rural areas where economic conditions were at their worst.

Here again the familiar story of Communist success in the East was repeated. The Indian Communists made little impression on the industrial population of cities like Bombay and Calcutta, where Western-trained Marxists would naturally look for recruits; their appeal found its target among poverty-stricken peasants and landless labourers in remote districts of South India, Hyderabad state and Bengal. Sir Archibald Nye, the last British Governor of Madras, attributed Communist success in South India to the zeal and energy of young men of intelligence who conducted their own newspapers and who preached the creed of expropriating landlords and distributing their land to needy and hungry labourers—just as the Chinese Communists did. The breakdown of law and order in parts of Hyderabad state during the inconclusive negotiations between the Nizam and the Government of India gave the Communists a chance to put their theories into practice. Taking advantage of a peasant rising in the Telengana district near Hyderabad's eastern frontier with Madras, they set up a miniature Marxist state by taking over village organizations and employing armed guerilla forces to expropriate landlords by terrorist methods.

When India achieved independence the Communists, still under a cloud for their criticism of Congress leaders during the war, gave tepid support to the Nehru government. Soon, however, the voice of Moscow described the Congress as a "reactionary *bloc* of Indian imperialists, landowners and princes" which had made a deal with "Anglo-American imperialism and Indian reactionaries". The signal for action was given by the so-called South-East Asian Youth Conference which met in Calcutta in 1948 and was in reality a gathering of international Communist agents. There issued from the meeting a programme for insurrection and civil war which was carried, with dire results, to all the countries of South-East Asia. India's Communists duly received the message, dismissed their veteran leader, Mr. P. C. Joshi, for "right deviationism" and elected Mr. B. T. Ranadive to lead the fight.

Violence and strikes broke out in various parts of the country, particularly in the rural areas where the Communists had entrenched themselves. The result is best portrayed in Mr. Nehru's words to the Constituent Assembly in February, 1952: "the Communist party of India has, during the past year, adopted an attitude not only of open hostility to the Government, but one which can be described as open revolt. This policy has been given effect to intensively in certain limited areas of India and has resulted in violence, murders, arson and looting as well as acts of sabotage." Drastic measures were taken to deal with the trouble; in several states, including West Bengal and Madras, the Communist party was outlawed and after a bitter struggle law and order were restored in Telengana, where the Communists staged a full-blooded revolt.

Telengana was to be their Yenan. "The Communist party has decided now to wage war," declared one of their pamphlets, "come you all and join in this final struggle." Although the outside world heard little of the fighting, for several years disorders and bloodshed occurred on a far greater scale than those in Malaya. Over 2,500 people were murdered between the time the Communists entrenched themselves in Telengana in 1946 and the final suppression of the revolt in 1950. Guerilla bands waged wholesale war against the police, landlords, and anyone connected with authority, disrupted communications, and indulged in arson and looting. Only a clean sweep of the whole region by the military and police, involving the break-up of guerilla bands and thousands of arrests, brought the rebellion to an end. The attempt to organize an Indian Yenan in Hyderabad had failed, primarily because Indian nationalism was too strong to tolerate another creed.

Then followed another Communist somersault. Early in 1950 the Cominform issued a new directive to its Indian followers announcing that the path pursued in China by Mr. Mao Tse-tung—whose success by this time had made him a hero in Moscow's eyes—was the right one, and that they should unite all parties in a fight against "Anglo-American imperialism". The militant leader, Mr. Ranadive, was expelled for "adventurism", and the Communists returned to the paths of political gradualism in time to participate as a constitutional party in the general elections of 1951–52. Their unexpected success in the regions where they had dug themselves in led to the defeat in 1953 of the Congress coalition government in the South Indian state of Travancore-Cochin, where the Socialists combined with the Communists to overthrow the ministry. As the Socialists refused to join a coalition with the Communists, fresh elections were held in 1954 but the result was much the same, both Communists and Socialists increasing their numbers, while the Congress remained the strongest single party.

Now, however tolerant Mr. Nehru may be of Communists abroad, he has no use for them at home, and Congress Party headquarters made its influence felt in arranging a coalition which kept the Communists out of the ministry. The Central Government had also to intervene in the Patiala and East Punjab States Union (PEPSU) where paralysis of the administration following the indecisive result of the general election led to Communists seizing power in villages by means of their own *panchayats*. By suspending the constitution and applying President's rule in 1953 the authorities were able to clean up the mess before fresh elections the following year brought into power a stable government.

The strength of the Communists in some rural areas is a serious problem for the Congress administration. In the new state of Andhra the Communists constitute a considerable element. In Travancore-Cochin is found the not unusual combination in the East of educated Marxist theorists and an economically depressed agricultural community, the one preaching a sort of new religion to the other. An American research worker[1] records that the main cause of the Congress failure to win the 1954 election was the neglect of the previous Congress coalition "to take the necessary steps to resolve the two major problems facing the state: providing alternative

[1] "Agrarian Unrest and Reform in South India," by Thomas Shea (*Far Eastern Survey*, July, 1954).

employment for hundreds of thousands of under-employed agricultural labourers, and solving the food problem". The lesson for the Congress, at any rate, is plain.

Two policies are competing for acceptance among India's Communists today. One, known as the "Tactical Line", has the blessing of Moscow; the other, described as the "Andhra Thesis", is the product of a group of young extremists belonging to the new state of Andhra which was formerly part of Madras. The "Tactical Line" was evolved at Moscow in 1951 as the result of the visit of a composite delegation of Indian Communist leaders representing both wings of the party in India. It is therefore a compromise, but it lacks little in pungency on that account. Its main objectives are the "complete liquidation of feudalism, the distribution of all land held by feudal owners among the peasants and agricultural workers, and achievement of full national independence and freedom". These objectives, the document states, "cannot be realized by a peaceful, parliamentary way" but only through "the overthrow of the present Indian state and its replacement by a People's Democratic State".

How is this to be achieved? The "Tactical Line" concludes that the Chinese method of all-out warfare cannot be followed in India because there is no Yenan with a standing army at its back; Indian communications, being much superior to those of China, would "swiftly concentrate big forces against partisan areas", and above all the "geographical position of India is such that we cannot expect to have a friendly neighbouring state which can serve as a firm and powerful rear". Therefore the policy advocated is a combination of two basic factors—"the partisan war of the peasants and workers uprising in the cities". In other words, the peasants in presumably selected regions are to be organized for guerilla warfare, while the city workers are to assist by strikes and riots. As regards foreign policy, the "Tactical Line" recommends support for (Nehru) government policies which hamper "the plans of the warmongers", coupled with condemnation of the government for its failure to oppose American and British "imperialism and colonialism".

Very different is the approach to the problem of the Andhra Thesis. This demands immediate concentration on Enemy No. One which is "British imperialism" because of India's membership of the Commonwealth and the fact that "more than 80 per cent of the foreign capital in India belongs to the British". The war against "British imperialism" would presumably take the form of strikes and sabotage in factories and other concerns which are either British owned or have a percentage of British capital.

Both policies were hotly debated at the third congress of the Communist Party of India held at Madura in South India in December, 1953. The draft political resolution did attempt a compromise by expressing the need "to intensify the fight against British imperialism, for quitting the Commonwealth and for the confiscation of British capital", but apparently the concession did not satisfy the Andhra group led by Rajeshwar Rao, the author of the Andhra Thesis, and its supporters. When the resolution was put to the vote it was found that only about half of those present endorsed it, 87 delegates from Andhra and Bengal declaring their abstention.[1] The significant point about the congress is that the right wing of Indian Communism still looks to Moscow for guidance as expounded by Mr. Harry Pollitt, the British delegate, while the left wing is presumably more inclined towards Peking.

At the close of the Congress Mr. Pollitt had some sarcastic things to say about the lack of importance given to the American "menace". "It is the U.S.A. which is the chief aggressor preparing a third world war. This is a challenge to your party and mine. Both Britain and India hold the key to world peace. I am pleading for both our countries because we are vulnerable".[2] Mr. Pollitt was, in fact, pleading for the latest Soviet policy of professing friendship with Britain in order to drive a wedge between Britain and America.

It would be a mistake to regard the divisions shown at Madura as proof of Communist ineffectiveness in India. The party, however divided it may be on American *versus* British "imperialism" as the first enemy, is still a potential menace because it is swift to utilize peasants' and workers' grievances as a means of promoting Communism. The opportunities afforded it are, unhappily, bound to be many in a country where the social revolution is not yet complete.

[1] *The Communist Party of India*, by M. R. Masani (Derek Verschoyle).
[2] Ibid.

In a series of articles, the Delhi correspondent of *The Times*[1] instanced several cases where the Communists were recently able to intervene successfully in labour and salary disputes. "Given time—usually about 24 hours—the CPI can (in Calcutta) change a legitimate and peaceful industrial dispute into a bloody riot. ... In every instance the state government was inadequate in the face of efficient Communist organization, supported by educated unemployed. The school teachers' strike this February was a classic example of successful Communist exploitation of legitimate disputes. . . . The state government refused to treat with them, and concentrated the entire police force in front of Government House where the teachers were silently squatting. Then the CPI intervened; simultaneously rioting broke out in many widely dispersed points in the city. The police were helpless, and for a day Calcutta was given over to hooligans, who murdered six people. When the state government subsequently met most of the demands the CPI naturally claimed the credit, saying that while other methods failed their own techniques had a consistent record of success".

Apart from its overcrowded state, Calcutta is faced with another problem, that of the educated unemployed. Graduates are being turned out by the colleges far in excess of the capacity of the professions and industry to absorb them. Again to quote *The Times* Delhi correspondent, "Communist ruthlessness could appear to them to be the only solution for their poverty and hopelessness," and may change "the nationalist antipathy towards the CPI if democratic government as practised by the Congress Party is found wanting. Should this happen it would amount to a desertion of the intellectuals—a prerequisite for revolution".

That ruthlessness in solving problems can find favour in the rural areas as well as in the cities is claimed by the Communists to have been proved in Telengana, where Communist candidates scored majorities in the general elections despite the Communists' murderous record. If the peasants are given land, so the argument runs, they do not mind the methods by which it is procured. In the words of the late Mr. M. N. Roy, the well-known Indian left wing leader, "The Communist Party still remains the dark horse of the Indian

[1] *The Times*, September 11, 1954.

political situation. . . . Barring the Congress, it alone has an effective organized machinery which, according to Lenin's description, can combine legal and illegal activities. The numerical strength of the Communist Party may be anywhere between 15,000 and 50,000, but it is a cadre whose strength is not to be measured by the number of its members only". With its expanding membership and the moving of its headquarters to Delhi, the Communist Party of India has now assumed the aspects of a national, rather than a regional, organization.

All this should not blind us to the fact that India under its present rulers has probably done more to meet the challenge of poverty and want than any other newly freed country in Asia. The food problem has been at least temporarily solved, and in many states drastic land reforms have been carried out. Planning for social and economic regeneration began before the British left; now a whole series of massive schemes is in progress. These include India's own Five Year Plan, the Commonwealth-inspired and supported Colombo Plan, and direct help from America, the International Bank, private agencies like the Ford Foundation and outside countries such as Norway. The Indian Planning Commission's Five Year Plan, which was approved by the Union Parliament in 1950, involves a total outlay between 1951 and 1956 of something approaching Rs. 22,000 million (about £1,650 million). America agreed to contribute $50 million towards an Indo-American Technical Co-operation Fund, the main purpose of which is to raise agricultural efficiency and to increase food production by means of irrigation and fertilizers.

Among the major projects covered by all these plans are the Tungabadra dam, capable of irrigating 700,000 acres in Hyderabad and Madras; the huge multi-purpose Damodar valley project in West Bengal and Bihar; the Bhakra-Nangal irrigation scheme in West Punjab designed to irrigate over three million acres and to generate electric power for the cities of northern India, including Delhi; the Hirakud irrigation project in Orissa with an irrigation capacity of nearly two million acres; and the Mayurakshi canal system in West Bengal capable of eventually irrigating nearly a million acres. At the end of the Plan period these vast schemes, together with a host of smaller ones, are expected to irrigate 8½ million acres, with double that figure as the ultimate objective. Most of the projects combine the generation of electric power with irrigation. In addition, there is a big Community Development programme intended to benefit villages in selected areas which will gradually be extended. By 1956 it is hoped to raise the national income by 10 per cent and to have done much to solve the problem of feeding India's rapidly growing population. To achieve that goal experts suggest it will be necessary to double the present 48 million acres of irrigated land within the next fifteen to twenty years.

On a somewhat similar scale is the industrial development programme, which envisages an expenditure of over Rs. 3,000 million for the expansion of nearly fifty industries. Prominent among them are iron, steel and aluminium, while three large new oil refineries are to be set up—two in Bombay and one in Visakhapatnam—by American and British oil companies.

Admittedly, the Five Year Plan is behind schedule. With under two years to go expenditure had reached only the halfway mark, and in some cases less. Moreover, huge as the Five Year Plan projects are, they do not, as experience in regions under Communist influence shows, cover the countryside as a whole. The Planning Commission's next Five Year Plan, mooted in 1954, is intended to reach every village in the country. That is a truly ambitious aim. On the skill, efficiency and speed with which it is tackled will depend the political complexion of the central and state governments after the next general elections. In the words of the *Eastern Economist*,[1] "If the Congress takes its stand on mere stability or consolidation it will not, it seems, win against the leftist opposition indefinitely".

Two things would help. The first is birth control; according to the Government's own census experts the country cannot support a population of more than 450 millions, a figure likely to be reached by 1969 unless restrictions are imposed. The second is more capital, both local and foreign, for private industry and its encouragement by labour regulations which do not, as at present, tend to frighten those willing to try tentative expansion.

[1] Delhi, March 10, 1954.

*Chapter Eleven*

# TROUBLED PAKISTAN

If Mahatma Gandhi was the founder of the Indian nation, Pakistan, the most populous Muslim state in the world, owes its existence to Quaid-i-Azam Mohammad Ali Jinnah. The remarkable thing about Mr. Jinnah is that he could not be called a devout Muslim; he was a successful lawyer who lived in Bombay, who conducted a lucrative practice for some time before the Privy Council in London, and who wore Western clothes with an elegance which was the envy of many an Englishman.

No two great national leaders could have been more unlike one another than Gandhi and Jinnah. While the Mahatma walked about in a loin cloth and—if the weather justified it—a shawl, the Quaid-i-Azam's silk suits of Savile Row cut were equally famous. Not until he became the hero of the Muslim masses did Mr. Jinnah adopt more orthodox Indian Muslim dress. There was about him an air of intellectual arrogance which set him apart from other men. His colleagues on the Muslim League Council might be prime ministers of provinces, men of great weight and importance, but if they displeased Mr. Jinnah he would rate them like schoolboys and like schoolboys they wilted before him. He had neither Mahatma Gandhi's lively sense of humour nor his willingness to argue with all and sundry.

Yet if ever a man was in earnest about his mission in life it was Mohammed Ali Jinnah. Once he made up his mind about Pakistan he held on his course with an unswerving determination which was almost frightening. Those who were not with him he considered to be against him; he broke up the Punjab Unionist Party—the most successful example of Hindu-Muslim-Sikh political co-operation in India—because for him there was only one party in India and only one aim for that party. Quaid-i-Azam Jinnah wanted to include in

Pakistan all the provinces in which the Muslims had a majority, including the two largest, the Punjab and Bengal, where they had just a bare majority. Only thus, he argued, could Pakistan be a viable state. But in the inflamed state of communal feeling which existed in 1947 there never was any hope of provinces with a large Hindu minority becoming part of Pakistan; both Bengal and the Punjab were split up according to their population ratios. Even then the Muslims were so scattered throughout the sub-continent that about 30 millions of them remain in India, just as a large number of Hindus are domiciled in Pakistan—about 11 millions of them in East Bengal.

Pakistan's greatest weakness is its division into two isolated sections. West Pakistan, comprising Sind, Baluchistan, West Punjab and the North-West Frontier Province, lies over a thousand miles from East Pakistan, consisting of East Bengal and part of Assam. Although West Pakistan forms six-sevenths of the total area of the state it contains only three-sevenths of the population, or 35 million people out of a total of 77 millions. The difference becomes even more striking when we record a population density of 775 to the square mile in East Pakistan compared with 92 to the square mile in West Pakistan, a fact which accounts for many of the country's present difficulties. Nor does the disparity end there. The people of East Pakistan are Bengalis, speaking the Bengali tongue; they are almost a different race and have nothing in common with the Punjabis and frontier tribesmen except their religion.

Small wonder, therefore, that Pakistan has had a chequered history since it came into existence. Many people imagined that so strangely divided a nation could not possibly last for more than a few years, yet Pakistan despite its troubles has confounded its Jeremiahs. Its founder and first Governor-General, Quaid-i-Azam Jinnah, died about a year after he assumed office; his doughty lieutenant and successor, Mr. Liaquat Ali Khan, perished by an Afghan assassin's bullet in 1951. The Muslim League, all-powerful throughout the state on partition, became subject to personalities, factions and inter-provincial jealousies.

No highly organized Communist movement ever existed in Pakistan, but Communists have always been quick to take advantage of trouble and disorder whenever and wherever they occurred.

They first showed their hand in an extraordinary and unexpected plot against the state in 1951. Known as the Rawalpindi conspiracy case, the plot involved a number of senior officers of the Pakistan army, including the Chief of Staff, and the editor of a leading daily paper who was an avowed Communist. Later another Communist leader, known to be a dangerous man, was arrested for complicity. As the trial took place *in camera* the full details were never made public, but official statements showed that the prime movers were a clique of military officers whose object was to seize power—not an uncommon thing in some Muslim countries—and that they had been in contact with a "foreign power" to secure the necessary armed support. From the fact that their fellow conspirators were Communists it was easy to guess the identity of the "foreign power".

Communists were again concerned in a much graver crisis in West Punjab two years later. Trouble began during a severe economic depression with the demands by a group of *mullahs* (religious leaders) that the Ahmadiya community to which Chaudri Muhammad Zafrullah Khan, Pakistan's then Foreign Minister, belonged should be declared a minority community because its tenets were not in accordance with orthodox Islam. Disturbances broke out all over West Pakistan; the revolt against the Central Government—which has its headquarters in Karachi, the Pakistan capital—became really serious in West Punjab, where the provincial Premier unexpectedly announced the support of the local Muslim League for the agitators.

Fortunately the Karachi cabinet took strong action. Martial law was declared in Lahore and after some time order was restored, the provincial Premier being replaced by a more reliable leader. Obviously religious feelings alone could not have stirred up the disorders; the central authorities were firmly convinced that Communists had taken an active part in fomenting lawlessness in an effort to bring about the fall of an administration which was blamed for the economic hardships of the people. The subsequent dismissal by the Governor-General, Mr. Ghulam Mohammad, of Kwaja Nazimuddin, the Prime Minister, because his government "had proved entirely inadequate to grapple with the difficulties of the country" brought to the head of affairs in Pakistan Mr. Mohammad Ali, at that time his country's ambassador in Washington.

Mr. Mohammad Ali's firm and efficient handling of affairs soon produced a change for the better, but it did not prevent another shock in 1954. This sprang from the general election in East Pakistan, which had been delayed until long after elections had been held, and Muslim League ministries again returned, in West Pakistan. Meantime the Muslim League ministry in East Pakistan had fallen into disfavour. The people of this densely populated and isolated part of Pakistan fostered many grievances; they suffered from all the economic ills which afflict an Asian community when pressure on the land is acute. Moreover, they felt that they had never received fair treatment from the federal government despite their population preponderance in the state. Earlier, rioting had occurred in East Pakistan because of fears that the Constituent Assembly in Karachi was weighting representation against Bengal in the upper house of the proposed new constitution, and because of the decision—since dropped—to make Urdu the official language of Pakistan, thereby ignoring Bengali.

Ill feeling had also been generated over industrialization. Much needed new jute, paper and other factories in East Bengal owed their existence to West Pakistan capital and naturally attracted a considerable number of executives and staff from the north. These "foreigners" were disliked by the East Bengalis, especially as they annexed jobs which the local inhabitants coveted. When the elections took place early in 1954 the Muslim League candidates, who had lost touch with their constituents, found themselves opposed by a mass of left wing elements. Nominally the leader of the left "United Front" was Mr. A. K. Fazlul Huq of the Praja Party, a former prime minister of undivided Bengal, who was supported by Mr. H. S. Suhrawardy, but the largest group in the coalition, the East Bengal Awami-Muslim League, owed allegiance to Maulana Bashani, who had attended a Communist-inspired "peace congress" in East Germany.

Aided by extravagant promises, including the nationalization of the jute industry, and a whole string of grievances, the United Front inflicted a crushing defeat on the Muslim League. Soon after Mr.

Fazlul Huq formed his ministry trouble began. Bloody riots which shocked both East and West Pakistan occurred at several of the new factories; they were undoubtedly inspired by the "anti-foreign" feeling among Bengali workers but, according to reliable reports, casualties soared because the police were deliberately prevented by East Bengal Government representatives from protecting the "foreigners".

On May 30 the Central Government took drastic action. The Fazlul Huq ministry was dismissed, and Major-General Iskandar Mirza, the strong-minded and energetic defence secretary, was appointed Governor with special powers to restore normal conditions. In a broadcast to the nation Mr. Mohammad Ali, the Pakistan Prime Minister, described Mr. Huq as a "traitor" who had advocated independence for East Pakistan and whose administration had failed to deal with "disruptive forces and enemy agents" aiming at the overthrow of the province by "sabotaging and destroying its economic progress".

How far the Communists were involved in the disorders is not clear, but they were known to have incited rioters against the "foreigners" and to have taken part in other subversive activities. At any rate the Pakistan Government harboured no doubts on the subject; it outlawed the Communist Party in both East and West Pakistan as a "danger to public peace" and arrested most of its leaders. Yet strong measures against Communists and lawless elements will not alone solve East Pakistan's problem. Much will depend on the implementation of schemes for economic betterment which are now being undertaken by the Central authorities, and on the growth of better relations between the people of Pakistan's two halves.

Pakistan's existence as a nation has been coloured by its exceedingly bad relations with India over Kashmir and the Punjab canal waters. At the time of partition, the Maharaja of Jammu and Kashmir, the Hindu ruler of a predominantly Muslim population, postponed accession to either India or Pakistan, both of which the state adjoins, until his hand was forced early in 1948. Inflamed by reports of savage reprisals by the Maharaja's troops against Muslim malcontents in Poonch, a part of the state bordering on Pakistan, well organized raiders from the North-West Frontier Province swept into Kashmir by way of the Jhelum valley. Had they gone straight to Srinagar, the Kashmir capital, in their motor transport they would probably have overthrown the government before the outside world realized what was happening, but their progress towards Srinagar developed into the looting and slaughter usually associated with tribal raids. Panic-stricken, the Maharaja and his advisers hastily decided to accede to India in return for military help, which was flown to Srinagar in time to save the capital and to drive the invaders out of the Vale of Kashmir. But they were not ejected from parts of the state lying next to Pakistan, where they rallied Kashmiris who had suffered under the Maharaja's rule. In these areas, now described by their occupants as "Azad (Free) Kashmir", Pakistan eventually intervened with armed support to protect—according to Karachi—its own frontiers.

In trying to sort out the rights and wrongs of the Kashmir affair the impartial observer must note one significant fact. Had, for example, the Nizam of Hyderabad acceded to Pakistan his action would have been hotly resented by his Hindu subjects; the Maharaja of Kashmir's accession to India, on the other hand, found favour in the eyes of the largest political organization in the state, the National Conference Party led by Shaikh Abdullah. The reason is obvious; Shaikh Abdullah's party had always received the support of the Indian National Congress in its fight for political progress, and indeed regarded itself as the Congress of Kashmir.

Whether the party does in fact represent the wishes of the majority of the state's inhabitants is still in dispute, since the plebiscite suggested by the United Nations, to which India appealed against Pakistan "aggression", has not yet taken place. Both India and Pakistan agreed to a plebiscite after a cease fire was effected by the Security Council, but Mr. Nehru's government insisted that as Kashmir had legally acceded to India the plebiscite should be held under the present Kashmir Government assisted by Indian troops, and that all other troops should retire from parts of the state which they still occupy. The Security Council's proposal, which has Pakistan's acceptance, is that the plebiscite should be under completely neutral supervision. In these circumstances the deadlock continues.

The issue was further complicated in 1953 by the sudden downfall and arrest of Shaikh Abdullah. For some time Shaikh Abdullah's growing advocacy of an independent Kashmir had been creating indignation in India, and eventually it reached a pitch where the premier found himself in a minority in his own cabinet. He was thereupon dismissed by the Sardar-i-Riyasat, the head of the state, and replaced by Mr. Bakshi Ghulam Mahommed, who put him under detention. At the instance of the new prime minister the Kashmir Constituent Assembly in 1954 declared the state's accession to the Union of India as "final and irrevocable". Delhi's official reaction was that the declaration made no difference to the state's accession as implemented in 1947, but Mr. Nehru maintained that India would still stand by her "international commitments"—by which he presumably meant the result of a plebiscite—although in a letter to the Pakistan premier he expressed the view that one could not go completely by a plebiscite.

Any hope of an agreement between the two Prime Ministers, which seemed just faintly possible after Mr. Mohammad Ali took office, was dashed by Karachi's acceptance of American military aid. In the course of official correspondence which was published in October, 1954, Mr. Nehru alleged that U.S. military help to Pakistan was a new threat to India because "it brings in the intervention of a foreign power". Mr. Mohammad Ali's reply that American aid could have no bearing on the issue if demilitarization was accepted failed to move Mr. Nehru, and the correspondence closed with the Pakistan premier's conviction that no scope was left for further direct negotiations and that the case must revert to the Security Council.

The whole affair has created the greatest bitterness in Pakistan, which is convinced—rightly or wrongly—that a neutrally conducted and supervised plebiscite would show a substantial majority in Pakistan's favour. Pakistani anger over the dispute extends even to the British Government, which is accused of favouring India by not taking more vigorous steps to ensure the enforcement of the United Nations plebiscite scheme. One aspect of the Kashmir situation which may well cause disquiet elsewhere is the pronounced left wing trend of the Kashmir Government since Shaikh Abdullah was replaced by Mr. Bakshi Ghulam Mahommed. Mr. Ghulam Mahommed Sadiq, the president of the Constituent Assembly, is a Communist whose fulminations against "Anglo-American imperialists" were quoted approvingly in *Izvestia*, and he is not by any means the only one among Kashmir's present leaders. Another disturbing factor is Mr. Bakshi Ghulam Mahommed's insistence that, in view of the Constituent Assembly's decision to accede to India, a plebiscite is now unnecessary.

Pakistan's quarrel with India over Kashmir is purely political. Much more serious because it is a life and death matter for millions of people in both countries is the dispute about the canal waters of the Indus basin. Here again partition proved the cause of trouble. It left Pakistan with 18 million acres of irrigated land and India with 5 million acres, but as each country has roughly the same number of people dependent on irrigation in the basin India went ahead with projects to increase her supply. She could do so only by tapping rivers which passed through Indian territory on their way to Pakistan, where they also constitute a vital source of irrigation.

For two years World Bank experts, to whom the problem was referred, tried to evolve an agreed solution. Pakistan demanded more time and data to consider the Bank's proposals; India construed Pakistan's attitude as a refusal and decided to go ahead with her own schemes, relying on an agreement reached with her neighbour in 1948. Matters came to a head when Mr. Nehru in the middle of 1954 opened the great new Bhakra-Nangal irrigation project on the Sutlej. A temporary agreement has been patched up, but the World Bank is still seeking to achieve a permanent settlement.

Pakistan's economic history has been as chequered as its political record. The British Indian Empire was a balanced economic unit; partition gave Pakistan a mainly rural economy by awarding to India the great industrial cities. Pakistan inherited the wheat and cotton growing areas of Sind and the Punjab, and the jute and rice regions of East Bengal which produce about 80 per cent of the world's jute crop, while the jute mills of Calcutta went to India along with the chief coal and iron mines. For some years Pakistan prospered owing to high commodity prices, particularly during the Korean war, but when that ended the situation was sharply reversed.

In 1953, owing to two poor monsoons, reduced water supplies from India-controlled canals and the cultivation of cash instead of food crops, Pakistan faced both bankruptcy and starvation. Only the gift of a million tons of wheat from America and help from Britain and other Commonwealth nations saved the country. Pakistan's plight was not eased by a virtual Indo-Pakistan economic war following Karachi's refusal in 1949 to devalue its rupee to accord with devaluation in India and Britain.

Rural betterment projects are in progress to prevent another food crisis, including schemes under the Government's Six-Year Plan, the Colombo Plan and direct help from America. The Six-Year Plan, which envisages an expenditure of Rs. 2,600 million, was amended to include a priority programme for projects aimed at making Pakistan self-sufficient in its basic needs. Big irrigation schemes include the Thal project in the Punjab to irrigate two million acres, and the Lower Sind Barrage at Kotri designed to increase the cultivable area by two and a half million acres.

Pakistan's main task, however, is to redress its badly balanced economy. "No country with an economy as heavily agrarian as ours," said Mr. Mohammad Ali, "can hope to raise the living standard of its people unless a pronounced swing is made towards industrialization." To help to implement this policy the Government set up the Pakistan Industrial Development Corporation, which is promoting essential industries by cooperation with private enterprise under the Colombo Plan and other agencies. Jute, cotton, woollen, paper, cement and chemical factories are already in operation or under construction; steel and coal production is being increased, and most valuable reserves of natural gas recently discovered at Sui in Baluchistan are being exploited. But the need for more foreign aid to strengthen Pakistan's economy led Mr. Mohammad Ali to pay a visit to America late in 1954.

Pakistan has taken an unexpectedly long time to devise its constitution, the delay being mainly due to the sharply divergent views of the two halves of the country. The Constituent Assembly had practically agreed to the details when a crisis, due to differences not only between East and West Pakistan but between sections of the Muslim League, led the Governor-General to dissolve the Assembly in October, 1954. Under the scheme approved earlier, Pakistan was to become an Islamic republic within the Commonwealth at the beginning of 1955, thereby acquiring the same status as India. While Mr. Mohammad Ali's Government refused to alter the composition of the Constituent Assembly after the Muslim League collapse in East Pakistan—an election result which rendered the Assembly unrepresentative—he earlier placated the province by giving East Pakistan a majority in the lower house and a minority in the upper house of the proposed federal legislature, but with the two halves sharing equally in the aggregate membership of both houses. He also agreed that Bengali should have an equal status with Urdu as a state language.

The constitutional structure built up laboriously over a period of seven years was, however, undermined by a revolt within the Muslim League caucus. Old disagreements based on East-West Pakistan and Sind-Punjab jealousies flared up afresh over the whole constitutional field; provinces and parties failed to agree on provincial representation at the centre, on the distribution of powers between the centre and the provinces, on state languages and on provincial boundaries. As there seemed no hope of agreement the authorities were faced with a rupture which might have split not only the Muslim League but the country. Cutting short his visit to the United States and Canada, Mr. Mohammad Ali hastened home, and soon after his arrival the Governor-General, Mr. Ghulam Mohammad, a powerful personality, declared a state of emergency, dissolved the Constituent Assembly, and promised new elections "as soon as possible". Simultaneously the Central Government was drastically reconstituted as a caretaker administration under Mr. Mohammad Ali, only two of the former ministers being retained.

The presence at the Governor-General's insistence of high officials, representatives of parties outside the League and of army officers in the caretaker cabinet was significant; it showed a leaning, not strange to those who know Pakistan, towards the army in the event of politicians failing to keep the country together. What was even more significant was the calibre of the officers selected; they were General Mohammad Ayub Khan, the commander-in-chief of the Pakistan army, and Major-General Iskandar Mirza, a former civil servant, who had earlier been sent to East Pakistan to "clean up the mess" following the suspension of the civil government. In order to lessen fissiparous tendencies in the northern half of the country, decisions were taken to weld the provinces and states of West Pakistan into a single province—as in East Pakistan—and to seek a provincial capital nearer to the heart of the northern region than Karachi. Pakistan's future will depend on a satisfactory settlement of the political problem in each of the two provinces, and their harmonious co-operation in the central government.

The implications of Pakistan's foreign policy fall more properly within the sphere of general trends in Asia today. All one need do at this stage is to note the marked—one might almost say dramatic—swing towards the West which has taken place in the last year or so. Although early in its existence Pakistan displayed friendship for Russia, Moscow's stock slumped to zero when Mr. Jacob Malik, the Soviet representative on the Security Council, intervened in the Kashmir debate in 1952 in a way suggesting strong support for India. Now official Soviet representatives in Pakistan are to have their movements restricted in the same way as Pakistan officials in Russia; friendly overtures have ceased.

As a Muslim state, Pakistan at one time tried to take a lead among the Arab states of the Middle East. An international Islamic economic conference convened in Karachi in 1949 had some success, but an invitation sent to twelve Muslim countries to attend a prime ministers' conference in Karachi three years later met with a poor response and was ultimately dropped. This rebuff cooled Pakistan's ardour towards the Middle East, and although Karachi continued to support the Arab League its politicians generally took the view that the Arab countries were too unstable to be satisfactory allies.

A new outlook in Pakistan's foreign policy became evident soon after Mr. Mohammad Ali's succession to the premiership. Early in 1954 announcements were made almost simultaneously that Pakistan had concluded a treaty with Turkey and had agreed to accept American military aid. Chaudri Muhammad Zafrullah Khan admitted that the Turkish pact could be called the first step in the direction of establishing a regional defence organization; the Prime Minister described the two agreements as "a momentous step for ward towards strengthening the Muslim world". India protested vigorously to both Washington and Karachi against what Mr. Nehru attacked as a form of intervention in Indo-Pakistan problems which was "likely to have far-reaching results" and would certainly encourage aggression. But while Delhi was perturbed over the effect of U.S. military aid on Indo-Pakistan relations, what struck the outside world as really significant was that the Turkey-Pakistan-America agreements contained the seeds of a Middle East defence arrangement to fill the vacuum caused by the withdrawal of British power from the Indian sub-continent. Pakistan's defence link-up with Turkey was the logical outcome of its situation, as Persia's neighbour, at the eastern end of the Russian frontage on the Middle East oil belt. All that now remains is to fill up the gaps in the centre, and already Iraq has joined with Turkey towards that end. Pakistan's alliance with the West was further strengthened by her signature of the 1954 Manila Treaty (SEATO) by which she agreed to co-operate in resisting Communist expansion in South-East Asia and the Far East.

*Chapter Twelve*

# INDEPENDENT CEYLON

CEYLON, THE LATEST member of the Commonwealth, appears on the map like a pendant dangling from the apex of the triangular land mass which constitutes India and Pakistan. Lying on the Indian Ocean flank of the sub-continent, it has always occupied an important position in Commonwealth naval strategy; in the last war its defenders inflicted decisive losses on a determined attack by Japanese carrier-borne aircraft which might have been the prelude to invasion.

Although Ceylon's eight million people are a drop in the ocean compared with the 360 millions of its giant neighbour, the Ceylonese keenly treasure their independence and have no more desire to be absorbed by India than by any other country. India's great epic, the *Ramayana*, tells the story of the conquest of the greater part of the island by the hero Rama who went to Lanka, as Ceylon is known in Brahmanical literature, in pursuit of his abducted wife. Certainly in historic times there has been no invasion of Ceylon on India's part except by the ubiquitous Tamil labourer in search of employment. Ceylon's invaders came from Europe, and were the same merchant adventurers who left their mark on the rest of Asia.

The Ceylonese people are an unusual mixture. There are low country and highland, or Kandyan, Sinhalese; Kandyans, whose stronghold lies in the old kingdom of Kandy in the centre of the sland; Ceylon Tamils and Indian Tamils; Burghers, who are descendants of Dutch settlers; and Moors, as the Muslims are known.

When the Portuguese reached Ceylon at the beginning of the sixteenth century the island was divided into seven kingdoms, each ruled by a separate monarch. It is interesting, in view of the trouble over Portuguese possessions in India today, to recall that the Portuguese directed their operations in Ceylon from Goa. Their rule was not popular; when the Dutch landed a century later the king of Kandy asked their help to get rid of the Portuguese. The Dutch accordingly took over the maritime parts of the island, but left the Kandyan kingdom alone.

History repeated itself in the closing years of the eighteenth century when the British, operating from Madras, invaded Ceylon and were welcomed by the Kandyan chiefs who handed over the kingdom to them voluntarily in order to get rid of a tyrannous king. That explains why the British obtained peaceful possession of the ancient kingdom of Kandy, whose picturesquely clad chiefs still appear in annual processions, as they did before Queen Elizabeth II on her Coronation tour.

Nationalism in Ceylon is largely the product of English education and the unifying influence of British rule. Until recent times the people were concerned with their own particular communities; they had little thought for the big world outside. To quote Sir Ivor Jennings,[1] "It is not an exaggeration to say that the Ceylonese as a people were invented in the present century. . . . The war of 1914–18 provided a great stimulus towards nationalism. . . . The wartime propaganda, unofficial as well as official, which asserted that Britain was fighting for the freedom of small nations, the right of self-determination, the prevention of imperialist aggression, and so forth, became for the nationalists propaganda for the 'freedom' of Ceylon. Everything said about 'brave little Belgium' could be adapted to 'brave little Ceylon', the essential difference being that brave little Belgium had been invaded in 1914 and brave little Ceylon in 1505. When President Roosevelt included among his Fourteen Points the right of every nation to govern itself freely, he enunciated a doctrine which the educated Ceylonese could hardly fail to apply to themselves".

Although the island had a Ceylon National Congress it never had a Gandhi, with the result that its nationalist movement at no time reached the fervour or relative magnitude of its massive Indian counterpart. Ceylon's balanced communities, coupled with a strong community feeling, undoubtedly contributed to a more sober type of

[1] *Nationalism and Political Development in Ceylon*, by Sir Ivor Jennings (Institute of Pacific Relations, New York).

nationalism than that which prevailed elsewhere; the Tamils, for example, have both a Ceylon Tamil Congress (for Ceylonese Tamils) and a Ceylon Indian Congress (for Indian Tamils). While nationalist leaders occasionally indulged in vigorous prodding of the ruling power, Ceylon's gradual advance to complete self-government under British rule was one of the smoothest transitions in colonial history. The association of the Ceylonese people with the administration of the country began in 1833 and expanded steadily until 1927, when a commission headed by Lord Donoughmore devised a constitution which came into effect in 1931. Under the Donoughmore plan communal electorates, which had caused a good deal of friction, were abolished and the administration was conducted by a board of ministers, only three of whom were officials. Thereafter the pattern of the island's political development followed closely that of the Indian sub-continent. Requests for dominion status in 1942 led to a declaration by the British Government that responsible government would be set up after the war, and the ministers were asked to prepare a draft constitution.

The result of their labours was examined and generally approved by a commission under Lord Soulbury in 1945; it provided for a cabinet system subject to reservations on defence and external affairs, but the British Government's statement issued the same year contained an implicit promise of full dominion status within a short period. Representations were renewed in 1947, and in December of that year the Ceylon Independence Act was passed by the British Parliament. The following February the new dominion came into being with Lord Soulbury as its first Governor-General. Six years later Lord Soulbury was succeeded by a Ceylonese, Sir Oliver Goonetilleke, whose appointment was announced by Her Majesty Queen Elizabeth II when, as Queen of Ceylon, she paid a triumphal visit to the island during her world tour of 1953–54. Not since the Kandyan dynasty was deposed in 1815 had a reigning monarch of Ceylon appeared in the island.

Ceylon's internal politics are intensely parochial. This is largely due to the island's varied communities, among whom caste, kinship and religion are still of more importance than political nomenclature. Yet nationalism is the thread which binds the majority of them together; it was largely the inspiration of Ceylon's first Prime Minister, Mr. D. S. Senanayake, "who was truly the creator of racial unity and parliamentary democracy in the Island and the chief architect of Ceylon's independence and full membership of the Commonwealth".[1]

Communism does not offer a serious challenge to nationalism; the local Communists are hopelessly split into Stalinists and Trotskyists, bedevilled by personalities as well as by ideological differences. Following Mr. Senanayake's untimely death in 1952 as the result of a riding accident, the first general elections since Ceylon's independence resulted in a still bigger majority for the ruling United Nationalist Party then led by the late premier's son, Mr. Dudley Senanayake, which captured 54 seats out of 92. The Communists, on the other hand, lost ground, particularly the Trotskyist Lanka Sama Samaj Party, whose chairman had to give up his position as leader of the opposition. There are two other Communist groups, one of them a break-away from the Trotskyists, which work together but have at present little significance.

Ceylon's relations with India, like those of Pakistan, are subject to stresses. Differences exist over the future of Ceylon's Indian population, numbering nearly a million, most of whom the Ceylon Government would like to return to their native country so as to provide more jobs for the island's indigenous inhabitants. As in other parts of South-East Asia, South Indian Tamils were imported to work on the tea estates, but others came to seek employment on their own account as clerks and shopkeepers. Colombo's main grievance against them, apart from Ceylonese unemployment, is that they do not regard the island as their home, using it instead as a means of acquiring money which they remit to India. Under an electoral law passed in 1949 Ceylon restricted the franchise to her own nationals, thereby disfranchising a very large proportion of Indians who indulged—with the Government of India's sympathy—in a non-violent civil disobedience movement at the time of the 1952 elections. An interim agreement between the new Ceylon Prime Minister, Sir John Kotelawala, and Mr. Nehru in 1954 provided for the expeditious registration of Indians who wished to acquire Ceylon

[1] *The Annual Register*, 1952 (Longmans, Green and Co. Ltd.).

citizenship, but those who did not or could not register—and Indians complained that the test was unnecessarily hard—were liable to be deported. It is over deportation that further tension between the two countries could arise. Sir John Kotelawala's attitude can be gauged from his declaration in the House of Representatives that he refused to be "bullied" by India on the subject. Late in 1954 the two Premiers agreed, in order to avoid deportation, to proceed as rapidly as possible with the process of registration, thereby progressively reducing the number of persons not accepted by either government. Their cases are to be reviewed again in two years' time, when the problem may not be as acute as it is now. Ceylon was prevailed upon not to take drastic action because the Colombo authorities realize that the Tamil tea estate labourers cannot be immediately replaced by Ceylonese who, like the Malays, do not relish work of this kind.

Yet, whatever may be Ceylon's domestic squabbles with her big brother, the Colombo Government takes a typical Asian line in foreign affairs. On issues such as non-involvement in power blocs and hostility to colonialism Ceylon's stand is unequivocal. Her feeling towards Communist governments is, however, less friendly than that of India, presumably because of Russia's persistent hostility in vetoing Ceylon's admission to the United Nations on the specious grounds that the country is not free because of its special defence agreement with Britain. When Ceylon for economic reasons, and much to America's displeasure, refused in 1951 to conform to the United Nations resolution banning the export of rubber to Communist China—by which in any case she was not bound—Sir John Kotelawala made it clear that his country's relations with Mr. Mao Tse-tung's Government were confined to trade affairs. He declined to receive a goodwill mission from China. Like Mr. Nehru, he has no use for Communists in his own country which, he says, they have betrayed. Also like Mr. Nehru, he is a strong supporter of the Colombo Powers, the first meeting of which he was largely responsible for organizing. Ceylon's desire to frame her foreign policy in accord with her Asian sympathies may lead her to declare herself a republic on the same basis as India.

Ceylon's economic problems are similar to those of her South-

East Asian neighbours possessing a mainly rural economy. Her chief cash crops, rubber and tea, have in recent years been subject to the fluctuations affecting all primary products. The island is particularly proud of its part in the Commonwealth Plan, to which Ceylon's capital gave its name; its purpose—in the Ceylon Premier's words—was to wage war on poverty in Asia as an effective reply to Communism.

Ceylon's contribution envisaged bringing under irrigation some three and a half million acres of potentially productive agricultural land and harnessing, where practicable, for electric power and irrigation purposes the abundant rainfall of the island. The somewhat ambitious expenditure contemplated earlier was curtailed in 1954 to Rs. 1,500 million on the advice of a World Bank mission; in view of the fall in commodity prices it is based on the availability of finance rather than on a rigid time limit. Apart from setting up certain essential industries, Ceylon's ambition is to increase her rice production so as to feed her growing population and thus to make herself less dependent on rice imports at present procured from China at cut rates under the rubber-rice trade pact. Like every other country which depends for its national wealth on primary products Ceylon at times passes through difficult periods, necessitating Western help and a wise use of her own resources.

*Chapter Thirteen*

# TERRORISM IN MALAYA

MY FIRST IMPRESSIONS of Malaya were, I suppose, much the same as those of every incomer who approaches it from the sea. As I gazed upon its amazing jungle greenness under a bright tropical sun I exclaimed to my neighbour, who happened to be a resident of Singapore, "this place looks like paradise". "Yes," was the "old hand's" reply, "it does, but there are a few large-sized serpents in this Eden".

That, unfortunately, is true. Since 1948 a grim and ceaseless war has been in progress with Communist terrorists, most of whom are not Malays but Chinese. During the last war they practised guerilla warfare against the Japanese; now they are in arms against the British and Malayan civil government, aided by the dense jungle which covers three-quarters of the peninsula. The proclaimed policy of the British Government is the achievement by Malaya of self-government within the Commonwealth. Nationalism is, however, a plant of tender growth in a country where the indigenous inhabitants are in a minority and where large sections of the people look elsewhere for their homeland. Malaya differs from many other Asian countries in that it does not suffer from over-population or from severe pressure on the land. Most of the peninsula lies under primeval jungle and in an area of some 50,000 square miles, including the island of Singapore, the total population does not exceed seven millions.

The Malays, who belong to the Indonesian ethnological group, are an easy-going people. They were once described to me as "Nature's gentlemen" in the sense that a bountiful Nature makes light the tasks of agriculture and fishing on which most of them depend for their living. In the old days they were certainly not interested in the drudgery associated with the exploitation of the country's tin and rubber resources. Mr. Nehru is reported to have said that the Indians, Chinese and Japanese are the most industrious peoples of Asia; few will quarrel with that assertion. For centuries Chinese traders and labourers have worked Malaya's tin mines. After the British introduced the rubber tree from South America *via* Kew Gardens, the vast expansion of the rubber estates led to the introduction of the Tamil *coolie* from South India, together with Indian merchants and bankers. Today there are in Malaya and Singapore over three million Chinese and three-quarters of a million Indians and Pakistanis. Malaya produces about half the world's supply of raw rubber and about a third of its tin; its value as a dollar earner to the Commonwealth can be judged from the fact that in 1950, for example, its rubber exports were worth 313 million dollars to the sterling block, and that in 1953 its total output of rubber and tin amounted in value to £105 million and £44 million respectively.

Originally Malaya became known to the West as a centre of the spice trade, which was at first in the hands of the Hindus. Early in the sixteenth century the Hindus were ousted by Muslims from the Coromandel and Malabar coasts of India, who converted the Malays to Islam, the religion they still profess. Then followed in the same old order the Portuguese, Dutch and British, all of whom used Malacca, a port on the straits of that name, for trading purposes. Penang island was purchased by the British from Kedah State in 1786; the island of Singapore, on which Sir Stamford Raffles founded in 1819 the famous city and free port, was acquired from Johore State. The three isolated possessions of Penang, with a stretch of coast called Wellesley province, Malacca and Singapore were ruled from India until 1867, when they became a Crown colony under the name of the Straits Settlements.

Meanwhile the interior of the peninsula continued to be governed by independent Malay sultans, and it was not until some years later —as a result of disorders caused by faction fights among Chinese tin miners—that Britain offered help, which was accepted, to Perak State. Thereafter all the other states became protectorates, suzerainty over four of them being ceded by Siam in 1909. Before the second World War Malaya comprised a strange administrative patchwork.

It included the Straits Settlements, four federated states—Perak, Selangor, Negri Sembilan and Pahang—and the five unfederated states of Johore, Kedah, Perlis, Kelantan and Trengganu. While the Straits Settlements were controlled by the Colonial Office, relations between the British Government and the states were regulated by treaties under which the rulers agreed to accept the advice of a British Resident except on questions of native custom and religion.

Before the last war political parties scarcely existed. The Malays were, on the whole, loyal to their sultans, whereas the Chinese and Indians concerned themselves with their own affairs, leaving the administration in the hands of the British who ruled with the aid of nominated legislative bodies. There was, however, one exception to the general rule; the Communist party took root in Malaya in the nineteen-twenties in the same way as the movement began in all other Asian countries. It is not altogether surprising that Marxist agents found sympathizers among the immigrant Chinese. Between the two wars there was a very large influx of settlers from China due, firstly, to world economic depression and, secondly, to disturbed conditions in their homeland following Japanese aggression. Many of the young immigrants had been in touch with left wing movements in China, especially during the period when the Kuomintang co-operated with the Communists against the war-lords.

Although the Malayan Communist Party was illegal it gathered recruits among students in Chinese schools and in labour unions until, just before the last war, it amassed sufficient strength to foment strikes and to organize anti-Japanese demonstrations after Japan's attack on China. The Communists did not, however, exercise as strong an influence on the Chinese community as the Kuomintang Nationalist Government, the activities of whose supporters also brought them into disfavour with the authorities. On the outbreak of war the Communists, in common with their comrades elsewhere, followed the usual party line of trying to obstruct the war effort, but changed their policy to co-operation with the Government as soon as Russia became involved.

Japan's occupation of Malaya came as a profound shock to all communities in the country, especially the Chinese. The invaders carried out a ruthless purge of the Chinese inhabitants, seeking to kill all who were active supporters of the Kuomintang, Communists who had taken a prominent part in the British war effort, and members of the Malayan armed forces who had not surrendered. Just before the fall of Singapore the British handed over arms to Chinese Communists, some of whom were released from prison, for guerilla purposes. These Communists organized and led the "Malayan People's Anti-Japanese Army" which, from its jungle hide-outs, fought against the occupation forces with great skill and courage. Guerillas were also furnished by the Kuomintang supporters, but they were not so effective.

Two lessons learnt during the Communists' campaign had a profound influence on their post-war tactics; they discovered how best to use the jungle for guerilla purposes and they established a sys tem, well understood by the Chinese, of levying blackmail on the civil population. Those who refused to supply the food, arms or money demanded of them were liable to be put to death as "collaborators". In this way there grew up a method of resistance in which the civil population was compelled, whether it liked or not, to play a part. During the war the Chinese naturally sympathized with the guerillas, and to help them became a habit. Today the urge is still in the same direction; the Japanese have departed but the Chinese Communists in Malaya are now members of the political creed which dominates a resurgent China.

This is not the only influence at work. In the words of two men[1] who have made a study of this problem:

> "No-one is likely to underrate the importance of the Occupation period in stimulating guerilla organization among the Chinese. But other effects may have been in the aggregate more important; the inculcation of the habit of paying extortion money; the vast increase in bribery and irregularity of all kinds; the undermining of the prewar respect for government and law; and the stimulation to fantastic extremes of the tendency among the South Seas Chinese to be steadfastly neutral on all political issues and concentrate attention on personal advancement."

The war was followed by a brief period of peace between the

[1] Nationalism in Malaya," by T. H. Silcock and Ungku Abdul Aziz (*Asian Nationalism and the West* (The Macmillan Company, New York).

reactivated British administration and the ex-guerillas, whose prestige and membership swelled immediately after the Japanese surrender. Some of the jungle fighters were awarded British honours and took part—rather to their astonishment—in the 1946 Victory Parade in London; among them was Chin Peng, who in 1954 was still secretary-general of the Malayan Communist Party and one of the principal organizers of the terrorist campaign. For the first year after the war the Communist guerillas, who were nominally disbanded and were supposed to have handed in their arms, concentrated on organizing trade unions of their own and in creating Communist cells in genuine labour bodies. They practised the sort of tactics which had served them well during the war; workers were terrorized into doing what the Communists ordered, and soon the inevitable harvest of strikes and unrest compelled the Government to intervene. All Communist-controlled trade unions were dissolved, many of their leaders being arrested.

A state of uneasy truce prevailed until the middle of 1948 when, in response to the notorious directive issued by the Calcutta conference of international Communist agents, Malaya's Communists—like their comrades in other parts of Asia—broke into open revolt. They resumed their guerilla warfare from the jungle, reverting to war-time methods of securing food and support by intimidating villagers. Government counter-measures appeared to be having effect in the year following the outbreak, but the success of the Communist revolution in China gave the terrorists, over 90 per cent of whom are Chinese, a new lease of life.

Meantime the nationalist movement was slowly taking shape. It received a fillip from the strange decision of the British Government in 1946 to impose on Malaya a constitution without first consulting its peoples. This constitution was the Malayan Union, which provided for the joining up of the nine Malay states and the settlements of Penang and Malacca in a single administration, with Singapore as a separate Crown colony. Although all the sultans signed away their powers when presented with the requisite treaties, there was a strong revulsion of feeling in the states when the details became known. For the first time Malay opinion manifested itself against what was regarded as an infringement of the rights of the states and their rulers; political bodies sprang up all over the peninsula and a joint conference held in Kuala Lumpur in 1946 saw the birth of the first really nationalist Malay association—the United Malay National Organization, with Dato Onn bin Jafaar as its president.

Almost immediately the new body achieved for the Malays a remarkable political success. Under pressure from UMNO and its friends Mr. Attlee's Government substituted for the Union, which never really functioned properly, a Federation giving greater autonomy to the states and ensuring the ascendancy of the Malays in the federal and state councils. One of the points in the Union scheme which aroused the wrath of UMNO, whose members represented the Malay aristocracy and wealthier classes, was the franchise; UMNO contended that it would make the acquisition of citizenship too easy for Chinese and Indians and would give the Chinese preponderant political power. Under the federation plan which UMNO sponsored, non-Malays found it much harder to secure the vote, a disadvantage which was deeply resented by both Chinese and Indians.

The Indian community, incidentally, developed during the war a political consciousness as a result of the Japanese occupation. Stimulated, as were the Malays, by the Japanese slogan of "Asia for the Asians" the Indians in Malaya came to regard themselves as the standard-bearers of Indian freedom outside India; they were represented in the fighting forces by members of the Indian army captured in Malaya whom the Japanese and their own fellow countrymen persuaded to join them. Both movements came to an unhappy end, as did Subhas Chandra Bose, their leader, but they gave the Indians a community sense which persists.

Despite Chinese and Indian opposition the Federation of Malaya came into existence in 1948. It consists of the two settlements of Penang and Malacca and the nine Malay states; it is administered by a High Commissioner assisted by a superimposed federal legislative council with a small unofficial majority, the non-officials being nominated by the High Commissioner until the electoral system is ready. Singapore is a Crown colony with a governor and executive and legislative councils, the council having an official and nominated majority over the elected representatives of 13 to 12. In 1954 proposals for liberalizing both the federal and Singapore constitutions were approved. The new federal legislature will comprise 52 elected members out of a total of 100. In Singapore the legislative council is to be replaced by a legislative assembly with 25 elected members out of 32, while the executive council will become a council of ministers with six elected members in a cabinet of nine responsible for all departments except external affairs, internal security and defence.

Non-Malays reacted to the Federation by attempting to mobilize a "united front" on as wide a base as possible among Chinese, Indians, Indonesians and even Communists. Efforts were made to give the front a nationalist flavour by incorporating Malays who stood for a united democratic Malaya in place of the patchwork arrangement of settlements and semi-autonomous states which someone described as the "joint design of Heath Robinson and W. S. Gilbert after a dinner at the Savage Club". Several bodies tried to fill the bill, including Communist-dominated organizations which either were dissolved or went underground when the terrorist campaign started, but eventually there emerged at the instance of the officially sponsored Communities Liaison Committee a movement entitled the Malayan Chinese Association. A parallel body to UMNO, the MCA, has for its objects not hostility to the Malays but a reasoned presentation of the non-Malay case and a claim for justice to all.

The leaven of nationalism began to work. By the end of 1950 Dato Onn bin Jafaar, recognizing that the co-operation of all races was essential in an independent self-governing Malaya, tried to transform UMNO into a non-communal body. Unsuccessful in this endeavour, he established the Independence of Malaya Party, which co-operates on purely nationalist issues with both UMNO and MCA, and has as the main plank in its platform the achievement of independence in ten years, leaving the question of whether Malaya should be outside or inside the Commonwealth to be settled later.

A notable step towards Malayan nationalism was taken in 1954 when UMNO and MCA, the latter led by Sir Cheng Lock Tan, a distinguished Chinese politician, united to demand that three-fifths of the members of the new federal legislature should be elected. When this was refused the alliance, after pressing its case in London, demanded an independent commission from outside Malaya to inquire into the whole question of constitutional reforms before fresh elections were held. The Colonial Secretary, then Mr. Oliver Lyttelton, referred the demand for consideration by the High Commissioner and the sultans, whereupon the alliance decided to withdraw its members from all administrative and legislative councils. Fortunately this drastic boycott was cancelled by the alliance on receipt of an assurance from the High Commissioner, Sir Donald MacGillivray, that he would consult the leaders of the majority among the elected members before making appointments to the five reserved seats in the new federal legislative council. Another sign of the times is the recent tendency of the Malay leaders to make to the Chinese franchise concessions which were unthinkable at the time the Federation was instituted.

All these are important developments. They point to a growing realization by the Malay and Chinese intelligentsia that an independent self-governing Malaya can be achieved only if all races and communities work together in harmony. The quicker that feeling spreads the sooner a case can be made out for the advance towards responsible government envisaged by the UMNO-MCA alliance. But there are real difficulties which cannot be ignored. The leaders of the Malay, Chinese and Indian communities may agree on the need for the fullest co-operation in the interests of the country they live in; their followers are unhappily far from that stage.

This is particularly true of the Chinese. Take the case of the Crown colony of Singapore, the population of which is 80 per cent Chinese, with recent immigrants from China forming the major part of the community. As an article in *The Times*[1] pointed out, in the problems of government these people take little interest. "It is not difficult to explain this seemingly nihilist attitude, for the whole structure of Chinese society is set against the tradition of self-government as it has developed in Europe and as it is being en-encouraged to develop in Singapore." The Chinese are usually opposed to anything which is intended to create a Malayan nation, such as service in the defence force, national schools, a common standard of examination in schools and a common language. They

[1] "The Reluctant Dragon," *The Times*, April 3, 1954.

recoil from any measure which seeks to deprive them of their essentially Chinese character. Unless or until their leaders can impress on them the necessity for taking an active part in the administration of their adopted country, the outlook for genuine Malayan nationalism is bleak. One bright spot on the landscape is the growing association in national schools of Malay, Chinese and Indian children. It is in these institutions that the key to genuine Malayan nationalism may be found.

Malaya's terrorists receive no outside material help except possibly a little over the Siamese border, but they obviously draw their inspiration from the Communist régime in China. The Federal Government of Malaya, with the help of leaders like Dato Onn bin Jafaar, have tackled the menace vigorously ever since it began, first by means of the Briggs plan for resettling Chinese squatters exposed to terrorist influence, and later by the trenchant but successful methods of General Sir Gerald Templer. An encouraging step was taken in 1954 when five members of the federal executive council, including two Malays and one Indian, accepted an invitation to sit on the anti-terrorist operations committee. Able-bodied men of all races are liable to two years' compulsory military service, and there are something like 350,000 Malayans of all nationalities in the security forces.

Much has been done to reduce terrorist activities, yet despite their heavy losses by casualties and surrender, the guerillas, whose numbers are believed to be about 5,000, still secure sufficient recruits to keep the fight going. How they do so is one of Malaya's mysteries. General Templer estimated that over one-third of the terrorists are professional bandits and about another third people escaping from justice, while the remainder constitute a hard core of fanatical Communists. They are known to have indoctrinated a number of jungle aboriginals who act as scouts for them; to counter this development use is being made of helicopters to attack jungle camps.

But the stark fact remains that the terrorists, as in war-time days, keep going because they are assisted with food and money by the local population either out of sympathy with the rebels or of fear of reprisals if they refuse. Lieutenant-General Sir Geoffrey Bourne, who was appointed Director of Operations in succession to General Sir

Gerald Templer, guaranteed to wipe out terrorist organizations within a year if the local inhabitants ceased to aid them. He also promised adequate protection for villagers if they furnished news of terrorists in their neighbourhood; information is one of the key requirements in the campaign.

Communist tactics have progressively changed since 1951. In that year the terrorists were ordered by their leaders to confine their activities more specifically to military objectives so as to avoid causing unnecessary popular resentment. Before he left in 1954 General Templer insisted that the real danger lay in Communist infiltration of "apparently harmless bodies like trade unions, political associations, youth clubs, even badminton clubs". The same year witnessed increasing indications that terrorists were becoming supposedly peaceful villagers, in which guise they could give unsuspected help to their armed comrades in the jungle.

It has been clear for some time that the answer to terrorism lies not in police or military action alone. General Templer rightly declared that the campaign must be fought on the social, economic, and political front as well as on the military one. Under the Colombo Plan, the Federal Government's own development schemes and other outside aid, the social and economic fronts are receiving a good deal of attention; village resettlement, education, social welfare, rural and industrial development, power and transport all figure in the programme. The International Bank has sent a mission to survey resources and needs. Village resettlement, forced on the authorities by the rebellion, is becoming a major welfare service; it is turning into orderly citizens thousands of Chinese squatters who, having lost their jobs in tin mines, settled on the fringe of the jungle as cultivators and were forced, willingly or unwillingly, to help the terrorists. Steps, hitherto encouragingly successful, are also being taken to win Communist-dominated aborigines over to the Government.

Progress is also essential on the political front, but here its speed and efficacy are dependent on the willingness of Malaya's multiracial inhabitants to grasp the opportunities afforded them. It is possible, for instance, that the future of the terrorists may be linked with the part to be played by the Chinese population in the future governance of the peninsula. This, in turn, depends on whether the

Communist leaders consider themselves an outpost of the Peking Government, or whether they merely represent a local urge for freedom. The evidence, unfortunately, suggests that terrorism is not a Malayan nationalist movement but part of the great world-wide struggle between Communism and democracy. Yet the authorities have no alternative but to press on towards the goal of responsible government and thereby to convince the people of Malaya—and of free Asia—that Communism, not colonialism, is the enemy. A notable step in that direction took place early in 1955, when the Labour Front won the Legislative Assembly elections in Singapore and its leader, Mr. David Marshall, became Singapore's first Chief Minister under the new constitution.

*Chapter Fourteen*

# KOREA'S AGONY

We come now to two Asian countries where a line has had to be drawn by international action between the Communist and non-Communist areas—Korea and Indo-China. In Korea the line came into existence almost fortuitously as a sequel to the first World War, but it brought upon that unhappy country a struggle in which the United Nations for the first time used force to resist aggression.

During the last hundred years the Korean people have certainly had a raw deal from their bigger neighbours. Up to the middle of the nineteenth century they had their own royal house, a troubled history and a rather tenuous political connection with the Chinese empire. An awakened Japan inevitably cast its eyes on the mainland country nearest to its shores, and in the latter half of the nineteenth century the Japanese Government imposed a trade treaty on Korea after the manner of the West in its dealings with Asian countries. The Sino-Japanese war of 1894 gave the invaders an opportunity of strengthening their hold on Korea; one of the victors' peace terms was that China should recognize the complete independence of the peninsula.

Korea's independence was, however, a mockery, for it soon became evident that the Japanese intended to exercise full control over the country. Their Korean activities brought them into conflict with Russia, which resented an incursion that brought the Japanese on to the Tsarist empire's far eastern doorstep. The Japanese tried to do a deal with the Russians, offering them a free hand in Manchuria in return for a free hand in Korea. Tsarist Russia haughtily refused Tokio's overtures; it had no desire to tolerate a rival in either Manchuria or Korea and the breakdown of the negotiations led to the Russo-Japanese war. Japan's surprising victory—surprising in the sense that it involved the defeat of a major European power by a relatively small Asian nation—created a sensation in Asia, where it stirred up widespread feelings of nationalism. Its immediate result, however, was to turn Korea into a Japanese protectorate. Some years later a Korean revolt led to savage repression, followed by the annexation of the country to Japan in 1910 and the abdication and virtual extinction of the ruling house.

No European country treated its Asian possessions as oppressively as did the Japanese in Korea. Their occupation resulted in an intense Korean dislike of the Japanese which is one of America's far eastern problems today. For thirty-five years Korea was subjected not only to political domination but to gross economic exploitation for the benefit of Japan; her industry and agriculture were expropriated and her people treated like serfs. The Koreans tried hard to get justice after the first World War, but it was not until the 1943 Cairo conference between President Roosevelt, Mr. Churchill and General Chiang Kai-shek that Allied war aims were declared to include "in due course" freedom and independence for Korea. President Roosevelt was of opinion—and this is important in view of what happened at the end of the war—that Korea might have to undergo a period of trusteeship in order to train her people to manage their own affairs after their long "enslavement".

At the Yalta conference in 1945 Marshal Stalin tacitly accepted the Cairo agreement and later, in view of Russia's participation in the war against Japan, it was agreed that Russia should occupy Korea north of the 38th parallel of latitude, leaving the Americans to take over the southern half. From the Western and Korean point of view this arrangement was most unfortunate. President Roosevelt undoubtedly regarded the splitting of the country as a temporary military expedient, but he reckoned without his collaborators in the north. At first all went well; an Allied conference in Moscow decided at the end of 1945 to set up a joint U.S.-Soviet commission whose task would be to form a provisional Korean government in consultation with Korean democratic parties and social organizations. A Four Power trusteeship was then to be instituted for a period not exceeding five years in conjunction with the provisional government, but this part of the agreement was strongly opposed by nearly all the political groups in Korea with the exception of the Communists, who obediently accepted what Moscow offered.

For two years a wrangle went on in the U.S.-Soviet commission over which Korean parties should be consulted. The Russians demanded the exclusion of all parties hostile to the trusteeship plan, thereby banning practically everybody except the Communists; the Americans naturally rejected so pro-Communist a move. Various schemes were suggested to resolve the deadlock. Finally Washington referred the issue to the United Nations, which set up a commission to supervise the elections to the Korean National Assembly. Russia and her satellites took no part in the voting, and when the commission reached Korea it was refused admission into the Russian sector. The deadlock was complete.

The continued partition of the country was bitterly resented by all Koreans. It proved definitely harmful to their economic interest, since, although the major part of the population lived in the south, the north contained the hydro-electric power works on the Yalu river, fertilizer factories, and iron and coal mines essential to the prosperity of the whole peninsula. It soon became evident that the North Korean Government under the Russians was purely Communist; in the south an administration was set up under President Syngman Rhee after the holding of elections supervised by the U.N. commission. By 1949 both Russia and the United States announced the withdrawal of their troops from their respective zones.

They left an unhappy state of affairs. Both Korean governments continued to demand the unification of the country on their own terms, with threats of violence. The triumph of the Communists in China and the return to North Korea of Korean units released by the Peking authorities increased the aggressiveness of the North Korean Government, and constant clashes occurred on the border. In response to South Korean requests the U.N. General Assembly agreed to continue the U.N. commission, adding to its functions the task of observing developments likely to lead to a conflict.

What eventually decided Kim Il Sung's North Korean Government to resort to war is not clear; it may have been Mr. Acheson's declaration—despite the generous civil and military help extended to South Korea—that the U.S.A. defence line ran through the Aleutians, Japan, Okinawa and the Philippines. Anxiety was certainly expressed in South Korea at Mr. Acheson's statement, and quite possibly it constituted one of the factors which encouraged the Communists to "have a go". No doubt there were others; America harbours a growing suspicion that Communist China instigated the attack. At any rate, when North Korean troops crossed the 38th parallel on a broad front on June 25, 1950, their action showed every sign of a well-organized invasion capable of subjugating an unprepared people. Fortunately for the South Koreans the U.N. commission was able to report promptly that the North Korean forces were the aggressors despite the fatuous but inevitable claims by the Communists that the South Koreans started the fighting.

For the first time in its brief history the U.N. found itself engaged in a war against an aggressor. By the end of the year some fourteen nations were involved in the war, with America providing the vast bulk of the allied forces. General Douglas MacArthur, appointed to command the U.N. army, handled the early part of the campaign in masterly fashion. The invaders were held along a line in the extreme south-east of the peninsula while a landing was prepared well in their rear. When this took place at Inchon, in the middle of September the North Koreans were completely routed. Seoul—the Korean capital—was recaptured, and by the end of the month the U.N. forces had reached the 38th parallel.

Then came a fateful decision. India, supported by other Asian member nations, urged the U.N. to review the situation before taking further action, basing her request on information obtained by her ambassador in Peking that if U.N. forces crossed the 38th parallel Communist China would consider her security directly menaced. No attention was paid to the warning; South Korean troops on the east coast crossed the line at the beginning of October and nine days later General MacArthur ordered his forces to advance on the implicit though not absolutely clear authority of a U.N. General Assembly resolution to set up a commission for the unification and rehabilitation of Korea.

By the end of the year the U.N. forces, after having neared the

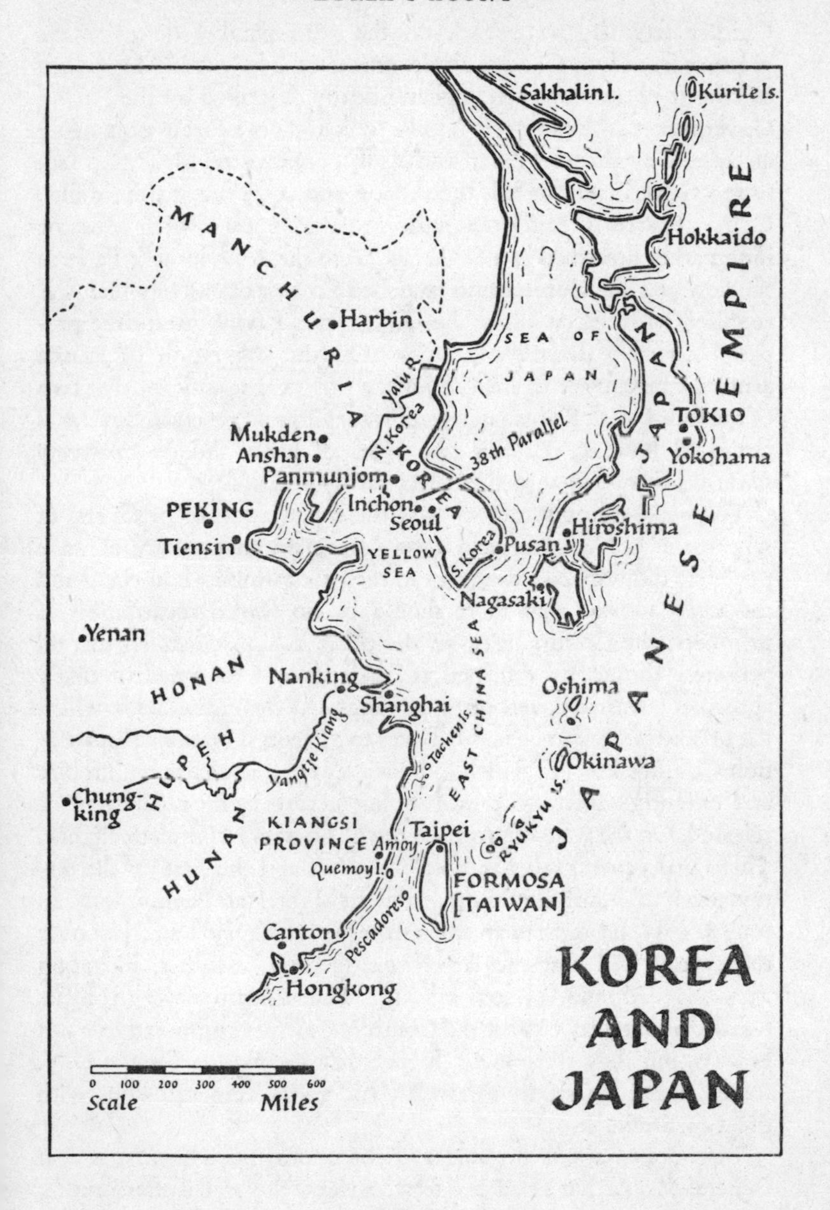


KOREA AND JAPAN

Chinese frontier, were back on the 38th parallel under severe pressure from four Chinese armies estimated by General MacArthur to consist of 200,000 men euphemistically described by the Peking Government as "volunteers". India took a leading part in organizing an appeal by thirteen Asian and Arab countries to Mr. Mao Tse-tung's Government to halt their forces and cease fire at the parallel. China apparently paid no attention to the appeal, which Moscow indignantly described as a device to "save the Americans". Early in the new year the Communists launched a major offensive which was repulsed with heavy losses, the U.N. forces having meantime prepared a strong defensive position. On the suggestion of Russia armistice talks were opened in June, and it was significant that two of the four North Korean delegates were Chinese generals. But it was not until June, 1953, after two years of bitter though relatively static warfare, that agreement was finally reached.

The main stumbling block was the repatriation of prisoners, of whom the U.N. forces held a very large number. Many of these prisoners did not want to return to their Communist homeland and the U.N. insisted that there should be no forced repatriation of prisoners; the Communists, on the other hand, demanded that all prisoners should be returned to their own country. Eventually agreement was achieved on lines suggested by India under which the prisoners were to be handed over to a Neutral Nations Repatriation Commission—of which India was appointed chairman, umpire and executive agent—for questioning before being repatriated or released. On the issue of prisoners the U.N. won a complete victory. There was general relief in both the West and the East on the termination of hostilities; the agreement signed at Panmunjom on June 8, 1953, brought to an end a struggle which had lasted just over three years and cost the Americans 142,000 casualties, including 23,000 killed and 14,000 missing. The Commonwealth losses totalled about 7,000. What the Communist losses amounted to is not known, but they were much higher than the figures for the U.N. forces; the Chinese, in particular, suffered severe casualties with great fortitude.

Two points about the war call for comment. The first is that General MacArthur's decision to cross the 38th parallel after routing the North Korean invaders was a mistake from the Asian point of view, although it would not be fair to blame the U.N. commander for a step which a U.N. resolution by implication permitted him to take. An undercurrent of hostility undoubtedly existed in Asia over the prompt manner in which the U.N., led by America, interfered in what could be regarded as a civil war in an Asian country. Nevertheless the U.N. decision that aggression had occurred and must be resisted was generally approved by the new Asian democracies, which saw in it an encouraging sign of a new order in world affairs.

That approval did not extend to the crossing of the 38th parallel. It was felt by most Asian countries, led by India, that the U.N. had achieved its object by driving the invaders out of South Korea, and that by carrying the war into North Korea it departed from the principles for which it stood. The U.N., these nations thought, would have enhanced its authority and prestige by confining itself to the bare necessity of repelling aggression; by carrying the war up to the Chinese border it asked for trouble. This feeling contributed to the refusal of a number of Asian states to vote for the resolution moved in the General Assembly in 1951 declaring Communist China an aggressor because of its intervention in Korea. India and Burma opposed the resolution, while Indonesia, Pakistan, Saudi Arabia and Afghanistan abstained on the grounds that the Peking Government had some justification for regarding the crossing of the 38th parallel as a threat to its security.

From the point of view of world peace the most unfortunate outcome of the event was to bring Communist China into direct conflict with the West, and especially with America, which bitterly regretted the ousting of the Kuomintang Government. America's attitude towards Communist China was bad enough before the Korean war; it is now one of marked hostility, aggravated by the memory of the casualties sustained in what Americans feel was completely uncalled-for intervention by the Chinese. Any hope there might have been of Washington changing its pre-Korean war views about the admission of Communist China to the United Nations has been most effectively dashed. The threat voiced in the American Senate that the United States would leave the U.N. if Communist China was admitted is painfully symptomatic of American feeling.

The second point worth noting was the embarrassment caused to the U.N. by the conduct of the South Korean President, Dr. Syngman Rhee. President Rhee was one of the most doughty opponents of the Japanese occupation of Korea; he studied in America as a student under President Woodrow Wilson and for many years held charge of the permanent commission for Korean independence established in Washington. He leads the Korean Liberal Party, but his views today are anything but liberal. When his first term of office expired in 1951 this aged fire-eater, by highly dubious and dictatorial methods which called forth protests from several Western governments, had the constitution altered so that he could be elected by the popular vote instead of by the national assembly. On an appeal to the people he was re-elected by an overwhelming majority, which testified to his personal popularity in the country.

His chief ambition is to conquer North Korea by force. He heartily disapproved of the armistice and wanted to go on with the war by himself; he nearly wrecked the cease-fire agreement by conniving at the escape of 25,000 prisoners who did not want to be repatriated to North Korea, and he threatened to attack the Indian custodian force which went to the demilitarized zone of Korea to look after prisoners awaiting disposal. When he visited the United States in 1954 at the invitation of President Eisenhower to discuss the future of his country he staggered even the American Congress and people by the violence of his demands for the extermination of all Communist governments and by his attacks on American policy, which he said had no "guts" and had "short-sightedly" prevented his army from "unifying Korea by force of arms". At a press conference in Washington Mr. John Foster Dulles, President Eisenhower's Secretary of State, described him as a "brave and patriotic man" whose "petulant criticisms" should not be taken too seriously, but Americans are inclined to think he does not sufficiently appreciate the help he has received both in blood and treasure.

The terms of the Panmunjom armistice included the appointment of representatives by each side to arrange for the withdrawal of all foreign forces from Korea and to confer on the peaceful settlement of the country. Czechoslovakia, Poland, Sweden and Switzerland agreed to supply neutral observers to witness the carrying out of the armistice provisions, but the Swiss and Swedish members were not allowed to enter North Korea. Up to 1954 nothing had been done about the armistice terms relating to Korea's future and unification. Delegates from sixteen nations involved in the Korean war who met at Geneva in June "for the purpose of establishing a united and independent Korea by peaceful means" in accordance with the armistice agreement found themselves in a complete deadlock. The non-Communist representatives adhered to two principles which the Communists flatly rejected.

These principles were, firstly, that the U.N. was empowered to take collective action to repel aggression and, secondly, that in order to establish a "unified, independent and democratic Korea" genuinely free elections should be held under U.N. supervision. The Communists denied the authority and competence of the U.N. in Korea, labelling that body an "aggressor", and on the subject of elections insisted on procedures which would (according to the U.N.) make genuinely free elections impossible. In these circumstances the conference ended, the U.N. delegates regretfully recognizing that the Communists had plainly "shown their intention to maintain Communist control over North Korea".

That, indeed, seems to be the stark truth. All evidence points to Chinese determination to convert North Korea into a province of Communist China. A new great underground defence line of immense strength is reported to have been constructed since the armistice behind the northern side of the demilitarized zone. Airfields are known to have been improved. Before the armistice it was estimated that Chinese troops in North Korea numbered about a million; many of these troops have not been withdrawn, but have been "rotated and replaced". Others are being settled on the land with their families to replace North Korean war dead or prisoners of war who refused to return.

Writing in the spring of 1954, the special correspondent of *The Times* in Korea[1] reported that North Korea's indigenous population of about nine millions had been reduced to three or four millions by flight, war casualties or removal to forced labour in Manchuria,

[1] *The Times*, April 21, 1954.

thereby leaving plenty of room for emigrants from China. North Korea's industrial resources are being restored with technical aid from Moscow and Peking. "In short", concludes *The Times* correspondent, "there is convincing proof that the Communists have established a stranglehold on North Korea, and that President Kim Il Sung and his Moscow-trained colleagues are willing collaborators in the sovietization of their country. That being so, any talk of 'neutralizing' North Korea is academic. . . . The conclusion must be that the partition of Korea is here to stay—until such time as the world-wide conflict between the two ideologies is resolved. Repugnant as this may be to champions of Korean freedom, it is the only realistic approach."

Even if Korea was unified at present, it could scarcely hope to escape falling under either an extreme right wing or an extreme left wing régime. Despite his notorious jingoism and dictatorial methods, President Rhee is popular in South Korea. His political position was strengthened by the general election to the national assembly in May, 1954, when his party improved its prospects by gaining a small absolute majority despite the large number of independents. Democracy as the West understands it may not be strong in South Korea, but the fact that the population includes nearly three million refugees from North Korea shows that it is definitely not Communist. Provided President Rhee and his government can be restrained from attempting to "march north", which they periodically threaten to do, stability would seem to be assured. Hopes are entertained that the cold douche administered to the president's belligerency during his visit to America after the failure of the 1954 Geneva conference will effectively curb his enthusiasm for unity by conquest. According to Mr. Dulles the truce agreement, like the cease-fire in Israel, is of indefinite duration unless broken by one of the contracting parties.

South Korea's military position is guaranteed by the U.N.; in August, 1953, it was announced in Washington that the sixteen powers with forces under U.N. command had signed an undertaking promptly to resist a renewal of armed attack, and that "in all probability it would not be possible to confine hostilities within the frontiers of Korea". Some perturbation was expressed by Labour members in the British Parliament about the implications of this addition to the ordinary resistance clause, but the explanation was given that there was nothing new in it. Obviously, however, it was inserted as a clear warning to Communist China. South Korea's security is also safeguarded by a mutual defence treaty with the United States under which American defence forces will continue to stay in the country.

Meanwhile U.N. and American aid is pouring into South Korea to restore its war-shattered economy. Factories are being built to replace those in North Korea which formerly supplied the country's needs in fertilizers and essential consumer goods. Farmers are receiving much-needed assistance in producing crops. These factors produced in 1954 an upsurge of hope and a general feeling that better days were on the way. In the absence of a settlement with the Communists, the U.N. aim must be to raise the standard of living in South Korea to a point where the people will not only resist Communism, but will make their way of life attractive to the North Koreans. Even in this beneficent task the Americans were disgusted by President Rhee's insistence on a grossly unfair currency exchange and rejection of U.S. conditions attached to a £250 million aid programme for 1955.

*Chapter Fifteen*

# RETREAT IN INDO-CHINA

"IT IS A FACT, though it seems almost incredible, that after all these years of French administration, the scores of military expeditions, the spending of thousands of millions of francs, the loss of tens of thousands of lives, Tongking is only 'pacified' so far as the delta is concerned."[1]

These words might have been written yesterday; actually they were penned by an English traveller in a book published in 1895—no less than sixty years ago. They tell something of the long and weary struggle which culminated in the Geneva agreement of July, 1954, by which Viet Nam—the largest and most populous of the Indo-China states—was partitioned in much the same way as Korea, with the Communists in power on one side and non-Communists on the other. In the Geneva pact provision is made for the holding of elections throughout the whole country by July, 1956, to decide its future. In Viet Nam there is the same intense desire for unification as exists in Korea. The next two years will show whether Viet Nam nationalism can assert itself, or whether Communist China will establish the same ascendancy in North Viet Nam as she has done in North Korea.

Before the second World War the French Union of Indo-China was a colonial patchwork. It consisted of the colony of Cochin China and the protectorates of Annam, Tongking, Laos and Cambodia. Annam, Tongking and Cochin China, which today constitute Viet Nam, stretch in a continuous line along the sea coast from China in the north to Cambodia in the south. The population of some 24 millions is chiefly concentrated in the Red river delta of Tongking in the north and the Mekong river delta of Cochin China in the south, both deltas being important rice-growing regions. Viet

[1] *The Peoples and Politics of the Far East*, by Henry Norman. (Unwin.)

Nam possesses language and, to a large extent, cultural unity. Laos is a land-locked mountainous country lying next to China in the north, Siam in the West, Viet Nam in the east and Cambodia in the south. Formerly part of Siam, its two million people are related to the Siamese, with whom they have strong religious and cultural affinities. Cambodia in by-gone days was subject to Indian influence and contains the ruins of the famous city of Angkor; wedged in between Siam and Viet Nam, it has a king, Norodom Sihanouk, who rules over about four million people.

French interest in Indo-China began in the seventeenth century when a French Roman Catholic missionary resided for some time in Annam and wrote an account of his experiences which proved very popular in France. He was followed by a missionary society whose activities led to a treaty between Louis XVI and the emperor of Annam. Previous to that the country had been for centuries under Chinese influence and occupation, although the Annamese at times asserted themselves by driving the Chinese out. Trouble over the persecution of French missionaries and their converts led to French military intervention in 1859. Saigon in Cochin China was occupied, and three years later Annam ceded the Saigon region to France. French power steadily expanded in the following years; Cambodia placed itself under French protection to escape Siamese and Annamese aggression, the western provinces of Cochin China were occupied, and in 1864 Annam itself signed a treaty accepting French suzerainty. French troops drove the Chinese out of Tongking in 1884, and by a treaty signed in Peking the Chinese Government recognized the status of the French in Indo-China. The last of France's Indo-China possessions was acquired in 1893 when Laos was ceded by Siam.

Annamese nationalism developed, as the quotation at the beginning of the chapter shows, in the nineteenth century and led to sporadic outbreaks of violence. French rule in Indo-China resembled in many respects Dutch government in Indonesia. It did much material good to the states in the Union; rice production in the Red river and Mekong deltas greatly increased with the draining of marsh lands, rubber was introduced and cultivated, roads and railways were built, industries started and public health vastly improved. But economically Indo-China was run for the benefit of France and

French investors, not to mention the mass of French officials who had a vested interest in the country. Political parties were forbidden, and there was no serious attempt, as in India, to build up a democratic system leading to self-government.

Yet nationalism persisted; in the nineteen-twenties it derived inspiration from Sun Yat-sen's movement in China, and in the absence of party outlet it expressed itself in a series of revolts. Communism appeared in organized form in 1930 with the formation of the Indo-Chinese Communist Party and although, like other parties, it was banned, it survived underground, looking abroad for its leadership. On various pretexts Japan occupied Indo-China during the second World War, but left the administration to the French officials in view of the Vichy Government's collaboration with the Axis. Led by Dr. Ho Chi-minh, a well-known figure, those who worked for the freedom of Viet Nam had perforce to conduct their campaign from China.

The Viet-minh (short for Viet Nam Doc Lap Dong Minh Hoi or League for the Independence of Viet Nam) was formed in China in 1941, its main constituent being the Indo-Chinese Communist Party. Its object was to fight both "French and Japanese fascism and imperialism". While other Viet Nam nationalist parties also existed in China, the Viet-minh was the only one to build up surreptitiously an organization in Viet Nam itself, particularly in the neighbouring province of Tongking which had always been susceptible to Communist influence. Towards the end of 1944 the Viet-minh took an important step by moving its headquarters from China into Tongking.

With the disappearance of Vichy France before the Allied offensive in Europe, the Japanese in the spring of 1945 overthrew the French administration in Indo-China and set up nominally independent states under the Annamese emperor Bao Dai in Viet Nam, King Norodom Sihanouk in Cambodia, and King Sisavong Vong in Laos. All three monarchs, presumably on Japanese instructions, issued grandiloquent proclamations announcing their independence, but pledging their loyalty to Japan's "co-prosperity sphere". Meanwhile the Viet-minh was biding its time; just before the Japanese surrender in August it ordered a general insurrection and seized control of Hanoi, the capital of Tongking. Dr. Ho Chi-minh, the Viet-minh leader, stepped into the vacuum created by the collapse of Japanese authority. So great was his prestige as head of an independence movement untarnished by collaboration with either French or Japanese that he gained control of the whole of Viet Nam in a few weeks. Bao Dai promptly abdicated, but appeared in the republican government which Viet-minh formed for Viet Nam as "supreme counsellor of state".

Under the Potsdam agreement the Japanese troops in the north of Indo-China were to surrender to Chinese Nationalist forces, and those in the south to British units of the South-East Asia Command, so as to prepare the way for the French. Serious trouble at once arose; nationalist feeling throughout the country revolted against a return to pre-war conditions. Paris, realizing that new conditions had arisen, negotiated through General Leclerc in March, 1946, an agreement with Dr. Ho Chi-minh whereby Viet Nam, consisting of Tongking and Annam, was to be recognized as an autonomous unit, leaving the question of the accession of Cochin China for decision by a plebiscite. Details were to be arranged later, but as part of the settlement Dr. Ho Chi-minh agreed to allow the return of French troops throughout the country for a period not exceeding five years.

The 1946 agreement throws a revealing light on Dr. Ho Chi-minh. That he was a Communist by conviction and training is not disputed; in the nineteen-twenties he was connected with the French Communist Party and spent some time in Moscow. He worked with Borodin, the Russian Communist agent in Canton, and for years took part in Communist activities in various parts of the Far East before organizing the Viet-minh in China during the last war. Yet he was clearly prepared to work with the French after the war for two possible reasons: firstly, as a Communist he could expect no help from the Kuomintang Government in China, and secondly, he wanted to secure the support of Viet Namese, including a considerable Roman Catholic population descended from French missionary converts, who were definitely not Communists.

His movement therefore became typical of many similar organizations in Asia in which nationalism and Communism were inextricably mixed up. Proof of Dr. Ho Chi-minh's moderation at this stage of his career is to be found not only in the liberal nature of the constitution which he set up, with its private property rights and religious freedom, but in the fact that he had to contend with extremists within his own party who wanted no truck at all with the French. Difficulty with some of his supporters probably made Dr. Ho Chi-minh a harder man to bargain with than he might otherwise have been. His visit to Paris in 1946 to settle details of his agreement had no result other than to keep the pact, with its special protection for French citizens and property, alive until negotiations could be resumed early the following year. It was known as the *modus vivendi* agreement. On his return to Indo-China Dr. Ho Chi-minh was faced with the task of justifying his dealings with the French; before forming a government in which he became president and foreign minister he arrested some of the wilder spirits among his followers who thought he had conceded too much.

Unfortunately relations between the new government and the French authorities deteriorated rapidly. Both sides were highly suspicious of each other; the Viet-minh contended that customs arrangements at Haiphong were a breach of the agreement and there was bitter resentment against the French High Commissioner, Admiral d'Argenlieu, who fostered a separatist movement in Cochin China aimed at prejudging the issue of unity with Viet Nam. The spirit which had made possible the General Leclerc-Ho Chi-minh concord vanished. From his dealings with the Viet-minh Admiral d'Argenlieu convinced himself that "the Viet-minh and Ho Chi-minh were no more than pawns in Moscow's struggle for global supremacy"[1] and that their removal from Viet Nam was the primary role and mission of France. Disputes and clashes broke out in various parts of the country. On December 19, 1946, Dr. Ho Chi-minh, who was under severe pressure from his extremist followers, openly revolted against the French.

Argument will go on endlessly as to whether Dr. Ho Chi-minh' moderation early in 1946 was genuine and would have led to a nationalist government, or whether he was merely using the agreement as a stepping stone to a Communist state. The plain truth is, of course, that he was never given a chance to prove his *bona fides*.

[1] *Le Viet-Nam Contemporain*, by Philippe Devillers.

Extremists on both sides, and especially the attitude of the French High Commissioner, wrecked all chances of a peaceful settlement. Dr. Ho Chi-minh's resumed discussions with the French Government after the inconclusive talks in Paris, which produced the *modus vivendi* arrangement, should have taken place in January, 1947. Instead, on what the French called the "St. Bartholomew's Eve of Hanoi", there began a struggle which lasted with many changes of fortune until the Geneva conference of 1954.

For the first two years fighting followed the guerilla pattern familiar in Asia since the end of the war. The French slowly expanded and consolidated their hold on the towns; the Viet-minh, based on the rural areas, conducted guerilla warfare against the French outposts. To the rest of the world the struggle was just another "colonial war" in which the French were trying to suppress a Communist rising in territory over which they had jurisdiction. But to the people of Indo-China the issue was not as simple as that. Dr. Ho Chi-minh and the Viet-minh might be Communists, but they were the spearhead of a nationalist movement which, with the blessing of their former emperor, for a brief period held power and produced a reasonably liberal constitution for a self-governing Viet Nam.

Not all who supported Dr. Ho Chi-minh were Communists; he had among his followers many genuine nationalists, some of whom were much less compromising towards the French connection than Dr. Ho Chi-minh himself. To people like these it was not enough for the French to declare that they must remove the menace of Communism from Viet Nam. This slogan had been used too often to arouse enthusiasm, as General Leclerc recognized when he said "Anti-Communism will be a useless tool as long as the problem of nationalism remains unsolved".

For some time after the start of guerilla warfare both sides expected a resumption of negotiations. Dr. Ho Chi-minh, whose position was not too strong, broadcast several requests to the French authorities and overtures were made by the French to the Viet-minh, but nothing came of these efforts partly because the Viet-minh, for propaganda reasons, had stepped up their demands. By the middle of 1947 the French High Commission in Indo-China reached two conclusions: (1) that no agreement with Dr. Ho Chi-minh was possible, and (2) that they must find a rallying point for Viet Namese nationalism if the country was to be saved from the Communists. They therefore decided to make an approach to Bao Dai, the ex-emperor of Annam, who was living in retirement in Hongkong.

In their negotiations with Bao Dai the French Government unhappily displayed the same niggardliness and tardiness which had characterized their dealings with Dr. Ho Chi-minh. In the words of a French professor:[1]

> "The time had arrived when a solution could have come about speedily if only the French had adopted toward Vietnam the same position which England had adopted toward India or the United States toward the Philippines: that is to say, if it had consented to recognize Vietnam's independence and unity, the country's right to an army of its own, to the conduct of its foreign relations, and to an autonomous economy. There would have been no difficulty in obtaining as a quid pro quo the guarantees which Frenchmen desired for their economic, cultural and military interests in Vietnam. Satisfied in its main demands, Vietnam would have been neither a dead weight nor a hotbed of hostile intrigue, not to say a plague spot, within the French Union. It should be remembered that Bao Dai's demands were not essentially different—one might say, they were exactly the same—from those put forward by Ho Chi Minh at Fontainebleau, a fact which goes to show that they were not only those of one of the parties but those of the whole nation."

Yet it was only after a great deal of haggling lasting some eighteen months that in March, 1949, an agreement was signed with Bao Dai in Paris providing for the eventual independence of Viet Nam within the French Union but with certain restrictions in the judicial sphere. Somewhat similar constitutions were framed for Laos and Cambodia. Bao Dai returned and set up a government in a Viet Nam which included Cochin China, and at the end of the year powers were transferred to him as the head of the state. The French, in short, were compelled by circumstances—since Bao Dai would take

[1] *Le Viet-Nam Contemporain*, by Philippe Devillers.

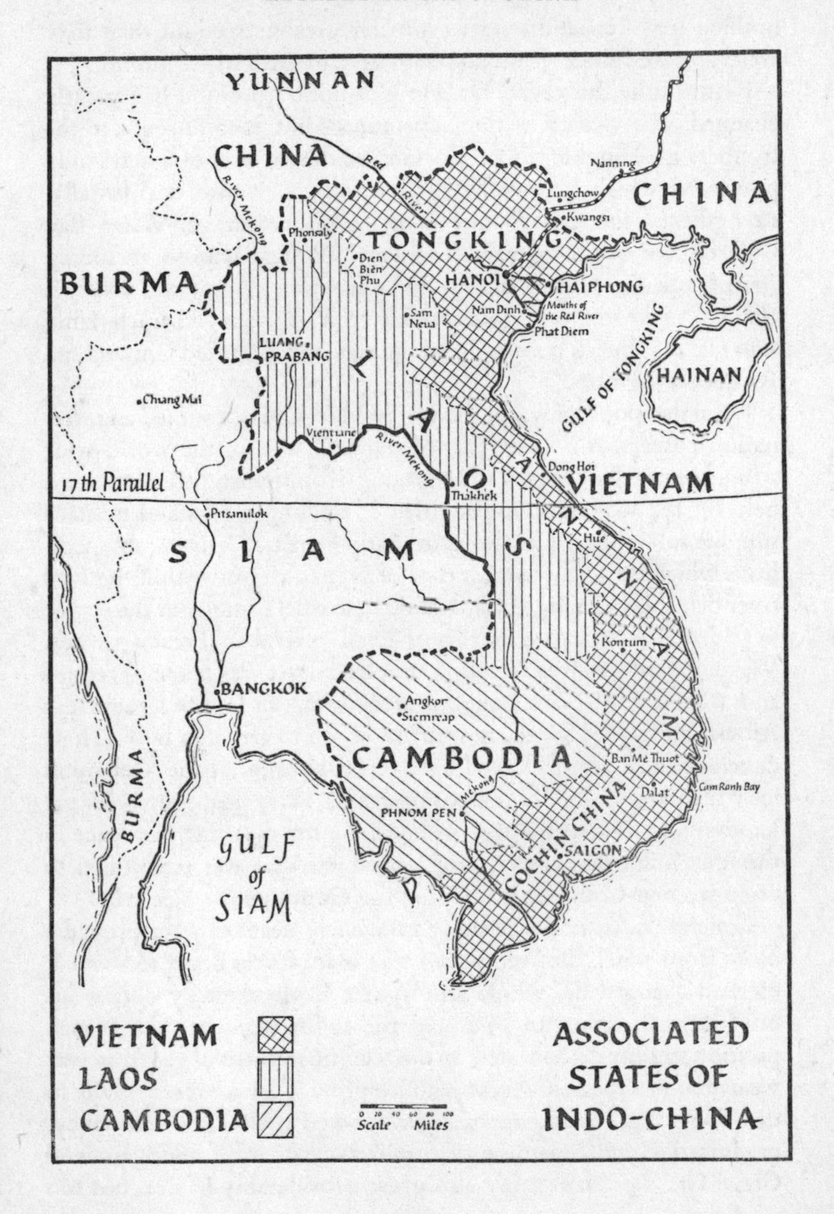
YUNNAN
CHINA
CHINA
BURMA
TONGKING
Nanning
Lungchow
Kwangsi
Phonsaly
Dien Bien Phu
HANOI
HAIPHONG
Nam Dinh
Mouths of the Red River
Phat Diem
Sam Neua
LUANG PRABANG
GULF OF TONGKING
HAINAN
Chiang Mai
Vientiane
LAOS
River Mekong
Red River
Dong Hoi
VIETNAM
17th Parallel
Thakhek
Pitsanulok
SIAM
Hue
ANNAM
Kontum
BANGKOK
Angkor
Siemreap
CAMBODIA
Ban Me Thuot
Dalat
Cam Ranh Bay
Mekong
PHNOM PEN
COCHIN CHINA
SAIGON
BURMA
GULF of SIAM
VIETNAM
LAOS
CAMBODIA
Scale Miles
ASSOCIATED STATES OF INDO-CHINA

nothing less—to hand over to him far greater freedom than they were prepared three years earlier to give to Dr. Ho Chi-minh.

By this time, however, Dr. Ho Chi-minh's position had greatly changed. The victory of the Communists in China brought to the frontiers of Tongking, Dr. Ho Chi-minh's stronghold, a friendly power on which he could rely for support. It also, incidentally, strengthened the Communist wing of his entourage. When Bao Dai's régime was recognized by several Western nations, including Britain and the United States, the Viet-minh riposte was swift; it claimed to be the real government of Viet Nam—characterizing Bao Dai as a French puppet—and immediately acquired Chinese and Russian recognition.

From that point onwards the war in Indo-China assumed an international aspect. It became part of the cold war, of the world-wide struggle between Communist and non-Communist forces. Chinese help for the Viet-minh in the form of training camps and military supplies soon showed its effects in vastly increased Viet-minh operations which led to the withdrawal of French troops within the Red river delta. The arrival of General de Lattre de Tassigny at the end of 1950 led to a vigorous but short-lived revival of French power. Viet-minh attacks were crushed, a belated start was made to recruit and train a Viet Nam national army and—at France's request—American supplies for the new army began to arrive in bulk. These developments were followed by a reorganization of the Viet-minh in which the Indo-Chinese Communist Party reappeared as the Laodong or Workers' Party and became the directing influence in the Viet-minh movement, while the Lien Viet was established to organize non-Communist support for Communist objectives.

General de Lattre de Tassigny's untimely death in 1952 proved a blow from which the French and Viet Nam forces never recovered. He had changed the whole atmosphere in the country during his brief term of office. In 1952 and the following years the French position steadily deteriorated, to the accompaniment of growing war weariness in France. Chinese help, reinforced by a railway built to the Tongking border, increasingly showed itself in the efficiency, organization and expansion of the Viet-minh army under General Giap. The Viet Nam army also grew considerably in size, but too late to be as effective a fighting machine as Dr. Ho Chi-minh's forces Moreover, it lacked enthusiasm; it was difficult for Bao Dai' Government to convince the Viet Namese people that it was truly nationalist, especially when in 1953 a Viet Nam "national congress" appointed by Bao Dai passed a series of resolutions demanding "complete independence". Asian opinion was equally dubious; India, for example, declined to recognize Viet Nam as an independent state.

Early in 1954 the war situation in Indo-China reached a crisis. New Viet-minh offensives began in northern Laos, aimed at the capital, Luang Prabang, and in Tongking, where General Giap's veteran divisions closely invested Dien Bien Phu, an outpost occupied by French parachute troops in 1953. Much criticism was later directed against the decision of General Navarre, the French commander, to hold this isolated fortress, which was cut off by land from the French troops in the delta and could be supplied and reinforced only by air, but the French commander's aim was to keep it as a base from which to harry the Viet-minh supply line to Laos. At this stage of the fighting the French were making more and more use of air power not only for offensive action but for air lifts to outlying garrisons in view of the dangers involved in road transport, particularly at night, from guerilla bands which operated even inside the delta area. Most of that air power came from America; in the later stages of the fighting the United States contributed about 80 per cent of the cost of France's Indo-China war on the grounds that a French-Viet Namese victory was important "not only to France and the Associated States but to the United States and the whole free world".

Where the French were caught napping was in the calibre of the forces employed by the Viet-minh in the siege of Dien Bien Phu. According to General Navarre, the fortress could have stood a siege of indefinite length by purely guerilla elements, but General Giap's army consisted of highly organized well armed troops backed by field artillery and anti-aircraft batteries. French air power found itself greatly hampered by effective anti-aircraft fire. The French and Viet Nam garrison of over 12,000 men under Brigadier-General de Castries put up a magnificent resistance lasting for fifty-five days of almost continual assault, but in the end—on May 7, 1954—the heroic defenders were compelled to surrender when the remains of the fortifications were overrun. The Viet-minh had scored their biggest and most spectacular success of the war.

Long before the fall of Dien Bien Phu peace talks were in prospect. By the beginning of the year the explosive possibilities of the war became increasingly evident as Chinese and American military aid poured into Indo-China. Fortunately the opportunity to hold peace talks arose in connection with the Berlin conference of the foreign ministers of the United States, Britain, France and Russia to seek a solution of the German and Austrian problems. The meeting was a failure, but arrangements were made for a conference at Geneva on Korea and Indo-China to be attended by representatives of Communist China, although Washington made it quite clear that its presence did not involve any recognition by America of Mr. Mao Tse-tung's government.

America, however, had little faith in any peace conference on Indo-China, and for a time Mr. Dulles, the American Secretary of State, ran a strange combination of policies. While agreeing with the Geneva conference he tried, on the plea of urgency, to get Britain to co-operate in more direct action. At the end of March Mr. Dulles made the first public reference to a scheme, fostered by America, for a South-East Asia Treaty Organization on the lines of NATO comprising countries willing to constitute a defence system against the spread of Communism in South-East Asia. During a visit to London a few days later he urged immediate united action by the West against the Viet-minh, one of his proposals being an air strike to relieve Dien Bien Phu. Sir Winston Churchill's reaction was to refuse to do anything which would prejudice the forthcoming Geneva talks, and to counsel patience until the result of the conference was known.

Meanwhile staff talks began in Singapore between military representatives of the ANZUS powers (America, Australia and New Zealand) as well as Britain and France with the object of laying the foundation of common action either to support a peace treaty on Indo-China or to take precautionary measures if the conference failed. The British Government's justified anxiety to secure the co-operation of non-Communist Asian countries in any Indo-China settlement was evident from Sir Anthony Eden's approach to the Colombo Powers—India, Pakistan, Burma, Ceylon and Indonesia—which held a meeting at Colombo just before the Geneva conference on Indo-China. Mr. Dulles's attitude differed sharply. He wanted to press on with the SEATO scheme and plainly had little use for Sir Anthony Eden's efforts to bring in the Colombo Powers so as to make the pact a truly Asian affair.

The Geneva conference on Indo-China opened with the hands of the Western governments weakened by the fall of Dien Bien Phu, which took place two days earlier. Mr. Chou En-lai, the Peking Foreign Minister, appeared for the first time at a conference in Europe; Mr. Molotov represented Russia and Sir Anthony Eden Great Britain. Although America was represented, Mr. Dulles did not attend; after the fall of Dien Bien Phu he announced that as Indo-China was in a state of flux it did not provide a suitable basis for armed American intervention—a view which by this time had become dominant in the United States.

M. Bidault, the French Premier, proposed that after a cease fire French-Viet Nam and Viet-minh troops should be concentrated in zones to be defined, and that Viet-minh forces should evacuate the occupied portions of Laos and Cambodia. The Viet-minh peace terms included the withdrawal of all foreign troops from Indo-China, the holding of elections and the recognition of the "Khmer" and "Pathet Lao" "governments" in Cambodia and Laos respectively. These so-called governments were really anti-French resistance movements which originated in much the same way as the Viet-minh. When the Japanese handed over power in 1948, the kings of Laos and Cambodia, like Bao Dai in Viet Nam, proclaimed themselves independent. With the return of the French they accepted the new situation, but some members of their governments did not; they started nationalist guerilla activities which eventually linked up with the Viet-minh organization in Viet Nam.

With Sir Anthony Eden and Mr. Bedell Smith supporting the French proposals and Mr. Molotov and Mr. Chou En-lai backing the Viet-minh demands the conference soon ran into difficulties. By the middle of June it had reached what looked like a hopeless deadlock.

From Washington Mr. Dulles thundered that the American people would meet any threat of intervention by Peking. At this critical stage Sir Anthony Eden left to attend with Sir Winston Churchill a conference at Washington; Mr. Molotov had already departed for Moscow, and Mr. Chou En-lai returned to Peking by way of Delhi and Rangoon where he had meetings with Mr. Nehru and U Nu. From Washington it was announced that Britain and America would press on with plans to meet either success or failure at Geneva. Simultaneously the ANZUS powers declared for "immediate action to bring about the early establishment of collective defence in South-East Asia".

This strange interlude in the Geneva proceedings certainly had a healthy effect. With the return of Sir Anthony Eden, Mr. Molotov and Mr. Chou En-lai, and the appearance at Geneva of a new French premier, M. Mendès-France, the tempo of the conference suddenly quickened. M. Mendès-France set the pace by stating on July 11 that if an armistice was not arranged in nine days he would resign. He was greatly helped by the change which had come over Mr. Molotov and Mr. Chou En-lai following their visit to their respective capitals. Both Moscow and Peking knew that France was willing to partition the country by evacuating the populous Red river delta; both were equally aware that if the conference failed America would take such steps to help the French as would render a general war almost inevitable. For that eventuality neither Russia nor China was prepared.

M. Mendès-France got his wish, and better terms than he had a right to expect in view of the daily weakening of the French-Viet Nam position in the delta. Agreement to end the conflict was achieved on July 20. The settlement provided for the partition of Viet Nam roughly along the 17th parallel just north of Hue, the old imperial capital of Annam, and for elections throughout Viet Nam within two years to decide the future of the country. India, Poland and Canada agreed to provide commissions to supervise the armistice in each of the states of Viet Nam, Laos and Cambodia, with the Indian representative as chairman in each commission. India's selection as chairman of the commissions was a tribute by both sides to the helpful attitude of Mr. Jawaharlal Nehru, who had long urged a settlement and who, in April, put forward a plan embodying six points for the achievement of peace. Most of his suggestions found a place in the truce terms. India was not officially represented at Geneva, but Mr. Nehru's "ambassador at large", Mr. V. K. Krishna Menon, actively assisted negotiations by his contacts with British and Chinese delegates.

Laos and Cambodia were left as neutral territories, though the north-east of Laos will remain until the elections in 1955 under the control of Laotian dissidents, Viet-minh troops being withdrawn. France agreed to recognize the full independence of the three states. The partitioning of their country is as bitterly resented by the Viet Namese people as the division of Korea is detested by the Koreans; both countries are the victims of power politics and the cold war.

For the non-Communist world two important concessions were achieved. Firstly, the two-year delay in holding elections in Viet Nam may redound to their benefit; had the elections taken place immediately as demanded by the Viet-minh the Communists would, almost certainly, have swept the board. Secondly, the virtual neutralization of Laos and Cambodia places a buffer between China and countries like Siam, Burma and Malaya, where local Communist movements constitute a menace. For Communist China the immediate gain was an increase of prestige and the creation of another buffer state, as in Korea, between her territory and the direct influence of the West.

For France the great benefit is release from a struggle which was no "little war". The Viet-minh had in the field in 1954 close on 400,000 troops, of whom 175,000 constituted a hard core of seasoned veterans; in seven and a half years' fighting France and her associates suffered casualties amounting to 92,000 dead or missing, 114,000 wounded and 28,000 prisoners.

The only one of the great powers which looked with disfavour on the Geneva agreement was America. To many citizens of that country Geneva seemed a second Munich. The United States delegation made it clear that, while they would not interfere in the new situation, they had no part in it, and would regard with "grave concern" any further Communist aggression. From American declarations it seems clear that if, in the future, south Viet Nam considered that the elections to decide the future of the whole country were not to be really "free" in the Communist-dominated northern half and refused to take part in them, the United States would support south Viet Nam in that decision even against the international control commission. Washington, with the example of Korea in mind, regards SEATO and not the Geneva agreement as the real solution.

*Chapter Sixteen*

# TODAY'S VITAL STRUGGLE: CHINA'S POSITION

THE VITAL STRUGGLE in Asia today is not, as I have already said, the battle for nationhood, which to all intents and purposes has been won. Western control of Asian countries is practically a thing of the past. While three former British possessions—India, Pakistan and Ceylon—remain of their own free will members of the Commonwealth, that in no way restricts their freedom, as Mr. Chou En-lai, Communist China's Prime Minister, is reported to have acknowledged during his visit to Delhi in 1954. In fact Mr. Chou En-lai "welcomed India's continued membership of the Commonwealth", an observation interpreted in India "as an appreciation of India's independent role and as conveying Mr. Chou's belief that the Commonwealth as a whole serves as a stabilizing factor in world affairs".[1] Indonesia's last political link with Holland, the Netherlands-Indonesian Union of 1949, was terminated by mutual consent in 1954, leaving relations between the two countries to be governed by ordinary treaties, and setting Indonesia free from any suspicion of "colonialism". There still exists a dispute over the future of Dutch New Guinea, which Indonesia claims to be part of her territory, but that is a matter for settlement between two independent nations. Apart from Dutch New Guinea and British Borneo, the only territory of any size under Western control is Malaya, where the difficulties of providing an agreed constitution for a multi-racial state are the main obstacle to the attainment of self-rule as promised by the British Government. But the goal for Malaya is not in dispute.

The real struggle is not Asian nationalism *versus* the West; it is Asian nationalism *versus* Communism. Even that battle would have been practically won today had it not been for an epoch-making

[1] *Manchester Guardian*, June 30, 1954.

event—the triumph of Communism in China. In all the newly liberated Asian states nationalist governments are in power with the exception of the northern half of Korea and the northern half of Viet Nam where Communists, backed by China, exercise control. In the words of *The Times*,[1] "The Communist victory throughout the length and breadth of China brought about the greatest swing in the balance of world forces since 1917. In many ways it was greater in its cumulative effect than the Bolshevist revolution of 1917, for then Russia was alone and weak, whereas the mass of China is now added to a Russia grown strong." Mr. Mao Tse-tung's success in firmly establishing a Communist régime in China creates a problem of tremendous concern for all the newly liberated Asian states. Each of these states contains a Communist movement of greater or less significance, but its importance has grown with the appearance of Communist China. There are something like ten million Chinese scattered throughout these countries, most of them in Malaya, Indonesia, Indo-China, Siam and Burma; they could become, as in Malaya, active fifth columnists of a dangerous type.

The situation is complicated by the undoubted admiration which all these non-Communist Asian governments feel for the triumph of Mr. Mao Tse-tung. They regard it as an exclusively Asian triumph; the victory of a man who, ignored by Soviet Russia as a "deviationist", led his peasant followers to overthrow a so-called nationalist government which was heavily backed by the greatest of the Western powers. Here indeed was a rousing assertion of Asia's rights! However much these non-Communist governments may disapprove of Communism in their own countries they cannot withhold their admiration for a man and a creed which struck so shattering a blow for the freedom of Asia from Western influence.

At one bound China replaced Russia in eastern eyes as the chief exponent of Communism. And within a few years of achieving power the Peking Government struck two solid blows against the West which immensely increased its prestige; it drove the United Nations forces, mainly composed of American troops, back from the Yalu river to the 38th parallel in Korea and pinned them there,

[1] *The Times*, May 17, 1954.

and it compelled France, another Western power, to evacuate the Red river delta in Indo-China despite the flow of war materials from America. Typical of Asian reaction was that of a non-Communist Chinese who, while disapproving of his country's action in Korea, yet exulted in pride that at last China, after years of humiliation at the hands of the West, had stood up to, and beaten back, Western armies in battle. Equally significant was the claim by a Peking newspaper after the Geneva conference of 1954 that China had already avenged four of the twenty-one national humiliations which she had suffered at the hands of foreigners. (I cannot vouch for the actual figures quoted, but the setting up of a score sheet is the point that matters.)

What, then, is the future of this new, powerful and aggressive Asian giant? In size China is colossal, with a population far exceeding that of any other country of Asia or the world. From a census taken in 1953 Peking claims that China's total population, including Formosa and an estimate of Chinese nationals overseas, is nearly 602 millions. Even if this figure is an exaggeration, the fact remains that China completely eclipses the 367 millions of her next biggest population rival, India, while her army, now reported to be growing to 175 divisions or two million men, dwarfs the forces which India or any other Asian country (Russia excluded) could put in the field. During the Korean war China's guerillas of the civil war were converted into modern positional fighters, equipped with automatic weapons and armoured vehicles. At the same time Soviet jet aircraft were acquired rapidly to expand the air force. The new China lags behind only in naval expansion.

China's policies are in the hands of a few inscrutable and resolute men in Peking; like those of their opposite numbers in the Kremlin, they are governed by certain long-term objectives. Sometimes Mr. Mao Tse-tung's tactics, following the example of Moscow, may seem to bear little relation to his ultimate aim. Communist China's main ambition is, of course, to become in every way the dominant nation in Asia, to take the place once held by Japan. To achieve that ambition, especially in the industrial sphere, she will require the sympathy and material support of Soviet Russia. It is therefore wishful thinking of a foolish and dangerous kind for the West to imagine that Moscow and Peking can be separated at this stage of China's development. That China will one day assert herself and develop along her own lines, Communist or otherwise, is obvious to all who know China and the Chinese people; signs of her growing assertiveness are already apparent. But that day is not yet. Mr. Mao Tse-tung, as we are frequently reminded, is no Tito. He is determined to build up China into a strong power in precisely the same way as Marshal Stalin established Soviet Russian strength, but at much greater speed. That is why Marshal Stalin is still a hero in Mr. Mao Tse-tung's eyes despite the scurvy treatment he received from the Kremlin in his Yenan days. Mr. Mao Tse-tung must follow Russia's example not only in the agricultural field, where the peasants have to be cajoled or compelled to produce more food, but in the much more important sphere of heavy industry. To quote an American newspaper correspondent in Hongkong[1] "The Chinese Communists, while working to build an impregnable position of international strength, are putting their major effort into mobilizing the country and people into a modern industrial state on the Soviet pattern". They have still a long way to go. In 1954 China was producing only two million tons of steel compared with Russia's forty millions, and only a quarter of the amount of Russia's coal output.

The emphasis in China's five-year plan is on heavy industry, together with communications, and on the development of technical and scientific resources. Already a notable start has been made with heavy industry in Manchuria, where there are coal and iron deposits, including the great steel works at Anshan. But Peking is not putting all its industrial eggs into one basket. According to the *People's Daily* of Peking (March 27, 1954) central China is to be the country's second industrial area; "Its mineral wealth provides almost all that is necessary for heavy industry, and China's second largest base for the iron and steel industries is to be built there." Three new industrial regions are to be developed in the provinces of Honan, Hupeh and Hunan where, the *People's Daily* states, the new iron and steel "industrial complex" will be larger than that at Anshan. Heavy industry is also being developed at Chungking, General

[1] *World*, New York, May, 1954.

Chiang Kai-shek's wartime capital on the upper reaches of the Yangtze-kiang river.

Equally significant is the impressive programme of railway construction, both commercial and strategic. The main south-west rail artery now links Hankow with Hanoi and the port of Haiphong on the Red river delta of Viet Nam; a new line under construction stretches into the province of Sinkiang in the far north-west, and a whole system of connecting lines is being either built or planned in the western provinces so as to connect these rich but hitherto isolated districts with one another and with the central plains. Of China's total estimated revenue in 1954 of about £4,000 million, something like £1,800 million, or 45 per cent, was earmarked for economic development comprising steel plants, coal mines, power stations, oil refineries and fertilizer factories. One of the coal mines which the British Labour Party delegation, headed by Mr. Attlee, saw in Manchuria in 1954 was a British pioneer effort expropriated by the Communists. Other illuminating details include 14 per cent for welfare and education, 21 per cent for defence and nearly 19 per cent for the cost of administration.

A striking picture of the new China was given by Mr. G. S. Gale, the special correspondent of the *Manchester Guardian* with the British Labour Party delegation which visited China in the summer of 1954. In a message from Hongkong after the departure of the delegation Mr. Gale wrote:[1]

> "although China is primarily an agricultural land, its whole economy revolves around its new industrialization. The industrialization of China is the true focus of all present Chinese activity, the true source of the unquestioning acceptance of Communist dictatorship. Factories, roads, railways, bridges—these are the true hard facts. Well over half of every yuan gathered in taxation goes into capital investment in heavy industry and transport. . . . There seems nothing to stop China from becoming a major industrial power within five years. China is already self-sufficient in pig-iron, and indeed is exporting it. A car plant of Coventry size is expected to begin production shortly. Anshan is now producing enough steel rails for China's railway

[1] *Manchester Guardian*, September 2, 1954.

programme, and that includes about seven hundred miles of new track to be laid down this year. Russian equipment is flooding in. And all the time the Chinese are voraciously learning the management techniques denied to them under Japanese occupation. Universities are transformed into technical colleges, the abler workers are sent to Russia and return as teachers. The ancient manual dexterity of the Chinese is now exercising fingers on lathes instead of in the decorative crafts."

Russia is not only the beau ideal of Communist China in respect of industrial development and economic self-sufficiency; it is the main source of China's supply for that development and for the technical training essential to its maintenance. Russian aid is all the more necessary in view of the restrictions laid by the United Nations on member states trading with China ever since the Peking Government was declared an aggressor in Korea; anything which is likely to increase China's war potential is banned. This state of affairs suits Russia, although it may not please China. The Kremlin's desire is manifestly to keep China tied to, and dependent on, Russia as long as possible. With that object in view Russia is thought to have deliberately spun out the Korea war for nearly a year longer than it should have lasted by savagely rejecting an Indian peace move which was justifiably believed by the Indian Government to have Peking's tacit support; it is a fact that the Peking Government knew the terms of the offer and made no objections to them while negotiations were in progress. Moscow knows that once China is on her feet she will not prove as amenable to Russian influence as her present circumstances dictate. Mr. Mao Tse-tung may walk respectfully behind Russia and in step with her at the moment, but the day will certainly come when Peking will claim full partnership with Moscow. A sign of China's increasing self-assertiveness was the Peking agreement of October, 1954, by which Russia agreed to restore to China by May, 1955, full possession of Port Arthur, which was under joint control, and to relinquish her share in joint enterprises formed to assist Chinese economic development in return for a long-term loan of 520 million roubles. China is too old and too proud a nation to play second fiddle indefinitely in any alliance.

All this means that Communist China must have a period of

peace in order to complete her economic reconstruction. Peking is therefore unlikely at present to provoke any major war in which China would be directly involved. How then, it will be asked, did the Chinese Communist Government allow itself to be implicated in major hostilities in Korea and to a much less extent in Indo-China. The answer in both cases is simple. A glance at the map will show that had the United Nations army reached the Yalu river it would have stood on the doorstep of China's new heavy industry area in Manchuria, with the steelworks at Anshan within easy bombing range.

The one thing that Communist China could not possibly countenance was to have the armed forces of the country she considers to be her greatest enemy, the United States of America, sitting close to a vital industrial region—vital for purposes of both war and peace. That explains why Peking, as soon as the U.N. forces neared the Yalu, unhesitatingly threw hundreds of thousands of Chinese "volunteers" into the fray so as to drive back the allied army to the 38th parallel. It also explains why north Korea is being converted into a Chinese province; Peking is taking no risks with President Syngman Rhee and his American friends. Mr. Mao Tse-tung would, of course, like to see American influence entirely eliminated from Korea, and to that end he may advocate some kind of Korean unity, just as the Russians plead for their own variety of German fusion, but it would be a unity acceptable to China.

To Mr. Mao Tse-tung and his government the Korean issue may well have seemed a matter of life and death for the new republic. The effort cost China heavily in men, in money, in material and in the dislocation of her industrial programme. It is an experience which China would not willingly want to repeat in her present stage of development, and it undoubtedly contributed to the Indo-Chinese peace settlement at Geneva on terms which France and the West could regard in the circumstances as reasonable.

China's troops were not involved in Viet Nam, but there was a heavy drain on her war material in support of Dr. Ho Chi-minh and the Viet-minh forces. Here again an important principle for China was at stake—Peking's policy of building up Communist buffer states on its frontiers as Russia did in Europe. The settlement gave

China what she wanted for the time being—a pro-Communist government in north Viet Nam and access to the important Red river delta port of Haiphong. Both Hanoi, the capital of Tongking, and Haiphong are linked by rail with the interior of China over the Tongking border, and the use of the port will prove most valuable to Peking as a trade outlet for south-west China. These gains are substantial; by themselves alone they justified Peking's policy of not pressing demands which might have led to a general conflagration.

The one big claim which Communist China has got on the West, and one which has highly dangerous possibilities, concerns the island of Formosa. This beautiful island, named Ilha Formosa by the sixteenth-century Portuguese explorers who discovered it, and known to the Chinese as Taiwan or "Terraced Bay", lies about a hundred miles off the south-east coast of China near Amoy. For many years in occupation by the Japanese, who seized it from China after the 1895 war, Formosa was handed back to China in 1945 in pursuance of the Cairo declaration on the Far East made by the allied powers two years earlier. It was taken possession of by General Chiang Kai-shek's nationalist government pending the Japanese peace treaty, and to it the bulk of his forces retired in 1949 following their defeat on the mainland. General Chiang Kai-shek was not the first Chinese ruler to seek retreat in Formosa in similar conditions; Cheng Chen-kung, the last of the Ming dynasty rulers to resist the Manchus, took refuge in Formosa and maintained its independence for twenty years.

The Kuomintang brought an addition of about two million people, including over half a million troops, to Formosa's population of about seven millions. At that time America adopted a watching brief because of its moral obligation to safeguard the lives of its protégé and his army. General Chiang Kai-shek was able to hold his enemies at bay because of his naval and air strength; for a period he attempted to blockade the mainland, and created much irritation by interfering with foreign shipping. The "blockade" was called off when President Truman, on the outbreak of the war in Korea, ordered the American fleet to "neutralize" the island. Washington's decision provided Peking with a convenient excuse for dropping loudly heralded operations for the conquest of Formosa in 1950, since it is most unlikely that the Communists had the naval craft necessary for invasion. America's "neutralization" policy was accompanied by renewed military aid to General Chiang Kai-shek in consequence of Communist China's intervention in north Korea.

Early in 1953 President Eisenhower issued an important and far-reaching policy directive; he cancelled his predecessor's order to the Seventh Fleet restraining the Nationalists from attacking the mainland. But simultaneously Mr. Dulles made it clear that the fleet—as a "primarily military decision"—would still protect Formosa and possibly some of the smaller islands connected with it. These small islands constituted a further complication. They include the Tachens, a few small islands close to the mainland about 200 miles north of Formosa, and the Quemoy group, comprising Quemoy, Little Quemoy, Big Tan and Little Tan, which lie just off the estuary leading to Amoy. Quemoy is strongly garrisoned by the Nationalists—there are said to be about 40,000 troops on it—and it is used as a listening post by General Chiang Kai-shek's intelligence staff in its contacts with the mainland. The other islands are the Pescadores, which lie about thirty miles off the west coast of Formosa and may well be considered part of the Formosan defences.

Just before the SEATO conference began, and probably inspired by it, the Peking authorities opened a propaganda campaign for the conquest of Formosa. "We must liberate our territory of Taiwan and eliminate the traitorous Chiang Kai-shek gang" declared the Peking *People's Daily* in August, 1954. "We shall not stop until this object is attained". About the same time Communist artillery carried out a heavy bombardment of Quemoy, which is only about four miles from the mainland, and other islands of the group, killing two American officers belonging to a military mission. The Nationalists retaliated by counter-battery action and air bombing of Amoy and its neighbourhood. For the next two months sporadic action and counter-action went on; they continued during the SEATO conference and the visit of the British Labour Party delegation to China, accompanied by insistent demands on the part of every Chinese leader from Mr. Mao Tse-tung downwards that Formosa must be "liberated". The Peking Government had presumably two main objects in view in carrying out the demonstrations: firstly, to test America's reactions to a threatened assault on these coastal islands, and secondly, to assert Communist China's determination to bring Formosa within its grasp sooner or later.

While it was axiomatic that America would defend Formosa in view of its importance to the Pacific defence chain running from Japan through Okinawa to the Philippines, there was for a time much speculation as to whether U.S. forces would aid the Chinese Nationalists to resist an attempt to seize Quemoy. Mr. Dulles in September declared somewhat oracularly that "the defence of Quemoy is primarily related to the defence of Formosa and it is being considered and studied in that light". Washington's aim was obviously to convey to Peking the impression that an attack on Quemoy might lead to U.S. intervention, a belief strengthened by unofficial reports that the American Seventh Fleet had been ordered to give "full logistic support" to the Quemoy defenders. Peking apparently took the hint, because by October hostile action ceased and excitement died down.

All doubts about America's attitude towards Formosa were removed by the signing in December of a mutual security pact between the United States and the Nationalist Chinese Government for the defence of Formosa and the Pescadores. Justifying the treaty, Mr. Dulles claimed that it took Formosa out of the realm of speculation and tended to stabilize the situation. That is doubtful because it still left two questions unanswered: would it commit America to the defence of the coastal islands held by the Nationalists, and to Nationalist attacks on the mainland? Mr. Dulles quite rightly admitted that the Quemoy and Tachen groups had never been taken over by the Japanese and could therefore be considered part of mainland China, but on the subject of their future he was again indefinite. Whether operations against them could be considered part of the defence of Formosa would, he said, "be a matter in the first instance for military advisers and finally for the President's decision". The general impression at the time of the signing of the treaty was, however, that the Nationalists' claim to the islands could not be defended provided America thought that Communist action was not part of an offensive against Formosa. U.S. Naval units assisted the Nationalist evacuation of the Tachens when these islands were attacked by the Communists early in 1955. But America's attitude towards the Quemoys was still uncertain up to that date, and was not made any easier by Peking's provocative assertions that the Communist offensive against the coastal islands was part of a campaign aimed at the "liberation" of Formosa. On the issue of Nationalist attacks on the mainland, the assumption was that the treaty gave Washington an excuse for discouraging General Chiang Kai-shek from undertaking needless pinpricks against the Peking authorities.

The plain fact of the matter is that so long as Formosa and its neighbouring islets remain under Western protection they will continue to be a thorn in the side of Communist China. One American view is that Formosa should be placed under U.N. trusteeship with the U.S. as the mandatory power. On his return from China Mr. Attlee, the leader of the British Labour Party delegation, declared that the Nationalists should be removed from the island, which should be handed over to the Communists after a period of neutrality. Whatever happens, one thing is clear. If America considers Formosa essential to her Far East defence system it should be neutralized. It is manifestly highly unfair, and asking for trouble, to allow General Chiang Kai-shek's government to harass the mainland in any unjustified way while the Nationalists are under American protection.

Opinions vary on the Nationalist administration of Formosa; it has been called a police state, although Mr. Chester Bowles, the former American ambassador to India, was told during his visit in 1953 that the Kuomintang authorities were moving towards local elections and "real democracy".[1] Mr. Bowles goes on: "Over and over again as I travelled around the island I thought to myself: If only Chiang Kai-shek's government had done as well on the mainland as it is now doing on Formosa it would still be there, and the world would be closer to peace. . . . With American assistance, the Nationalists are determined to turn Formosa into a model of economic development for Asia". Professor W. G. Goddard, an Australian who visited the island in 1954, wrote in *The Times* of August 30:

[1] *Ambassador's Report*, by Chester Bowles (Harper and Brothers, New York).

"I spent three months in Formosa earlier this year and I was amazed at the freedom enjoyed by the people, considering that the country is in a state of actual war". Tragically enough, the only hope of the Kuomintang lies in a third World War, which might give its troops an opportunity of reconquering the mainland with American help. An ageing army, they constitute at present no real threat to Communist China, a fact of which Peking is presumably well aware.

Until her internal strength is built up, Communist China can have no desire to embark on a major war, involving America, for the conquest of Formosa. But the island holds highly explosive possibilities for several reasons. Its possession is a matter of prestige for Peking; it is a subject on which the Communists can raise a patriotic rallying cry—a very valuable asset to them—in the same way as they did over Korea. Moreover, in any attempt to bring Formosa under its sway Peking would have the sympathy of most Asian countries and of quite a number of people outside Asia. The danger is that a spark may set off a conflagration which neither East nor West wants. Hence the extreme importance of America insisting on complete neutrality by General Chiang Kai-shek so long as her wings are over the island.

In foreign policy the Chinese Communists have two main objectives. The first is to isolate America from her Western friends. To that end Britain is being wooed assiduously after a period of diplomatic aloofness on Peking's part in strange contrast to the promptitude with which the British Government accorded recognition to the Communist régime. That aloofness was due, it is believed, to Peking's conviction that Britain was America's "stooge" in the Anglo-American partnership; the differences displayed by London and Washington in their approach to the Geneva conference acted as an eye-opener to Mr. Chou En-lai. But whatever the reason, the change was most marked. A flattering reception was accorded to the British Labour Party delegation which, under the leadership of Mr. Attlee, visited China during the 1954 autumn parliamentary recess. They were feted and entertained by Mr. Mao Tse-tung and his colleagues in the most lavish fashion, with speeches of welcome extolling the virtues of co-existence. The same flattering attention is being paid to Japan with the same object in view.

Another aspect of this anti-American campaign is the suggestion mooted by Mr. Chou En-lai in recent talks with Colombo Powers representatives that all Asian countries should unite to free themselves from every trace of Western influence. By Western influence the Peking premier undoubtedly meant in the first place American influence, since that is the biggest obstacle to China's domination of the Far East and South-East Asia. The idea of wiping out all Western connections is certainly not one that would appeal to the majority of the Colombo Powers, apart altogether from states like Siam and the Philippines which look to SEATO for protection against Communist aggression. India, for example, wishes to steer clear of all power *blocs*, whether Eastern or Western, and in that view Mr. Nehru does not stand alone.

Peking's second main objective is to create around China, as Russia did, a series of satellite states. China has not forgotten, any more than her neighbours, that centuries ago the Chinese empire extended into Indo-China, Siam, Burma and even across parts of what is now India's north-eastern border. As far east as Burma the Chinese form a not inconsiderable element of the population of various countries. A Canadian observer,[1] writing in 1954, emphasizes that the Chinese Government indoctrination classes envisage China "liberating her friends", and he goes on: "Indo-China, Thailand, Malaya, Indonesia, Burma and India are all in the next line of threat from China".

The nature of that threat can well be imagined. Since Asian Communists now tend to look to China for leadership, Peking could—without open aggression—stimulate the Communists in those countries to work for the overthrow of their governments, using some at least of the Chinese inhabitants as a fifth column. That is what is really worrying the newly liberated democracies of Asia today.

[1] *China Under Communist Control*, by Stewart Allen (Canadian Institute of International Affairs).

*Chapter Seventeen*

# THREAT TO SOUTH-EAST ASIA

FROM THE POINT of view of nationalist governments in South-East Asia—and the West—the supreme value of the Geneva settlement was that it restrained, temporarily at least, a grave Communist threat. Had the Communists overrun the three Associated States of Indo-China, the whole of South-East Asia would have been imperilled. So great an impetus would have been given to Communist and "Free Thai" elements both outside and inside Siam that the government of Field-Marshal Pibul Songgram would have been swept away. The way would then have been clear for intensified support for the Communists still fighting in Malaya and Burma. That in turn would have led to pressure on the Assam region of India in the north and Indonesia in the south. Communist penetration would have followed the line of the Japanese advance in 1941–1942, when country after country fell to the invaders on the house of cards principle. With the weight of Communist China behind infiltration and local risings, progress would have been no less sure even if it might have been slower.

Communist China could simultaneously, had she wanted, have exercised pressure on India along the whole frontier of Tibet, and especially across the borders of Nepal, which is an independent state but under Indian influence. Since the overthrow of the traditional ruling class, the Ranas, the Communists have become a factor to be reckoned with in this beautiful hill state. Most of these countries, notably Siam and Tibet, have their own Communist leaders and movements functioning inside neighbouring Chinese territory just as Dr. Ho Chi-minh and his Viet-minh nucleus were given sanctuary in Kwangsi province across the Tongking border. China, as a reference to the map will show, is peculiarly fitted to conduct a Communist infiltration campaign. From its massive interior it can thrust outwards along thousands of miles of land frontier.

Although the Communist danger to South-East Asia has been reduced by the agreement to end the war in Indo-China, it has not been removed. Can, for example, the southern half of Viet Nam pull itself together sufficiently in the next two years to win the election due to be held to decide the future of the whole country? The omens in 1954 were not too good. Feeling among the anti-Communist Viet Namese at the conclusion of the armistice was one of despair; they considered themselves badly let down by the French. For a time it looked as if Viet Nam morale would completely collapse in the face of Viet-minh propaganda, which proclaimed the taking over of the Red river delta as a preliminary to the acquisition of the whole country. But after the tumult and the shouting had died down, signs of a reaction began to appear. Chinese help, which was welcomed by the Viet-minh during the fighting, seemed less desirable when peace was declared; the traditional dislike of the Viet Nam people for Chinese overlordship started to assert itself even on the Viet-minh side of the 17th parallel. The Viet Namese could not forget their domination in past centuries by the former Chinese empire and the fact that they had achieved their freedom by throwing the Chinese out.

On the southern side of the armistice line an immediate breakdown of morale was prevented largely by the courage displayed by Mr. Ngo Dinh Diem, the head of the Viet Nam Government and a Roman Catholic nationalist, who rallied Roman Catholic resistance. Opinion was sharply divided on what course to pursue. One school of thought felt they should follow the example of President Syngman Rhee of Korea by organizing the southern half of Viet Nam into a unit for the reconquest of the north; another section aspired to develop South Viet Nam as a model democratic state with U.N. help, while a third group was prepared to co-operate with the Viet-minh in the hope of winning them to the democratic cause.

Much will depend on the type of government which the southern Viet Namese succeed in establishing and whether it can unite, and acquire the confidence of, the people as a whole. The southern Viet Namese include some strange politico-religious sects with private armies which did not always see eye to eye with pre-armistice administrations—the Cao Daists of Cochin China, the Buddhist Hoa

Haos and the Binh Xuyen army of General Le Van Vien. The Cao Daists were described by Mr. Graham Greene[1] as an "amalgam of Confucianism, Buddhism and Christianity", with a pope, a holy see, female cardinals, canonization of Victor Hugo, and prophecies by a kind of planchette.

Control of these sects, with their private armies, led to trouble between Mr. Ngo Dinh Diem and the former chief of staff of the Viet Namese national army, General Nguyen Van Hinh, which was described as a "rivalry for personal power" on the part of the civil authority and military leadership. Bao Dai's dismissal of General Hinh and the inclusion of representatives of the sects in the Government settled—at least on the surface—the quarrel between the civil and military authorities. Unfortunately the truce did not last long. Open warfare between Government and two of the sects, the Binh Xuyen (which is little better than a gangster organization) and the Hoa Haos led early in 1955 to much damage and loss of life in Saigon and its neighbourhood. The Prime Minister's position had been strengthened late in 1954 by the promise of direct United States aid to south Viet Nam "in order that a strong, solid state, capable of resisting subversive temptations or armed aggression, may be developed or maintained". President Eisenhower also hoped that the counterpart of the aid would be the carrying out by the government of "indispensable reforms". The American aim is clearly to encourage the south Viet Namese to build up a strong nationalist state, capable not only of resisting Communism but of voting against it when election day for the whole country arrives.

Uncertainty existed after the armistice about the future of the emperor Bao Dai; there are republican tendencies among a section of the Viet Namese who hold Bao Dai partly responsible for the Viet Nam failure to overcome the Communists. Given a government capable of uniting and enthusing the people, about half a million of whom are Roman Catholics from the Red river delta, the south Viet Namese could face the future confidently with American assistance. But if they are rentby factional rivalries and do not organize themselves on a solid anti-Communist basis, their chances of prevailing against Viet-minh methods and propaganda in

[1] *The Sunday Times*, March 21, 1954.

an election contest are bound to be bleak. Surveying the scene towards the end of 1954, a special correspondent of *The Times*[1] lately in Indo-China found much to depress him in the shape of apathy, lack of inspiring leadership and lack of practical idealism. By 1955 the situation was still bleaker owing to the fighting between the Government and the sects.

The French appear to be planning to make the best of both worlds. According to General Ely, Commissioner-General at Saigon, French policy towards the Viet Nam Government—now established in the historic Norodom palace in Saigon—which the French authorities recognize as the only legal government of the whole country, is based on the twin ideals of total independence and complete support. Total independence became effective at the end of 1954; France was then ready to give the free government all aid, economic and otherwise, necessary for the progress and development of the country. France was also prepared to assist in the creation of a Viet Nam army which would make the presence of French troops unnecessary. But by the beginning of 1955 French participation was giving way to increasing American aid, and French policy was being subordinated to U.S. initiative. This tended to add to the confusion in southern Viet Nam, since it bore no relation to the French attitude in the northern half of the country.

In the north the French Government took the significant step immediately after the armistice of appointing as their representative with the Viet-minh Government M. Jean Sainteny, a personal friend of Dr. Ho Chi-minh; with General Leclerc, M. Sainteny negotiated the first agreement between France and Viet-minh. His purpose is to look after French people and French business interests in Tonking, but there can be no doubt that he will maintain as close contact as possible with the Viet-minh authorities as a sort of insurance for the future. He has already achieved economic and cultural agreements with Dr. Ho Chi-minh. France is obviously determined to have a foot in both camps.

Although the situation in Laos is simpler than that in Viet Nam, nevertheless the Laotian frontier with Viet-minh territory and the terms of the Geneva settlement render the country liable to

[1] *The Times*, October 27, 1954.

Communist infiltration. Under the agreement the pro-Communist members of the "Pathet Lao" forces, as the Laotian rebels were known, were concentrated in the northern Laotian provinces of Phong Saly and Sam Neua. The Pathet Lao forces originally comprised a mixture of anti-French nationalist guerillas, Communists, and a sprinkling of "Free Thais" from the north. When the independent Laotian government established by three royal brothers prior to the Japanese surrender was broken up by the French on their return to the country the three brothers fled to Siam, but one of them, Souphanou Vong, returned to lead a nationalist guerilla movement against King Sisavong Vong's government at Vientiane, the capital of Laos, which had French backing. This government had as its chief minister another of the brothers, Souvanna Vong, who accepted office on the French assurances of self-government in 1949.

Eventually the Pathet Lao forces made contact across the Viet Nam border with the Viet-minh, which hailed them as brothers, invaded northern Laos in their support and helped them to set up a Pathet Lao "government" at Sam Neua. After the Geneva agreement the Laotian Government appealed to all genuine nationalists in the Pathet Lao forces to leave the rebel army and settle down in the state, but one of the less satisfactory aspects of the settlement was the concentration of Pathet Lao dissidents in Phong Saly and Sam Neua, thereby permitting the northernmost portion of Laos bordering on Viet-minh territory to be occupied by Communist elements until elections were held. Measures are being promulgated for the special representation in the Laos Government of these two provinces after the withdrawal of the Viet-minh.

The danger now is that from behind the scenes the Viet-minh will work to secure the admission of their own agents in the shape of Viet-minh indoctrinated Laotians as dissident representatives in the Laotian administration. Only one thing can prevent that happening—a reconciliation between the two royal brothers, one of whom heads the royal government and the other leads the Pathet Lao forces. If they cannot agree it means that the Pathet Lao movement is so closely tied up with the Viet-minh that the door to Laos will be open to the Communists.

Although the population of Laos is only a million and a half, the country occupies a key position as a buffer state between Viet-minh territory and Siam. Should Viet Nam go Communist, the position of both Laos and Cambodia as independent states would become impossible. But even under the Geneva agreement it is open to Communist agents to infiltrate Laotian territory and, by way of northern Laos, to cross the border into Siam at a point where there is a considerable population of Laotians and "Free Thais".

The danger here is obvious. Siam, or Thailand, has long lived under the shadow of Communist influence. Since the abolition of royal absolutism in 1932 power in the country has revolved round two outstanding figures, Field Marshal Luang Pibul Songgram, representing the right wing elements, including the armed forces, and Nai Pridi Panomyong, leader of those whose political creed is to the left. When the Japanese army invaded the country in 1941 there was much talk of fighting for freedom but, in the words of an eastern journalist, the battle was over before breakfast and Field Marshal Songgram, who was then prime minister, co-operated heartily with the Japanese. His rival, who led an underground anti-Japanese resistance movement during the war, came into power after the defeat of Japan, but in 1947 Nai Pridi Panomyong had to flee the country as the result of a *coup d'état* which restored Field Marshal Songgram.

For a time the Field Marshal's supremacy hung in the balance; several attempts, fostered by Nai Pridi Panomyong's followers, were made to overthrow him, and his position was further weakened by the success of the Communists in China and their activity in the neighbouring states of Indo-China and Malaya. Strong Communist elements inside the country also proved an embarrassment. These were mostly Chinese, who constitute a sixth of Siam's 20 million people, and after Mao Tse-tung's triumph the Chinese press in Bangkok, the Siamese capital, became blatantly pro-Communist in tone.

Faced with a multitude of Communist worries Field Marshal Songgram's Government in 1950 abandoned Siam's traditional policy of neutrality and definitely aligned itself with the Western democracies in the cold war. Siam sent a contingent to the U.N. forces in Korea. This gesture stimulated American interest in the country, and after a visit from United States economic and military missions,

Field Marshal Songgram signed agreements with Washington providing for the supply of arms, equipment and military instructors.

The Siamese Premier spent the next few years consolidating his position. In 1951 he abolished the post-war constitution which provided for free elections to the National Assembly, and reverted to the 1932 constitution whereby half the Assembly members are nominated by the king; in actual fact, of course, by the party in power. Having thus ensured his unquestioned authority, the Field Marshal imposed increasingly restrictive controls on the Chinese community in Siam and on all forms of Communist activity. Strong anti-Communist legislation was rushed through the National Assembly in 1952 following the discovery of what the Government described as a Communist plot to seize power and to compel the king to abdicate.

These measures earned the Bangkok Government the mounting hostility of Communist China, and in 1953 Siam suffered from the depredations of Malayan terrorists in the south and from an influx of refugees from Laos in consequence of the Viet-minh invasion of that country. Bangkok declared a state of emergency in nine eastern and north-eastern provinces, simultaneously despatching military reinforcements to the Laos border. In May, 1954, Siam decided to ask the U.N. Security Council to send observers to her frontiers in view of the possible dangers to her territory of the Indo-Chinese war, a move which the British Government feared might embarrass the Geneva negotiations then in progress. This particular threat disappeared with the signing of the Indo-China armistice.

Another source of danger to Siam is the "Free Thai" movement. In 1953 Peking announced the establishment in the province of Yunnan, due north of Siam, of a "Thai Autonomous Region" which Bangkok interpreted as a centre for Communist penetration of neighbouring Burmese, Laotian and Siamese areas and as a meeting place for dissident Siamese political groups. A strong racial affinity exists between the people of Yunnan and the inhabitants of the Burma Shan states, Laos and the northern districts of Siam, and the boundaries of a "Free Thai" republic would certainly include the northern Siamese provinces, of which Chiengmai is the principal town. From there it would be easy to conduct a Communist campaign to the South.

Bangkok's alarm at this development was heightened by the appearance in China of Nai Pridi Panomyong, Field Marshal Songgram's exiled rival. In an article in the Peking *People's Daily* Nai Pridi Panomyong called upon the Siamese to "wage a struggle against American imperialism and its puppets, the Government of Siam", the Americans being denounced for "using Siam as a base for aggression" in South-East Asia. Nai Pridi was careful, however, not to call for a Communist revolt; his main theme was that Siam should have a government (presumably led by himself) which would work in close co-operation with the Colombo Powers and especially with India and Burma. Since the article obviously had Peking's approval, its chief interest to the outside world lay in its revelation of the type of government in Siam which would prove acceptable to Communist China. Although Nai Pridi Panomyong's link-up with the Chinese was calculated to do him harm in Siam, where national feeling is strongly hostile to any hint of Chinese domination, the policy he advocated was bound to find a hearing, especially among intellectuals who hold him in esteem. Official Siamese disquiet grew as reports reached Bangkok that Nai Pridi Panomyong had gone to Yunnan.

In these circumstances Field Marshal Songgram's response to the invitation to attend the proposed South-East Asia Treaty Organization conference convened by the Western Powers in the Philippines in September, 1954, was not only cordial but insistent; he demanded that SEATO should not merely have teeth but teeth strong enough to protect Siam from any form of invasion. Scarcely was the ink dry on the SEATO agreement when the Siamese Government announced that it believed "aggression to be imminent from supporters of the 'Free Thai' army".

Despite the assurance which Siam has received under SEATO and the economic and military aid which America is pouring into the country, her internal position cannot be described as satisfactory. Siam is the largest exporter of rice in the world—a fact which gives her special importance in the eyes of Communist China—but she is faced with a deepening economic depression owing to a fall in export prices and a rise in the cost of living. Distress in 1954 was worst in the north-east provinces, where the people are most accessible to Communist propaganda from over the Laotian border and where Communist "cells" are known to be active. Under the 1951 constitution ten years must elapse before there can be a wholly elected National Assembly, but meantime, as political parties are banned, no training in democracy is possible.

To all intents and purposes Siam is a dictatorship, suffering from all the defects usually associated with unrestricted power, including corruption which stifles trade and hinders relief measures for the mass of the people. According to a "correspondent lately in Siam" writing in the *Manchester Guardian*,[1] "As constituted at present the Government is quite unable to enforce such measures because it depends for its support upon a system of concessions, privileges, and bribes to Government officials and business men who in turn pass on a percentage to an even wider circle of friends and minor officials".

Although Siam is a member of the Colombo Plan, she has no comprehensive development programme, but several development projects are in hand or are planned. These include irrigation, power, water supply and rice research schemes. In recent years Siam has had little contact with her neighbours, the newly liberated nations of South-East Asia. In August, 1954, a *Manchester Guardian* correspondent summed up his impressions of the country's foreign relations as follows:[2]

> "Thailand's attitude towards America might be compared with the traditional attitude of Montenegro to Russia. There used to be a saying in Montenegro that 'we and the Russians are two hundred million strong'. Even today, when most thoughtful people in Bangkok realize the importance of military preparedness and welcome military aid from America, there is a tendency to regard the matter as essentially a Siamese concern depending more upon co-operation with America than with the Colombo Plan countries. This could do much harm to collective security in this part of Asia, as these countries may hesitate to support a defence organization in which Thailand appears to have a special role as a close satellite of the United States. Even in Thailand, where there is almost unanimous support for acceptance of

[1] *Manchester Guardian*, August 17, 1954.
[2] *Manchester Guardian*, May 31, 1954.

American military aid, there is some reluctance to consider the establishment of actual American bases completely under American control".

For Siam's determination to ward off Communism there can be nothing but sincere sympathy and support; the only question that arises is whether Field Marshal Songgram's Government is going the right way about it from a long term point of view. Even an American admirer of the country, Mr. Chester Bowles,[1] had to admit after a visit to Siam that the present government "has no strong roots among the people. Lacking the tradition of national struggle which supports Nehru and U Nu of Burma, the leaders of Thailand are constantly in danger of being supplanted by a military coup. . . . The Communist party is outlawed and not yet strong, but the young people of the country who are studying abroad are increasingly dissatisfied with the system of strong men". What Mr. Bowles might have added is that behind the national struggle of India and Burma lay the British parliamentary system which taught the people the rudiments of democratic government. Siam's great need today is the training of her people in that system, and it is devoutly to be hoped that her rulers will increasingly devote their attention to the building up of a sound democracy which is the surest guarantee against Communism.

The value of Siam to the free world of Asia cannot be sufficiently emphasized. It is an all-important gateway. Were Siam to go Communist either from internal upheaval or from external intervention, the way would be clear for the application of direct Communist pressure towards two great Asian democratic fields—Burma, East Pakistan and India in the north-west, and Malaya and Indonesia to the south. Here again the path of Communism would follow the route taken by the invading Japanese armies in the second World War. On the whole the Siamese authorities have done their best to seal off the frontier of Malaya from Communist infiltration; it is acknowledged in Kuala Lumpur that the Malayan terrorists receive little or no help from outside.

If, however, Siam fell to the Communists it is easy to imagine not merely the practical stimulus which this development would give

[1] *Ambassador's Report*, by Chester Bowles (Harper and Brothers, New York).

to Malaya's terrorists, but its psychological effect on the people of Malaya as a whole. Control of Malaya would be a terrific prize for Communist China; its wealth of rubber and tin, which is vital to the Commonwealth, would immensely strengthen Peking's economic resources for purposes of both peace and war. And if the whole of the mainland facing the South China Sea came under Communist domination, the multiple-island republic of Indonesia would fall like a ripe plum into the Communists' lap. A heavy responsibility, both internal and external, rests on Siam's army of 50,000 men now being rapidly expanded to double that number with American help.

Burma, Siam's western neighbour, is the gateway to India. The country has a very long frontier with Siam, extending for nearly a thousand miles from the isthmus of Kra to the state of Laos on the upper reaches of the Mekong river. The Shan states carry the border for about 150 miles along the northern part of Laos, where Communist Laotian dissidents were concentrated after the Geneva agreement, and thence for nearly a thousand miles along the frontier of the Yunnan province of China, where the "Free Thai" movement is located. Communist infiltration could therefore be applied to Burma not only from Siam but from northern Laos and Yunnan through which, incidentally, the famous Burma Road passes. Burma is also involved in the "Free Thai" campaign owing to the racial affinity between the Thais of Yunnan and the people of the Shan states.

All this explains the anxiety of the Burma Government to secure assurances from Communist China that the country's territorial integrity will be respected, and that subversive movements, which have plagued Burma ever since the war ended, will not be encouraged. One of Burma's main dangers in the past few years has been not Chinese Communists but Chinese Nationalists. Although 2,000 of Chiang Kai-shek's troops which escaped across the Yunnan border into the Shan states were evacuated in 1953, large numbers of these men are still scattered throughout Burma's hilly north-eastern region. Fortunately for the country, the main centre of Communist revolt lay in the Irrawaddy delta and the central stretch of the river, well removed from Burma's eastern frontier. Yet if Siam fell a victim to Communist pressure, Burma would be most vulnerable, a fact fully appreciated by U Nu and his Government. Between them, Siam and Burma would represent another rich prize for the Communists, constituting as they do the two great rice granaries of South-East Asia.

A bridge between India and her eastern neighbours, Burma and China, is provided by the Indian state of Assam. Not long ago Communist activities in Assam and in the frontier states of Tripura and Manipur caused grave concern in Delhi, particularly because local leaders were in close touch with Burmese Communists on the other side of the frontier. "Peking", said *The Times of India*[1] in 1951, "may not harbour expansionist desires, but Communism is potentially expansive and explosive, and anxiety is heightened by the Union Home Minister's reference to encouragement for the Assam terrorists from across the border. The Communist Party Congress in Calcutta three years ago served as a useful cloak for transborder contact men".

In 1954 the Government of India approved a considerable expansion of the security intelligence services for Assam's eastern and northern border, where Communist agents were reported to be active among local tribesmen who are susceptible to Communist influence because of their dislike of central authority. The Nagas, for example, who loyally supported the Indo-British war effort against the Japanese, have embarrassed the Delhi Government by demanding a separate Naga state. Experience shows that these remote frontier areas can be used for Communist infiltration not only into India but into East Pakistan, where Communists were recently involved in large-scale disorders which led to the suspension of the provincial government.

Another source of Communist infection on India's borders is the kingdom of Nepal. This beautiful hill state, famous as the birthplace of Buddha, extends for 500 miles as a sort of buffer between India and the former semi-independent state of Tibet, now the "Tibet region" of Communist China. Its people are Mongolian in origin but for centuries they have been ruled by Rajputs from India who fled from Chitor on its capture by the Muslims in 1503. The leading Rajput families established their authority over the whole country,

[1] *The Times of India*, February 28, 1951.

constituting a hierarchy which provided the ruling dynasty and the hereditary occupant of the offices of prime minister and commander-in-chief. Over a hundred years ago the head of the powerful Rana family secured from the then king the "perpetual right" to the office of prime minister, a right which was enjoyed by his descendants until the revolution of 1951. Up to that time the king was a mere figure-head, occupying a semi-divine position similar to that of the emperor of Japan under the shogunate.

For long Nepal proved an aggressive neighbour. Late in the eighteenth century a Nepalese invasion of Tibet led to armed intervention by the Chinese empire, which repelled the invaders and claimed jurisdiction over both Tibet and Nepal. Another war between Nepal and Tibet in the middle of the nineteenth century ended in a treaty under which Tibet agreed to receive a Nepalese ambassador and to pay an annual tribute to Nepal of Rs. 10,000. Up to 1953, strangely enough, the payment was continued despite Chinese Communist mastery of Tibet, but the following year it stopped for the first time in 97 years. A Gurkha incursion into India was finally defeated by General Ochterlony of the East India Company in 1816, after which there ensued uninterrupted peace and most friendly relations between the British Government in India and the Nepalese authorities.

Nepal was recognized as an independent kingdom, but by a special agreement the Government of India recruited Gurkhas—the short sturdy hillmen of Nepal—for the Indian army. Two world wars in which 200,000 Gurkhas took part familiarized both East and West with these fine fighting men, whose characteristic felt hats, cocked jauntily on their heads, and *kukris*, heavy curved blades worn at the belt like bayonets, achieved world fame. By a treaty between the British Government and the Government of Nepal enacted after the separation of India and Pakistan, Great Britain retains the right to recruit in Nepal eight battalions of Gurkhas for service with the British army, the British Brigade of Gurkhas being mostly employed in Malaya. This right of recruitment is strongly criticized by left wing elements in both India and Nepal, yet its economic advantages appeal to the Nepal Government, which in the past derived a steady income for its peasantry from military service abroad. It is estimated that half a million sterling goes into Nepal each year in the shape of pensions and family remittances.

The authority of the Ranas remained unquestioned until 1950. For many years Nepalese exiled from their native country because of their political activities organized themselves in India in alliance with the Indian National Congress, but the British India Government prevented them from interfering in Nepalese affairs and the state continued to lead an isolated feudal existence, cut off from the outside by the absence of road and rail transport. Delhi's attitude towards the Nepal exiles altered after the Indian National Congress came into power on the British withdrawal. When treaties of peace, friendship and trade were signed between the two countries in 1950 Mr. Nehru made it clear that he had advised the Nepal Government "to the extent that a friendly power can advise an independent nation" to bring itself more into line with modern democratic trends.

About the same time the Nepalese National Congress, which met at Patna in India under the presidentship of Mr. M. P. Koirala, passed a resolution affirming its determination "to fight the tyranny of one-man rule in Nepal till a democratic form of government is established". Simultaneously it was decided to organize a mass movement against the authorities inside Nepal itself. Disorders occurred throughout the country. They were suppressed by the state forces, but a crisis developed within the government between the Ranas and King Tribhuvana, who favoured the Nepalese Congress idea of a democratic government of which he would be the constitutional head.

Tension rose to such a pitch that the king with his family took refuge in the Indian embassy in Katmandu, the capital, whence they received permission to fly to Delhi. Declaring that King Tribhuvana had abdicated, the Rana government proclaimed his second grandson, who had been left behind, as king. Complete deadlock ensued; the Indian Government refused to recognize the boy king and after months of negotiation the reformers won a striking victory. The principle of democratic government was accepted, with the king having the right to appoint ministers on the advice of the premier and with the cabinet divided equally between members of the Rana family and the Nepal Congress until such time as a constituent assembly could be elected to frame a new constitution. The half-Rana half-Congress Government did not last long. Following friction and a spate of resignations in 1951 the king reconstituted the cabinet under Congress leadership, thereby ending the long hereditary premiership of the Rana family.

Nepal's political troubles were, however, far from being at an end, and the country had to pay the price of an all too sudden change from autocracy to a form of self-government in which neither rulers nor ruled had any experience. In a country of valleys separated by mountain ranges and with practically no modern communications, separatist tendencies asserted themselves. Branches of the Congress in remote regions demanded local autonomy, but a more dangerous movement was led by Dr. K. I. Singh, who aimed at the overthrow of the Katmandu Government in favour of a Communist state. With the aid of Indian forces, which co-operated at the request of the Nepal Congress Government led by Mr. M. P. Koirala, the Communist revolt at Bhiratnagar near the Indian frontier was smashed and Dr. Singh imprisoned.

Early in 1952 Mr. M. P. Koirala's administration narrowly escaped violent destruction when Dr. Singh and his fellow prisoners were released by their guards and for some hours were masters of the capital until the revolt was quelled by the army. Dr. Singh fled into Tibet, where he and his henchmen now constitute a continual menace to the peace of Nepal. Hardly had Katmandu recovered from the shock of Dr. Singh's escape than a fierce quarrel broke out between the Prime Minister and his half brother, the irrepressible Mr. B. P. Koirala, the Nepal Congress leader. Popular government had to be abandoned in favour of a cabinet of advisers and, after a brief interval, this policy was continued by King Mahendra after his father's death early in 1955.

Nepal suffers from poverty and a bad land system. Help to build up the country's economy is being given by the Government of India, by the United States Administration under Point Four of the foreign aid programme, and under the Colombo Plan. Indian experts are reorganizing and training the Nepal civil service. Vigorous measures are also being taken to modernize Nepal's communications, the lack of which seriously restricts the authority of the Government over outlying districts, and renders possible the development of Communist cells. A big step forward was taken in 1954 with the opening, thanks to Indian enterprise, of the first road linking Katmandu with the railhead at Amlekganj, a distance of eighty miles over highly mountainous terrain.

The need to improve Nepal's communications, its land system and its economy generally is urgent in view of the activities of Communist agents both inside and outside the country. Communism obtained a foothold among some of the intelligentsia and peasantry in the days of Rana absolutism; Dr. Singh's rebellion in 1951 showed its strength in the remoter areas, while its influence in the cities was illustrated by the success of Communist candidates in the Katmandu municipal elections. During one of his visits to the capital before he left India in 1953, Mr. Chester Bowles, the American ambassador in Delhi, records seeing "a party of three thousand young men in Katmandu, marching through the streets with clenched fists. While most of these young men were not Communists, they were certainly Communist-organized and led. Whether this smoldering Communist movement grows more powerful or not will depend to a major degree on whether the new Government is able and willing to move swiftly and distribute land to the villagers".[1] In April, 1953, Communist strength among the lecturers and students at Katmandu was so considerable "that they were able to call a joint strike of professors and the Communist-dominated student organization".[2]

Communists are well established in the Nepal Terai, the stretch of low-lying marshy and malaria-ridden but fertile country which extends between the plains of India and the main Himalaya range. According to the Delhi correspondent of *The Times*,[3] "Indian Communism does not stop at the frontier; in fact, it appears to be as strong in the Terai as in Bengal or Travancore-Cochin. In jute mills and factories built in Bhiratnagar to avoid Indian taxation and labour regulations, Indian workmen are well organized. The

[1] *Ambassador's Report*, by Chester Bowles (Harper and Brothers, New York).
[2] *The Communist Party of India*, by M. R. Masani (Derek Verschoyle).
[3] *The Times*, July 8, 1954.

Communist flag flies over many buildings; and in shops the portrait of Mr. Stalin has a place of honour among pictures of Hindu deities. . . . The Terai is as much a stronghold of Indian Communists as it is of the less responsible Indian industrialists and business men".

Fears are expressed that as communications between the Terai and the towns in the interior of Nepal are extended there will be a link up between the Communists of the plains and those of the hills. Nor must it be forgotten that so long as Dr. Singh and his adherents are allowed to function without interference across the Tibetan border there will always be plenty of stimulus for the local Communists. Incidentally, there appears to be a struggle going on among the Nepalese Communists as to whether they should take their lead from Moscow through the Indian Communist Party, or look to Peking for guidance now that Dr. Singh is in Tibet.

Yet however divided they may be in their allegiance they are quick to exploit political feeling against foreign aid as "interference" and "turning Nepal into a colony" of India or America. Again to quote Mr. Chester Bowles: "The continued presence of Chinese Communists on its northern border makes what happens in Nepal all the more important to India, and to the whole non-Communist world. If Nepal should fall before an invasion from Tibet, or from an internal Communist revolution, the Communists would be poised right on the Indian border, above the great heartland of the country, and less than four hundred miles from Delhi".[1] The battle between nationalism and Communism in Nepal requires for victory not only adequate material help but the spread of democratic institutions and a sense of responsibility among anti-Communist Congress groups.

[1] *Ambassador's Report*, by Chester Bowles (Harper and Brothers, New York).

*Chapter Eighteen*

# INDIA AND CHINA

MUCH MISUNDERSTANDING EXISTS in the West, and especially in America, on the subject of India's relations with Communist China. It is sometimes assumed that Delhi leans towards Peking either because India favours the Communist world, or because she is scared of it and wants to appease her powerful new Communist neighbour. A third reason occasionally advanced is that she does it out of sheer "cussedness" in order to spite the West for the way it treated Asia in the past. None of these reasons is the right one. India's friendship with China has nothing to do with the form of government existing in that country; it is based on a desire to work harmoniously with a great and free Asian state with which India has always lived in peace. As Mr. Chou En-lai put it in reciprocating Mr. Nehru's sentiments in his speech at the state banquet during his visit to Delhi in the middle of 1954, "between India and China there has existed for over 2,000 years traditional friendship".

Mr. Nehru's Government was prepared to extend the same goodwill to General Chiang Kai-shek's Nationalist China as it does today to the Communist China of Mr. Mao Tse-tung. Hardly had Mr. Nehru become Prime Minister of India immediately after the war than he extended an invitation to the Generalissimo and his charming wife, Madame Chiang Kai-shek, to come to Delhi. They did so, and there is no doubt that plans were discussed for the co-operation of the two countries after India had achieved its independence. Chinese Nationalist delegates attended the picturesque Asian conference held in Delhi in 1946. Their manner, it is true, was friendly, but it was touched with *hauteur*, as if they wished to remind India that it was still a "colonial" state compared with China, which they obviously regarded as the proper country to lead the new Asia. But there was no mistaking Delhi's genuine wish to be on the friendliest possible terms with Nationalist China after the departure of the British. Mr. Nehru sent to General Chiang Kai-shek's capital as his ambassador Mr. K. M. Panikkar, whom he regarded as one of his top-ranking diplomats, and it is significant that on the Generalissimo's eclipse Mr. Panikkar was despatched to Peking as soon as India recognized Mr. Mao Tse-tung's Government in 1950.

Mr. Nehru does not like Communism; he has said so publicly time and again. He has denounced India's Communists in the strongest and most opprobrious terms and his Government sternly suppressed the Communist risings which occurred in India in 1948. Yet he was prepared, like Britain, to recognize that the Communist régime had established itself in China and that it was frankly ridiculous to pretend that the real rulers of the country were located in an island off the Chinese coast.

No special reason existed why Delhi should be more friendly to Mr. Mao Tse-tung than it had been to General Chiang Kai-shek. Indeed, in the same year that India acknowledged the Peking Government a strange episode occurred affecting Mr. Mao Tse-tung's relations with Indian Communists. In reply to a message from the Indian Communist Party conveying its apologies for having earlier described him as a "deviationist"—this was done under the guidance of Moscow which similarly admitted its mistake—Mr. Mao Tse-tung cabled an assurance of the full support of the Chinese people for the Indian Communists in their "struggle", and expressed the hope that the day was not far distant when "India, too, would be liberated by the Communist Party from the oppression of Anglo-American imperialism and its Indian lackeys".

Although he must have known of it, Mr. Nehru tactfully took no official notice of this somewhat devastating message. His Government continued to press for the admission of Communist China to the United Nations on the grounds that its absence from that body was one of the principal reasons for the deterioration of the international situation as exemplified in Korea and elsewhere. While India supported the initial action of the Security Council by recognizing that aggression had been committed in Korea and sent an ambulance unit as a token contribution to the U.N. forces there, the Delhi Government strongly opposed the crossing of the 38th parallel by General MacArthur's troops, its ambassador in Peking having been plainly told that by such action Communist China would consider her security directly menaced. Delhi took the view, quite rightly, that once North Korean aggression had been pushed back to its own borders an attempt should be made to settle the Korean problem by negotiation before further military steps were undertaken.

Two developments which occurred after these events rather shook India's faith in Mr. Mao Tse-tung's Government. The first was the Chinese invasion of Tibet, where India had inherited from the British certain old-established rights, including an agent in Lhasa, the Tibetan capital, trade agencies in Gyantse and Yatung, post and telegraph offices on the trade route to Gyantse and a small military escort for their protection. These arrangements were for the mutual benefit of both countries; they suited India admirably, and Delhi quite frankly had no wish to see its semi-independent neighbour overrun by forces which would bring Communism to the frontiers of both India and Nepal.

When Mr. Nehru's Government expressed to Peking their deep regret that "in spite of friendly and disinterested advice repeatedly tendered by them, the Chinese Government should have decided to seek a solution of the problems of their relations with Tibet by force instead of by the slower and more enduring methods of peaceful approach", Peking's reply was bitterly uncompromising. Tibet, it declared, was an integral part of China and no foreign interference would be tolerated. "The Chinese People's Liberation Army must enter Tibet, liberate the Tibetan peoples and defend the frontiers of China". Peking's attitude and actions aroused considerable resentment in India, particularly as China somewhat gratuitously suggested that India had been influenced "by foreign agents hostile to China in Tibet". In public speeches Mr. Nehru demanded to know from whom the Tibetan people were to be liberated, and when asked about a Chinese map showing part of northern Assam as Chinese territory he angrily declared that India would defend her frontier, "map or no map".

The second shock happened in connection with the Korea peace negotiations. While Mr. Nehru agreed that aggression had occurred in Korea, India voted against the modified American resolution in the United Nations Political Committee branding Communist China as an aggressor, her reason being that to do so would extinguish all hopes of a peaceful settlement. The war in Korea, like the war in Indo-China, was a matter of intense concern to Mr. Nehru, who rightly feared that from these struggles might spring a conflagration in which the whole of Asia, including India, would be involved. In 1952 the Government of India, after months of careful sounding of all the interested parties, brought before the U.N. Political Committee a seventeen-point draft resolution for a truce in Korea. Russia's flat rejection of the plan disappointed India, but her disappointment changed to surprise and chagrin when Peking also uncompromisingly turned down the resolution.

The Chinese attitude puzzled Delhi, because Peking had been kept fully informed of developments during the formative stages of the plan and had at no time indicated disapproval. There was a good deal of public anger at the unceremonious way in which India had been treated by a country she had so consistently championed in the United Nations and elsewhere, but the Indian Government took comfort in the thought that Russia was the villain of the piece, and that had Russia not intervened so drastically Peking would have accepted the Indian proposals. Subsequent events tended to confirm India's deductions. It was significant that after Marshal Stalin's death the following year China agreed to truce plans which differed little from those propounded by the Indian delegation in the U.N. Political Committee at the end of 1952. International recognition of India's part in securing peace was accorded when that country was asked by the United Nations to be chairman, umpire and executive agent of the Neutral Nations Repatriation Commission at Panmunjom.

India's continued support of Communist China after these rebuffs might lead Westerners to imagine that Delhi's policy, so far as China is concerned, is one of appeasement. That, however, would be a wrong assumption. In its attitude towards the handling of Eastern countries by the West, Mr. Nehru's Government is at least consistent; India has no cause to love Japan, yet Delhi annoyed America by refusing to sign the Japanese peace treaty because its terms did not concede to Japan "a place of honour, equality and content among the community of free nations", especially in regard to continued American occupation of the Ryukyu and Bonin islands. Delhi later signed a separate peace treaty with Tokio.

Meanwhile the Chinese "liberation" of Tibet, which had aroused Mr. Nehru's ire, proceeded slowly but surely. At Peking's request the sixteen-year old Indian mission in Lhasa became a consulate-general and all direct relations with Tibet ceased. For centuries Tibet had been a feudal theocracy. Its religion, Lamaism, is a corrupt form of Buddhism, with the chief lama, known as the Dalai Lama, nominally exercising supreme authority both in civil and religious affairs. By a convention dating from 1907 both Britain and Russia recognized China's suzerainty over Tibet; in 1910 the Chinese empire despatched an army which occupied Lhasa, but the revolution of 1911 destroyed its authority and in the succeeding years Tibet managed its own affairs. In 1945 General Chiang Kai-shek said he would give Tibet "a high degree of autonomy", but his agents, too, were expelled by the Tibetans when his régime collapsed.

Communist China's occupation of Tibet was a carefully planned operation. In order not to outrage the religious feelings of the inhabitants, since the spiritual supremacy of the Dalai Lama as the viceregent or incarnation of Buddha exists not only throughout Tibet but in parts of Mongolia and China, Communist agents infiltrated Tibetan monasteries and won over Tibetans living in China, including the Panchen Lama, the second most powerful lama of Tibet, who agreed to work for them in return for the strengthening of his position against the Dalai Lama. The Tibetan army, such as it was, could do little against the invaders, and by the end of 1950 the Tibetian hierarchy had no option but to negotiate an agreement. The young Dalai Lama with his retinue fled from Lhasa to Yatung on the Indian border, but by a show of reasonableness on the part of the Chinese representatives he was persuaded to return to his capital.

Chinese policy in Tibet is that of the iron hand in the velvet glove. While the old forms of priestly authority remain, in actual fact all power rests in the hands of the Communists. Tibet has autonomy, but "under the unified leadership of the Central People's Government". A steady attempt was made to undermine the prestige of the Dalai Lama and to build up that of the Panchen Lama; in 1954 the Dalai Lama was invited to go to Peking for the obvious purpose of demonstrating Chinese overlordship; he and the Panchen Lama appeared in public in China as a sort of prize exhibit. Chinese army units are employed in constructing various public utility works, including the building of three major roads into Tibet—two of which were completed in 1954, thereby ending the country's isolation—and the production of enough food to make the country self-sufficient.

Nevertheless there has been a good deal of friction caused by food shortages due to the influx of a large body of Chinese troops, demands for the services of men and pack animals, and higher taxation to meet increased government expenditure. According to *The Manchester Guardian*,[1] the "Resistance Movement in Tibet" recently issued a manifesto complaining among other things of the "sacrilegious behaviour of the Communists who defile our monasteries and chapels by hanging their washing and soiled socks and underwear on the altars", which "shocked even the most tolerant of us". Despite these and other more serious grievances, all signs point to the Peking Government steadily expanding and tightening its authority over Tibet.

The Chinese occupation of Tibet had one most important result so far as India is concerned. It led to an agreement between Delhi and Peking which enunciated certain guiding principles in the relationship of the two countries. The agreement, which was signed in Peking on April 29, 1954, was prefaced by a statement that it was based on the following five principles accepted by both countries—(1) Mutual respect for each other's territorial integrity and sovereignty; (2) Mutual non-aggression; (3) Mutual non-interference in each other's internal affairs; (4) Equality and mutual benefit; and (5) Peaceful co-existence. True, all one-sided privileges formerly enjoyed by the Government of India in what was referred to as the "Tibet region of China" disappeared. The Indian military escort had to be withdrawn, all Indian Government rest houses, buildings, post, telegraph and telephone services had to be handed over to the

[1] *Manchester Guardian*, September 9, 1954.

Chinese, and in return for trade facilities in Tibet Delhi had to grant to the Chinese Government similar trade facilities in India.

In some Western countries, notably America, the agreement was regarded as a climb-down for India, whereas in actual fact it was merely the recognition of the new state of affairs in China. No other country, including Britain, could in the circumstances have acted differently. Chinese suzerainty over Tibet, although seldom exercised, had always been recognized, and when the Peking Government in 1950 decided to assert its authority there was really nothing the outside world could do about it short of challenging China's right to manage her own affairs. On the other hand, Delhi secured from Peking agreement to a set of international principles which were later to assume great significance.

The signing of the Sino-Indian agreement on Tibet marked a distinct change in Communist China's attitude to India. This was dramatically illustrated at the end of June, 1954, when the Chinese Premier, Mr. Chou En-lai, paid a three-day visit to Delhi on his way to Peking from the Geneva conference on Indo-China. For a total of ten hours the two prime ministers were locked in close consultation, and at the end of the talks a joint *communiqué* stated that the main purpose of the visit—which came as a surprise to East and West and even, it is reported, to Mr. Nehru himself—was "to arrive at a clearer understanding of each other's point of view in order to help in the maintenance of peace, both in co-operation with each other and with other countries". This clearer understanding was detailed in the next paragraph of the statement which read: "The Prime Ministers recognized that different social and political systems exist in various parts of Asia and the world. If, however, the above-mentioned principles (in the preamble to the Tibet agreement) are accepted and acted upon and there is no interference by any one country with another, these differences should not come in the way of peace or create conflicts".

Shrewd observers in Geneva saw in Mr. Chou En-lai's unexpected call on Mr. Nehru and later on U Nu, the Prime Minister of Burma, a well-timed effort to wean away their respective countries from the projected South-East Asia Treaty Organization which was then being mooted by America. That, undoubtedly, was its object, but the visit was significant as representing Communist China's first overt act of friendship towards two South-East Asia democracies which up to then she had treated with something approaching contempt. For India, however, the main result was to give Mr. Nehru a convenient yardstick by which to measure the sincerity of Chinese professions of peaceful co-existence. Mr. Nehru, as the record of events up to this stage showed, had no illusions about Communism or Communist China. He dislikes Communism and he was fully aware of the massive violence and bloodshed—repugnant to a disciple of Mahatma Gandhi—employed by Mr. Mao Tse-tung and his régime in establishing control of the country. He was also aware of the menacing possibilities of Chinese expansion—the potential threats to South-East Asian countries which could involve his own frontier from Assam to the state of Uttar Pradesh. No Indian government, he said, in 1950, could tolerate the invasion of Nepal from anywhere, and on his visit to the state the following year he referred to the Himalayas as "the guardians and sentinels of India", whose "white-capped peaks welcome friends and are a warning to those of hostile intent". He was similarly aware of the Communist movement in India, of its desire to found another Yenan within the remoter parts of India's frontiers, and of the encouragement which open or underground Chinese support could give its subversive activities.

All these factors must have been present in Mr. Nehru's mind when he discussed the five principles of co-existence with Mr. Chou En-lai in Delhi, one result of which was that the two prime ministers agreed to drop the word "mutual" in the second principle, making it read simply "non-aggression". Of transcendent importance to Mr. Nehru were the first and third principles, "mutual respect for each other's territorial integrity and sovereignty" and "mutual non-interference in each other's internal affairs". Here, indeed, at its face value, was a valuable guarantee to India and the rest of the newly liberated Asian countries struggling with Communist minorities.

The essential thing to remember about these principles is that they are of Chinese origin; they were repeatedly emphasized by Mr. Chou En-lai during his visit to Delhi both in his speeches and at his press conference. According to Mr. Chou En-lai, the five principles provide a new basis for close co-operation and constant contact between the two governments and peoples for the cause of world peace. In reply to a question at his press conference, he went on to expand his government's general attitude towards foreign countries in the following words:

> "It is our view that on the basis of the five principles . . . all nations of the world can peacefully co-exist whether they are big or small, strong or weak, and no matter what kind of social system each of them has. The rights of the people of each nation to national independence and self-determination must be respected. The people of each nation should have the right to choose their own state system and way of life without interference from other nations. Revolution cannot be exported; at the same time outside interference with the common will expressed by the people of any nation should not be permitted. If all nations of the world put their mutual relations on the basis of these principles, intimidation and aggression by one nation against another would not happen and peaceful co-existence of all nations of the world would be turned from possibility into reality."

All these statements meant a great deal to Mr. Nehru. They gave him a public assurance that Communist China would not lay claim to any part of India's territory for the purpose of "liberating" its inhabitants, nor interfere in India's internal affairs by, for example, encouraging subversive Communists movements. Whether Mr. Nehru and Mr. Chou En-lai will interpret the five principles in precisely the same way in any given situation is another matter, but Mr. Nehru and the Indian people will be able in future to judge all China's actions by the standard of those principles and by Mr. Chou En-lai's assurances publicly stated in Delhi. These are bound to have far-reaching effects on India's future relations with China. If Peking takes action which is contrary to the five principles, or which seems clear in Indian eyes to be contrary to them, then Mr. Nehru's Government may have radically to readjust its ideas in respect of both China and the West. And Mr. Chou En-lai must know that too. The onus of living up to the standard of peaceful co-existence now very definitely rests on China.

One other important point should be noted. Mr. Nehru longs

ardently for peace in Asia and throughout the world, but he has no intention of joining any Chinese or Russian *bloc* which is antagonistic to the West. Here again he is consistent. His policy of non-involvement, which will be explained in the next chapter, does not permit such a step, nor have Mr. Nehru and his Government any desire to see the world divided into two irreconcilable halves. Their main object is to reduce all causes of international friction, particularly in Asia and the neighbouring continent of Africa. There is no racialism in Mr. Nehru's attitude. His methods may at times appear suspect to Westerners, especially Americans, who regard Communism as an evil thing which should be banished from the earth, but his sincerity cannot be questioned.

*Chapter Nineteen*

# THE COLOMBO POWERS

THE NAME "Colombo Powers" is now applied in a political sense to the group of recently liberated Asian states, with the addition of Indonesia, which formed the bulk of Britain's eastern empire. Between them they represent about 550 million people. They comprise India, Pakistan and Ceylon, which chose voluntarily to remain members of the Commonwealth after obtaining their independence; Burma, which is closely linked with them; and Indonesia, formerly the Dutch East Indies. The expression originated in the fact that the inaugural meeting of the Colombo Plan for Co-operative Economic Development in South and South-East Asia—generally known as the Colombo Plan—took place in Colombo in 1950. At the first meeting the only Asian nations concerned were India, Pakistan and Ceylon, but soon others were added until today there is scarcely an Asian democracy which is not a member of the Plan. Nevertheless the name Colombo Powers, which has nothing to do with the Colombo Plan, stuck to the group of which Colombo is the geographical centre. The Colombo Powers have a common background in that they were formerly under Western control; they were involved in the second World War and two of them, Burma and Indonesia, experienced Japanese occupation. All of them achieved independence after the war. They are democracies of the Western type, and each has had to contend with subversive Communist movements which in Burma and Indonesia led to civil war. Their common background and geographical proximity encourage political friendship and an identical outlook; in the early stages of their association their attitude towards the two world power *blocs* in the "cold war" was strikingly similar. For obvious reasons they share a common dislike of colonialism, on which they tend to be ultra-sensitive, regarding it as a bigger menace than Communism. These factors naturally colour their foreign policy in a way that is puzzling to the West, where the distinction between Communism and democracy is startlingly clear.

By far the largest country of the group, and the holder of a key position in it, is India. India's foreign policy is typical of most, but not all, of the Colombo Powers. It is one of non-involvement, not neutrality, as India's official spokesmen are careful to point out on all possible occasions. Mr. Nehru was at great pains to explain the difference during his tour of the United States in 1949. While stressing India's desire not to align herself with a particular nation or group of nations, he emphatically declared that "where freedom is menaced or justice is threatened, or where aggression takes place, we cannot, and shall not, be neutral". In his presidential address to the 59th session of the Indian National Congress in 1954 he elaborated his views, which may be taken to represent the sincerely held feelings of the vast majority of his fellow countrymen:

> "Two powerful blocs of nations confront each other, each trying to play a dominant role. . . . Those who refuse to join either of these groups are criticized as sitting on the fence, as if there could be only two extreme positions to take up. Our policy has been one of non-alignment and of development of friendly relations with all countries. We have done so not only because we are passionately devoted to peace, but also because we cannot be untrue to our national background and the principles for which we have stood. We are convinced that the problems of today can be solved by peaceful methods and that each country can live its own life as it chooses without imposing itself on others. . . .
>
> We can never forget the great teaching of our master that the ends do not justify the means. Perhaps most of the trouble in the world today is due to the fact that people have forgotten this basic doctrine and are prepared to justify any means in order to obtain their objectives. And so, in the defence of democracy or in the name of liberation, an atmosphere is created which suffocates democracy and stifles freedom and may ultimately kill both.
>
> We claim or desire no right of leadership anywhere. We wish to interfere with no country just as we will not tolerate interference with ours. We believe that friendly and co-operative relations are

essential among the countries of the world, even though they may disagree in many ways. We do not presume to think that by our policies, or by any step that we might take, we can make any serious difference to the great world issues. But perhaps we might sometimes help to turn the scales in favour of peace and, if that is a possibility, every effort to that end is worth while. Peace is not merely an absence of war. It is also a state of mind. That state of mind is almost completely absent from this world of cold war today. We have endeavoured not to succumb to this climate of war and fear and to consider our problems as dispassionately as possible. We have felt that even if some terrible tragedy should overtake the world, it is worth while to keep some area of the world free from it to the extent possible.

Therefore we have declared that India will be no participant in a war, and we have hoped that other countries in Asia would likewise keep away from it, thus building up an area of peace. The larger this area is, the more the danger of war recedes. If the whole world is divided up into two major and hostile camps, then there is no hope for the world and war becomes inevitable. It is not our way to live in or by fear. We should not live in fear of aggression from any country. If, by misfortune, there is any aggression, it will be resisted with all our strength."

My excuse for quoting Mr. Nehru's views at such length is that, whether the Western world agrees with them or not, they represent a settled factor in Asian and world affairs which must be clearly appreciated. India's foreign policy is based on two fundamental principles. The first is that nationalism needs a generation to establish itself economically. In his analysis of India's attitude, Mr. Chester Bowles[1] refers to India's conviction that "her first order of business must be to create internal stability and build a solid base for industrial expansion. . . . 'If the Communists moved into Burma or the Middle East', an Indian political leader said to me, 'our future would be threatened, but if we fail to build a modern nation here in India, the Communists will take over and that will be the end'." This is a view widely held in India, and again, whether Westerners agree with it or not, it must be accepted as a fact.

[1] *Ambassador's Report*, by Chester Bowles (Harper and Brothers, New York).

The second principle is that by joining any particular group of nations India invites attack by the others. This contention is founded on the teaching of Mahatma Gandhi during the second World War. He maintained that if the British left India—hence the slogan "Quit India"—the Japanese, who were then in Burma, would have no reason to invade the country. It was no use pointing out to him (as I frequently did) that a neutral independent nation like Siam had been overwhelmed and occupied; he merely repeated that if the Japanese wantonly invaded a free India, the duty of the Indian people was to practise mass *satyagraha* (civil disobedience) against them. The Indian people, he said, were a peaceful people and had no other remedy.

That attitude, it will be noted, is not the policy of India today. Mr. Nehru specifically says that if India is attacked she will defend herself to the utmost, but she will follow Mahatma Gandhi's precept of avoiding any foreign entanglements which might give offence to any country. To Americans who complain about India "sitting on the fence", as many of them have done since India became independent, the average Indian can quote the foreign policy of America for the first century and a half of its existence. In his neutrality proclamation of 1793 President George Washington specified the reasons for his declaration; they included American weakness and national interest. Indians contend that their foreign policy today bears a striking resemblance to the isolation and non-involvement which the United States pursued until the second World War. To the American retort that the free world was not then menaced by the appalling evil of Communism from which it must now be protected at all costs, the Indian reply is that they do not see Communism in quite that light, nor is armed force the real answer to Communism.

One other aspect of India's foreign policy demands attention. Mr. Nehru is a firm believer in the Commonwealth, and he has stoutly and consistently defended India's membership against critics both outside and inside his own country. Although he is opposed on this issue by both Communists and Socialists, he undoubtedly has on his side the great majority of the Indian people. Mr. Nehru finds the Commonwealth attractive because it is an association of free peoples, who meet to discuss their problems in a friendly spirit, who do not seek to impose their will on one another, and who co-operate where possible. All these attributes are in complete accord with the Indian Premier's concept of international relations.

In explaining India's belief in the Commonwealth to an American audience, Mr. G. L. Mehta, the Indian ambassador in Washington, put the position in this way: "There was no attempt in the Commonwealth to impose overall leadership either on the basis of priority, wealth, size or population. Mutual equality and respect among its members are what makes the Commonwealth so important an international experiment. And India is glad to be a party to this organization wherein, when differences arise, they are accepted with tolerance and mutual respect". In the Commonwealth, he said, "we are not continuously asked to proclaim ourselves on the side of the angels"—a pointed reference to the American demand that India should unequivocally join the anti-Communist *bloc*.

As a matter of general principle the other two members of the Commonwealth within the group—Ceylon and Pakistan—agree with India on the Commonwealth issue. By keeping together within the Commonwealth these countries feel that they can increase their influence in the world and thereby avoid being drawn too much into the American orbit. Commonwealth membership enables them, they argue, to stand up to the American giant in a way which would be impossible if they were merely individual nations, and as proof of their contention that it strengthens their voice in world affairs they quote their claim to have persuaded the British Government to recognize Communist China at the time it did. The Commonwealth is therefore, in Mr. Nehru's eyes, an association definitely helpful to India and to the cause of world peace. Moreover, the Asian members acknowledge the *bona fides* of Britain in her relations with colonial peoples; they themselves are testimonies to the British Government's fulfilment of its self-government pledges.

India's foreign policy is a model for most, although not all, of the Colombo Powers. There are marked differences of emphasis. Indonesia, owing to her government's dependence on the local Communist party, does not go as far as Mr. Nehru in criticizing Communism. The country's outlook is frankly tinged with racialism; both President Soekarno and his Prime Minister, Dr. Sastroamidjojo, want to get rid of all Western influence and connections, including the considerable Dutch commercial interests in Indonesia, and to unite with the African people and Arab states of the Middle East in an anti-Western *bloc*. Indonesia aims at the transfer of the centre of international affairs from Europe to Asia. The Indonesian leaders cannot understand, and are highly critical of, India's connection with the Commonwealth; in Jakarta in 1954 President Soekarno told Mrs. Pandit, Mr. Nehru's sister and the then President of the United Nations General Assembly, that he and his Government were surprised both by India's non-violence and by her Commonwealth membership. On the whole, however, the present Government of Indonesia is content to work with India, and is in fact much more closely associated with India's foreign policy than any other member of the Colombo group.

Ceylon, for religious reasons, is more openly critical of Communist China than her big neighbour, but agrees with India's policy of non-involvement. Sir John Kotelawala, the Prime Minister, told the Ceylon parliament that his aim was to make Ceylon the "Switzerland of Asia" in the matter of neutrality, and Colombo the "Geneva of the Orient". Ceylon also shares India's support of the Commonwealth for somewhat different reasons. Sir John Kotelawala's Government has for years had serious differences with India over the island's Indian inhabitants, most of whom he wants to get rid of, and he has on several occasions loudly declared that his Government will not be bullied or threatened on this issue. Ceylon, in short, is somewhat nervous of her huge neighbour, and values her Commonwealth membership because she regards it as a kind of guarantee that she will not be swallowed up.

In an amazingly frank statement Sir John Kotelawala gave voice to this fear in defending his Government's policy of granting naval and air bases to the British at Trincomalee and Katunayake. Speaking to the Ceylon House of Representatives in September, 1954, he said: "We respect Mr. Nehru; we love him; we accept him as an honourable and honest man who wants peace in the world. But suppose he is no more—human beings must die—and if South India goes Communist, as it is going now, and invades us, can we by ourselves, with 300,000 people we have to fight for us, fight against these South Indians? We must have friends to support us at all times. That being so, I will stick to the Commonwealth as long as I can, or until they say they do not want us or insult us. Till such time we must have trust in them; we must have faith in everybody who wants to help us". To satisfy her *amour propre*, Ceylon may discard British titles and become a republic, but her loyalty to the Commonwealth is not in doubt.

With every justification, Burma is more apprehensive about Communist China than India. Her north-eastern frontier adjoins the Chinese province of Yunnan where a "Free Thai" movement threatens her control of the Shan states; she has still in open revolt Communist elements which would welcome Chinese support, covert or otherwise, and she is worried by the residue of Chinese Nationalist forces which fled into her territory from Yunnan a few years ago. It was believed to be at Mr. Nehru's request that Mr. Chou En-lai went to Rangoon after his visit to Delhi in 1954 with the object of quieting U Nu's fears of Chinese expansion. Nevertheless U Nu's Government is firm on non-involvement; in a speech at Rangoon the same year the Burmese Prime Minister declared that while he did not like Communism and had done his best to prevent its spread within Burmese territory, he paid tribute to Mr. Mao Tse-tung, whose unification of the Chinese people had earned the respect of many foreigners and had gratified Asians.

The only one of the Colombo Powers which has departed from the strict policy of non-involvement is Pakistan. Here the reason lies in Pakistan's unhappy relations with her closest neighbours, and the two-way pull inherent in the widely separated halves of the country. To the north of West Pakistan is an unfriendly Afghanistan which, ever since the partition of the sub-continent, has fomented the demand for a separate Pathan state south of the hilly frontier inherited by Pakistan from the British. The agitation shows no signs of dying down, and it has been a sore point with Pakistan for years. Both regions of Pakistan border on India, from which the Karachi Government is estranged owing to the Kashmir, canal waters and other disputes.

While East Pakistan has its Communist threat from the direction of China, West Pakistan naturally looks towards a possible Russian effort to reach the Arabian Sea and the Persian Gulf, a threat which in the days of the British rule was at times a major concern to the Government of India. Islamic Pakistan, at loggerheads with India, seeks comfort among the Muslim states of the Middle East. In February, 1954, Mr. Mahomed Ali's Government unexpectedly entered into a treaty with Turkey, one of the NATO countries, to study methods for the achievement of close collaboration in political economic and cultural spheres and for "strengthening peace and security". Asked whether the pact could be called a first step towards establishing a regional defence organization, Chaudri Zafrullah Khan, Pakistan's then Foreign Minister, replied "In a way, yes", but added that everything would depend on how the agreement worked out.

Any annoyance which India might have felt at this departure of one of the Colombo Powers from the general policy of non-involvement was drowned in the wave of indignation that swept over the country when the Pakistan Government almost simultaneously announced its acceptance of military aid from America under the mutual security programme. Mr. Nehru was deeply grieved at the shattering of his hopes that the Colombo Powers would form the beginning of a steadily expanding Asian "peace area". He protested vigorously to America that her action would disrupt peace and bring another war nearer; that it would advance the cold war to India's borders because Pakistan became part of a great group of nations lined up against another; that it was part of an American attempt to dominate Asia, and that it was a form of intervention in Indo-Pakistan problems which was likely to have more far-reaching results than previous types of intervention.

President Eisenhower's soft answer certainly did not turn away Mr. Nehru's wrath. The President assured the Indian Premier that American military aid to Pakistan was in no way directed against India, and as proof of his *bona fides* he offered similar assistance in addition to the substantial economic and technical help which India was receiving from the United States. But Mr. Nehru refused to be mollified; in his reply he made it plain that his views and suspicions about American action remained unchanged, and he brushed aside

President Eisenhower's offer with the remark that acceptance of such aid would make Indians "hypocrites and unprincipled opportunists". Mr. Nehru defended India's receipt of economic and technical help from America on the grounds that it was devoted to purely civil purposes.

Pakistan's reactions to the treaty were a sad commentary on Indo-Pakistan relations. So radical a departure from the country's non-involvement policy created a certain amount of public criticism, especially in East Pakistan, but the voices in opposition were soon hushed by India's condemnation. "If India attacks American military aid"—so ran the argument—"it must be a good thing for Pakistan". The official reason for Pakistan's request was declared by Mr. Mohammad Ali, the Prime Minister, to be the adequate strengthening of the country's defences without having to impose a heavy burden on an economy devoted increasingly to measures of social welfare.

But the real reasons lay deeper. They were a reaction to Mr. Nehru's domination of Asian affairs and the feeling of frustration which assailed the country over the continued deadlock in Kashmir. In 1952 and 1953, according to Mr. Mohammad Ali, Pakistan had no firm ally outside the Commonwealth, even among the Muslim states; the treaties with America and Turkey would in future be described as the "turning point in Pakistan's history", and "an event of especial significance to the entire Muslim world. . . . The country was on the threshold of a new era which promises greater security, more rapid progress and expanding prosperity". American aid and the Turkish treaty would enable Pakistan "to make an important contribution to the strength and stability of the region".

Finally—and here's the rub—Pakistanis privately took the view that American military help would strengthen them against India. Mr. Mohammad Ali had always made it plain that its object is to protect Pakistan not necessarily from Communist aggression, but from "any aggression". Pakistan's long period of strained relations with her nearest neighbours, and the feeling—however mistaken it may have been—that the British Government listened more to the Indian point of view than her own, contributed to a sense of isolation which the Pakistan Government finally decided to remove. It is not without significance that Mr. Mohammad Ali, whose administration negotiated both agreements, spent some years in Washington as Pakistan's ambassador before he became prime minister.

Pakistan's new orientation did not prevent her from attending the first formal meeting of the Colombo Powers at Colombo just before the opening of the Geneva conference on Indo-China in the summer of 1954. Pakistan has no more use for Communism at home than either India or Burma. She is as strongly "anti-colonial" as any of the Colombo Powers—her special *bête noire* being the French possessions in Africa—and both inside and outside the United Nations the Pakistan delegation has vigorously attacked France's policy in Tunisia and Morocco. The 1954 Colombo conference was called by Sir John Kotelawala, but it is generally believed that Mr. Nehru was its chief inspiration, his immediate object being to bring pressure to bear on the Geneva conference to end hostilities in Indo-China. In some of the countries concerned great things were expected from the gathering of the five prime ministers; there was talk of forming a regional organization for political and economic co-operation which would enable the Colombo Powers to play a much more effective part in world affairs.

These hopes were not fulfilled, partly because of internal quarrels —Pakistan's Premier wanted to raise the Kashmir issue—and partly because of differences in outlook on relations with the West and with Communist powers. In the words of a London newspaper, there was no light from the East. By an act of sound statesmanship, Sir Anthony Eden, the British Foreign Minister, tried from Geneva to get the Colombo Powers to participate actively in an Indo-China settlement. In a cable to the three Commonwealth prime ministers Sir Anthony, after expressing the hope that peace would be achieved, asked whether the three countries could join in a guarantee to assure the future of Indo-China or whether they could take any other action to reinforce a settlement. While the Commonwealth premiers were highly appreciative of Sir Anthony Eden's approach, none of them was prepared to back any guarantee which might involve them in any kind of military commitment; Mr. Nehru did, however, state after the conference that his Government would be willing to be associated with a guarantee provided India was invited to do so by both sides.

Pakistan opposed the Indian suggestion that the Great Powers should be called upon not to intervene in the Indo-China war either directly or indirectly—this would have involved a ban on American military aid to the French and Viet Namese armies—and eventually the conference concentrated on a resolution calling for a cease-fire, immediate direct negotiations between the combatants and other parties invited by agreement, and the granting of complete independence by France to the Associated States. It was further suggested that all the countries concerned, including China, Britain, the United States and Russia, should agree on the steps necessary to prevent a recurrence or resumption of hostilities—this being a concession to Mr. Nehru's anxiety for non-participation in the war by the Great Powers.

Issues on which the conference found unanimity included the use of the hydrogen bomb, the need for Communist China's admission to the United Nations, and condemnation of colonialism. Lively differences occurred over the conference's attitude to international Communism. Ceylon and Pakistan wanted a forthright denunciation of Communism, but Indonesia—for obvious reasons—and India would not agree, Mr. Nehru arguing that an outright condemnation of Communism would in effect be a declaration in favour of the West. The resolution was accordingly watered down to suit Indian and Indonesian tastes, but it constitutes a political testament which is worth quoting:

> "The Prime Ministers affirmed their faith in democracy and democratic institutions, and, being resolved to preserve in their respective countries the freedoms inherent in the democratic system, declared their unshakable determination to resist interference in the affairs of their countries by external Communist, anti-Communist or other agencies. They were convinced that such interference threatened the sovereignty, security and political independence of their respective States and the right of each country to develop and progress in accordance with the conceptions and desires of its own people".

It was notable that during the conference U Nu's contributions to the discussion were moderate and weighty; according to the special correspondent of *The Times*[1] "he acted as though he was an honorary member of the Commonwealth", thereby confirming Burma's close liaison with her former British Empire associates, India and Pakistan. He impressed Mr. Nehru by his outspoken opinion that while the danger to Asia from colonialism was decreasing, the risk of Communism was definitely increasing, and he asked what guarantee they had that the withdrawal of French rule from Indo-China would not be followed by Communist infiltration. The only really disruptive elements were the raising of the Kashmir question by Mr. Mohammad Ali of Pakistan and Mr. Nehru's counter-charge regarding Pakistan's acceptance of American military aid. Mr. Mohammad Ali insisted that it was unrealistic to talk of peace in Indo-China when the Kashmir issue was still undecided. While the conference naturally desired to achieve harmony by the settlement of its internal problems, the bitterness engendered by the Mohammad Ali-Nehru clash compelled a postponement of inter-Asian differences. Little headway was likewise made with Burma's suggestion that economic co-operation and joint planning should be discussed. The conference decided that fuller details were needed and referred the matter to the governments concerned for consideration.

When the Geneva conference succeeded in reaching agreement on Indo-China, Sir John Kotelawala on behalf of the five Colombo Powers sent a message of congratulation to Sir Anthony Eden. He described the settlement as "a notable contribution to the consolidation of peace in South-East Asia", to which the Colombo Powers extended their firm support. Since Mr. Nehru's conditions for participating in the Geneva arrangement were fulfilled, India accepted the chairmanship of the neutral commissions charged with supervising the details.

It is easy to emphasize the differences among the Colombo Powers and to complain, as a London newspaper did, that the Colombo conference shed no light from Asia. Despite their internal quarrels and their divergent outlook on certain aspects of the cold war, there does exist among these countries a strong community of interests

[1] *The Times*, May 3, 1954.

which makes for continued close co-operation. The Colombo Powers are united in resenting any kind of Western interference in Asian affairs, and any form of colonialism either in Asia or Africa. Most of them are nervous of Asia being made the battle ground of the power blocs by the U.N. or especially by the United States. They demand the admission of Communist China to the United Nations on the grounds that it would "promote stability in Asia, ease world tensions and assist in bringing about a more realistic approach to problems concerning the world, particularly in the Far East". Although West Pakistan's preoccupation with Middle East affairs may tend to swing the Pakistan Government more definitely towards the West, Karachi cannot very well disentangle itself from the Colombo group even if it wanted, since East Pakistan, which belongs well and truly to South-East Asia, contains more than half the population of the country and Pakistan's key product, jute.

Nor can Britain and the rest of the Commonwealth forget that India, Pakistan and Ceylon are fellow members of that Commonwealth, forming an Asian unit with a population of over 450 millions, a figure vastly in excess of the total number of people in the rest of the Commonwealth and Empire combined. With Burma, they represent a bridge between East and West. They have inherited the British parliamentary system which they are determined to defend. They form a freedom *bloc* which, if they can achieve their economic and social salvation, will provide the only real answer to Communism in Asia.

These constitute good reasons why their views deserve the most sympathetic consideration of the British people and the people of the rest of the Commonwealth, why their common aims should be supported whenever possible, and why they should receive the maximum of economic help from the West. The fight they are putting up for democracy in Asia is the biggest thing in the democratic world today.

*Chapter Twenty*

# THE MANILA TREATY (SEATO)

PLANS FOR THE defence of South-East Asia had been canvassed ever since the emergence of Communist China as a major factor in Asian and world affairs. Before the second World War the need for a joint system of protection against the then possible aggressor, Japan, was not considered necessary. British naval power, backed by a strong British Indian army, extended as far east as Singapore and Hongkong. France and Holland looked after the defence of French Indo-China and the Dutch East Indies respectively, while America was responsible for the Philippines. Not until Japan struck westwards and southwards did a South-East Asia Command come into being, but by then it was too late to defend the outlying parts of the area with any hope of success. France was out of the running, the Dutch—owing to the German occupation of Holland—had only their local forces, Britain was heavily involved in Europe and Africa, and America in the early stages of the Asian war was too far away to be effective. Nevertheless the South-East Asia Command persisted; from its headquarters in Ceylon it directed the liberation of Burma, and had Japanese resistance not collapsed before the American assault from the Pacific its armies would have gone on to free Malaya, Siam, Indo-China and Indonesia.

After the war suggestions for some kind of defensive organization were mooted from time to time by countries like Siam, the Philippines and South Korea, which considered themselves menaced by Communists both inside and outside their frontiers. Nothing practical was achieved until, on the initiative of General de Lattre de Tassigny, a conference between the Far East military commands of Britain, France, and America was held at Singapore in 1951, General de Lattre de Tassigny's contention being that France's battle in Indo-China was really a fight for the preservation of South-East Asia from Communism in which other interested powers should help. Communist aggression in Korea and the Peking Government's aid for Dr. Ho Chi-minh began to worry not only America but the other ANZUS powers, which saw the dangerous possibilities of a Chinese thrust towards the Pacific. A continuation of the Singapore talks, attended by chiefs of staff, took place in Washington the following year; the countries participating included Australia, New Zealand and Canada in addition to those represented at Singapore.

Nothing very conclusive resulted from these talks, but early in 1953 Sir Winston Churchill proposed to the new Eisenhower administration in America that the principle of the North Atlantic Treaty Organization should be extended to South-East Asia. The British Prime Minister's purpose was clear; he wanted to enlarge the ANZUS pact, Britain's exclusion from which had given rise to much annoyance in London. In this project he had the support of France. America was at first dubious about Sir Winston Churchill's proposal. She feared, quite rightly, that a defence organization on these lines would be regarded by the Colombo Powers as a means of protecting and perpetuating British and French colonial interests in Asia.

Increasing bitterness against Communist China over the Korean war and alarm at the rapid deterioration of France's position in Viet Nam led, however, to a dramatic change of front by Washington. In April, 1954, Mr. John Foster Dulles, the American Secretary of State, flew to London and at his urgent request Britain and America agreed to examine the possibility of establishing a collective defence system similar to NATO for South-East Asia and the neighbouring Pacific regions. The hurried nature of the agreement almost immediately became evident in differences of view between London and Washington over the proposed participants. Oddly enough, the earlier attitudes of both governments were reversed. In his haste to set up a South-East Asia Treaty Organization, or SEATO as it came to be called, Mr. Dulles wanted to ignore the Colombo Powers. Sir Anthony Eden, on the other hand, very wisely insisted on including them since, he said, "without their understanding and support no permanent South-East Asia defence organization could be fully effective".

Fresh differences arose. Mr. Dulles, by this time fearful of a "sell out" by France in Indo-China, wished to use SEATO as a weapon in the Geneva peace negotiations. Sir Anthony Eden, anxious to secure the co-operation of the Colombo Powers, feared that to confront the Geneva conference with a *fait accompli* in the shape of SEATO would upset not only the Colombo Powers but the Chinese, and prejudice all chances of success. Washington's annoyance was aggravated by Sir Anthony's references in the House of Commons to the possibility of non-aggression treaties of the Locarno type existing alongside SEATO, an idea which seemed to fit in with Mr. Nehru's support for bilateral peace agreements among the Asian powers.

What America wanted without delay was the British Government's signature to a hastily conceived military project, the details of which were to be discussed later. The idea of treaties on the Locarno model was repugnant to Mr. Dulles, who considered they would be used to strengthen demands for Communist China's inclusion in the United Nations and would imply recognition, for example, of the Chinese occupation of North Korea. But the British Government remained adamant in its refusal to commit itself to any military arrangement in South-East Asia until the result of the Geneva conference was known; both sides meanwhile agreed to continue SEATO consultations, America with Siam, the Philippines and the ANZUS group, and Britain with the Colombo Powers.

Within three weeks of the Geneva agreement on Indo-China a SEATO conference was summoned to meet at Baguio, the Philippines health resort, on September 6. To America the surrender of northern Viet Nam to the Communists made essential the drawing of a line along which the Communists advance could be contained. Australia and New Zealand were scarcely less anxious to see a definite limit put to Communist expansion; Britain's abandonment of the Suez Canal base combined with the Communist success in Indo-China to produce in the two dominions a feeling of isolation and danger. Before long, said Mr. Menzies, the Australian Premier, in a statement to the House of Representatives in Canberra, "the Communist frontier might be regarded as lying on the southern

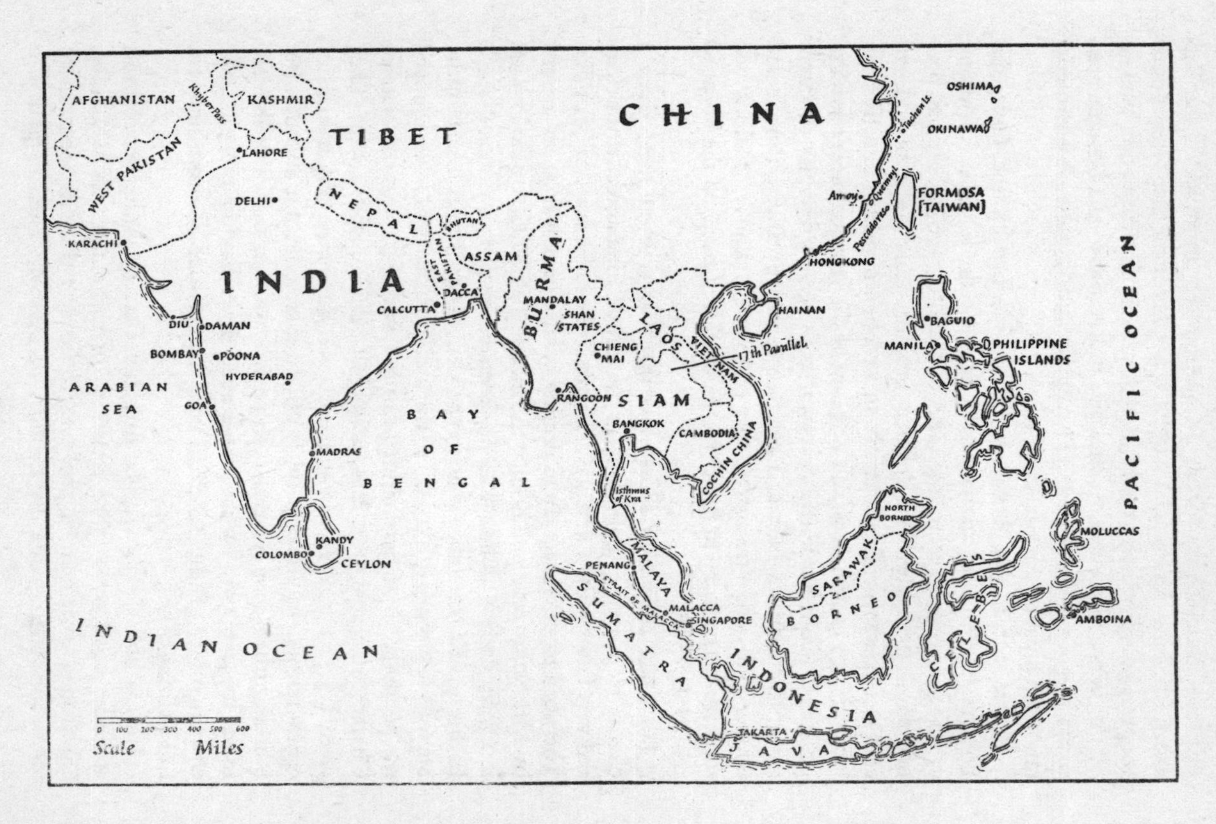
CHINA
TIBET
INDIA
KASHMIR
AFGHANISTAN
WEST PAKISTAN
Khyber Pass
LAHORE
DELHI
NEPAL
BHUTAN
ASSAM
EAST PAKISTAN
DACCA
CALCUTTA
BURMA
MANDALAY
SHAN STATES
RANGOON
CHIENG MAI
LAOS
VIET NAM
17th Parallel
SIAM
BANGKOK
CAMBODIA
COCHIN CHINA
HAINAN
HONGKONG
Amoy
Quemoy
Pescadores
Tachen Is.
FORMOSA [TAIWAN]
OKINAWA
OSHIMA
PHILIPPINE ISLANDS
BAGUIO
MANILA
PACIFIC OCEAN
MOLUCCAS
AMBOINA
CELEBES
NORTH BORNEO
SARAWAK
BORNEO
INDONESIA
JAKARTA
JAVA
SUMATRA
MALAYA
MALACCA
SINGAPORE
PENANG
STRAIT OF MALACCA
Isthmus of Kra
BAY OF BENGAL
MADRAS
KANDY
CEYLON
COLOMBO
INDIAN OCEAN
ARABIAN SEA
KARACHI
DIU
DAMAN
BOMBAY
POONA
HYDERABAD
GOA
0 100 200 300 400 500 600
Scale Miles

shores of Indo-China within a few hundred air miles of the Kra isthmus". Like America, Australia was convinced that Communist progress could be halted only by a display of determination backed by the Western powers, Australasia, and as many Asian countries as could be got to join. Both the Philippines and Siamese Governments favoured a pact "with teeth in it".

It was left to Sir Anthony Eden to approach the Colombo Powers. He sent an invitation to each of them either to attend or send an observer to the SEATO conference to discuss participation in a regional defence organization. As expected, all except Pakistan declined. Mr. Nehru replied in a long and friendly letter, in the course of which he restated the basis of India's foreign policy, explained his attitude towards the five principles of international conduct which had been agreed to by India, Burma and China, and, while he agreed that collective action by nations was sometimes necessary in the U.N., he preferred pacts on the Locarno model for Asia.

His main theme, in short, was that China should be given a chance to prove her good faith in the Indo-China agreement before she was faced with a defence arrangement on the lines of SEATO. The need to move slowly in dealing with China was again stressed by Mr. Nehru, as it had been at the meeting of the Colombo Powers in April. India's policy was, in essence, one of "wait and see". In his public utterances, however, Mr. Nehru was much more uncompromising. In a speech to the Indian Parliament he denounced the proposed treaty as contrary to the spirit of the United Nations Charter, and gave three reasons for India declining to attend. They were (1) that SEATO would not promote peace but would increase tension and insecurity; (2) that India could not abandon her non-alignment policy; and (3) that it would be incompatible for India to take part in the conference after having accepted the chairmanship of the International Supervisory Commission for Indo-China.

Burma and Ceylon agreed in general terms with Mr. Nehru's attitude; both were more conscious of the danger from Chinese Communism than India professed to be, but they decided not to attend. Indonesia naturally strongly backed Mr. Nehru's policy.

The only exception amongst the Colombo Powers was Pakistan. A mixed variety of motives, including the country's Western commitments, governed Karachi's acceptance of the invitation, but the main reason was undoubtedly Pakistan's continued resentment against India over the Kashmir issue and her general feeling of frustration. The fact that India refused the invitation was sufficient to make Pakistan accept it. Another compelling influence was Pakistan's determination to make any treaty signed at Manila a guarantee against not merely Communist aggression but aggression of any kind—a development which India regarded as unmistakably aimed at herself. So strongly did Chaudri Zafrullah Khan, Pakistan's Foreign Minister, press this point before the conference that he was able eventually to secure agreement on it.

Following the precedent created by the Colombo Powers at their meeting on the eve of the Geneva conference, Sir John Kotelawala proposed to call another Colombo Powers gathering to discuss the invitations to the SEATO talks, but the idea was dropped mainly at the instance of Mr. Nehru who, owing to Pakistan's attitude and the doubts entertained by Ceylon and Burma, did not welcome a conference which might well have resulted in an open split in the group. When the SEATO conference of eight powers—the United States, Britain, France, Australia, New Zealand, Pakistan, Siam and the Philippines—met at Baguio at the beginning of September, some comment was caused by the absence of Sir Anthony Eden, whose place was taken by his deputy the Marquis of Reading. Rumours went around that Sir Anthony was not keen to attend owing to the attitude of India and Ceylon, but the official explanation that the crisis in Europe, following France's rejection of the European Defence Community, compelled him to stay in London was generally appreciated.

The conference proved to be one of the smoothest and swiftest on record. It reached its decisions in three days, due mainly to the American draft, the premature publication of which by a Manila newspaper caused some embarrassment but which was adopted with minor amendments. Australia received an assurance beforehand from Mr. Dulles that SEATO would not be merged with ANZUS or allowed to dilute the more specific provisions of the Pacific treaty. Both Siam and the Philippines emphasized the need for as strong a treaty as possible based on the NATO model. Chaudri Zafrullah Khan's insistence on the Pakistan view that aggression from any quarter was the concern of the conference resulted in the deletion of the word "Communist" before "aggression" in one of the vital clauses, a decision which forced Mr. Dulles to add a note to the treaty pointing out that America adhered to the original draft. An attempt by the Philippines delegation to insert a provision for the immediate grant of independence to countries like Malaya was shelved as being outside the scope of the conference.

The treaty in its final form bore strong evidence of the desire of the signatories to make it as acceptable as possible to the missing Colombo Powers—India, Burma, Ceylon and Indonesia. It was declared to be in accordance with the United Nations Charter, and to provide that the signatory countries should "separately and jointly by means of continuous and effective self-help and mutual aid will maintain and develop their individual and collective capacity to resist armed attack and to prevent and counter subversive acts from without against their territorial integrity and political stability". In furtherance of these objectives the parties "undertake to strengthen their free institutions, and to co-operate with one another in the further development of economic measures, including technical assistance, designed both to promote economic progress and social well-being, and to further the individual and collective efforts of governments towards these ends".

The key article in the treaty, No. 4, deals with the procedure to be followed in cases of aggression. In the event of armed aggression against any of the signatories to the treaty, each member would act to meet the common danger "in accordance with its constitutional processes". If the sovereignty or political independence of any member is threatened "in any way other than by armed attack, or is affected or threatened by any fact or situation which might endanger the peace of the area", the parties "shall consult immediately in order to agree on the measures which should be taken for the common defence". Then follows the important proviso that no action can be taken on the territory of any member state "except at the invitation or with the consent of the government concerned".

Means to implement the treaty are to be decided by a council representing all the signatories, which would also provide for consultation with regard to military and any other planning.

Clearly the South-East Asia Collective Defence Treaty, as SEATO is officially known, is a much more flexible instrument than either NATO or ANZUS. Its provisions excluding action unless the government concerned demanded it was designed to avoid offending the Colombo Powers; Mr. Nehru had inveighed against the idea of a protective mantle being thrown by Western powers over Asian countries "whether they wanted it or not". The treaty has no automatic commitments. No demand is made for the establishment of American bases in Asia, although they are not precluded if asked for. Added to the treaty is a reservation by Washington that its undertakings refer only to "Communist aggression", although it would consult with the other parties in the event of other aggression or armed attack. A protocol designates Cambodia, Laos and south Viet Nam as areas to which the treaty is applicable both in respect of protection and economic benefits; a way was thus found to provide for help to the Associated States without infringing the Geneva agreement, which authorizes them to belong to a defence pact on condition that its terms are in conformity with the U.N. Charter. They do not have the right to permit foreign bases on their territory unless they consider their security is threatened.

But the most unusual feature of the treaty, and one which may give rise to much controversy, is its provision against subversive action from either without or within. As an American senator pointed out, this might mean the refusal of the signatories to allow any kind of revolution or governmental change, even if the people desired it, in any of the countries concerned, since the present rulers could use the treaty to bolster up their régime indefinitely. Mr. Dulles's contention is that a difference exists between "indigenous" revolutions and those fomented from outside by, for example, Communists, but Mr. Dulles had to admit that the two might sometimes get mixed up. The danger is that the treaty may be used to secure Western support for certain types of régimes in a manner reminiscent of "colonialism", thereby damning it in the eyes of most Asians.

The door is left open for other countries to join the treaty by a clause which permits any state in a position to further SEATO objectives and contribute to the security of the area to become a party by the unanimous agreement of the other members. Of all the signatories, the country most likely to demand immediate help is Siam, which had already declared itself to be threatened by the "Free Thai" movement on its northern border. Korea, Japan, Formosa and Hongkong are excluded from the treaty area. Korea is the continuing concern of the United Nations, Japan is covered by her peace treaties with America, while Formosa and Hongkong look to the United States and Britain respectively.

SEATO cannot be regarded as a treaty with many teeth, since it possesses little in the shape of external strength on the spot beyond the American Seventh Fleet and the Okinawa garrison. Its main purpose is to act as a clear warning to Communist China that any Asian state covered by the treaty can appeal for help either against armed attack or "subversive acts from without". To that extent it is valuable as an attempt to draw a line for the protection of nationalist democracies against Communist aggression. Its weaknesses are twofold. It does not include India, the next biggest Asian country to China, nor Burma, Ceylon and Indonesia—all very important members of the democratic fold. Secondly, it cannot protect a country from underground Communist infiltration. It might indeed tend to isolate from the people a government suspected of being the creature of Western imperialism, and thereby provide a fertile breeding ground for Communism. To combat these eventualities countries must still protect themselves, with or without Western help, by building up an economic and social system in which Communism cannot flourish.

Reactions to the treaty in South-East Asia followed the usual lines. The Pakistan Government ratified the treaty in January, 1955. Some of the reasons which weighed with the Karachi authorities were outlined earlier by official spokesmen who drew attention to what were regarded as satisfactory provisions from their point of view, namely, that the treaty was the culmination of the Prime Minister's policy of winning more friends for his country, that it would consolidate Pakistan's position externally, and at the same time would act as a deterrent to countries "which might harbour aggressive designs against Pakistan"—a thinly veiled allusion to India. This broad hint was promply taken up by the Indian Press, which openly declared Pakistan's adhesion to the treaty to be a move against India. Mutterings were heard about the advisability of India withdrawing from the Colombo Powers in view of Pakistan's action.

Mr. Nehru's criticism was mainly directed against the problems of Asia being discussed by non-Asians who wanted to protect other countries "even after they had shouted that they did not want any such protection". He did, however, in a speech in the Indian parliament, refuse to subscribe to the view propounded by the Communists that SEATO was intended as an instrument of aggression. He was prepared, he said, to believe that the intention behind the treaty was good, but he considered the method of fulfilling that intention to be ineffective and even dangerous. Other official Indian views described SEATO as really a diplomatic move since it did not have sufficient land forces to deal with China; it was regarded more as an attempt to draw some South-East Asian countries away from their former partners into the American orbit. (Obviously Pakistan was one country the spokesmen had in mind.)

Burma's attitude was explained by U Nu in a speech at Maymyo the week after the signing of the treaty. "We do not," he said, "stop at non-involvement: we do our utmost to shun any activity which is likely to create misunderstanding in any quarter". The Ceylon Prime Minister was not so forthright in his objections as U Nu. Until it had time to consider the implications of SEATO, he said, the Ceylon Government's main objection was that it should have been considered necessary to conceive the treaty in the spirit in which it had been conceived. Nevertheless Sir John Kotelawala noted with "great satisfaction" that the original spirit of the treaty had been greatly modified. The fact that governments both inside and outside SEATO had the right to say whether they wanted help in the event of aggression, subversive or otherwise, could not—in his opinion—be regarded as "gratuitous or meddlesome offers".

SEATO can never be the complete answer to the Communist menace in South-East Asia. It is a makeshift arrangement in that it excludes four Asian democracies with a total population of something like 475 millions. In the words of Mr. Chester Bowles,[1] the participants in the treaty "make up less than 15 per cent of the population of free Asia. To rely on an alliance of these nations would be like trying to hold Europe with a NATO consisting of Spain, Portugal and Greece, with the rest of Europe sitting on the sidelines. It would be welcome assistance, but it could hardly be decisive". That may seem a harsh judgment, but it contains more than a grain of truth. The treaty does not cover Formosa, one of the most explosive factors in Asia. It does offer economic help, but obviously not on a scale adequate to the needs of Asian countries. It cannot prevent internal rot from destroying a country's democratic institutions. All this is said not in disparagement of SEATO, the merits of which have already been noted. But its limitations are patent; it does not apply, and it may never be asked to apply, to the vast majority of the people of South-East Asia. That is the probem which faces both the democratic East and the democratic West.

[1] *Ambassador's Report*, by Chester Bowles (Harper and Brothers, New York).

*Chapter Twenty-one*

# THE CRUCIAL ISSUES

HOW, THEN, IS THE future of these 475 million people belonging to four newly liberated Asian democracies to be assured? Indonesia, which would like to see Western influence banished from the continent, is turning to an alliance with Africans on purely racial lines. This idea was mooted at the first meeting of the Colombo Powers in the middle of 1954. After the signing of the Manila treaty Dr. Ali Sastroamidjojo, the Indonesian Prime Minister, returned to the charge, presumably with the blessing of President Soekarno. When he visited India in September to discuss other matters with Mr. Nehru, including his country's relations with Communist China, he got the Indian Premier to agree to the holding of an Asian-African conference at Bandung, in Indonesia to be preceded by a meeting of the Colombo Powers to draw up an agenda.

Dr. Sastroamidjojo's aim was to interest the Arab states of the Middle East in the project so as to make Bandung the venue of a gathering representative of countries from Egypt to the China Sea, with delegates from African states, some of whom might be observers from colonial territories. The object of the conference was nominally to increase the "peace area" and to discuss colonialism, but other motives lay behind the Indonesian move.

President Soekarno and Dr. Sastroamidjojo clearly approve of Mr. Chou En-lai's recent suggestion that all Asian countries should unite to free themselves from every trace of Western influence; the Indonesian Prime Minister told a press conference in Delhi that he would like to see an economic as well as a political shift from Europe to Asia. "We like to look forward to the day," he said, "when we shall not receive assistance any more from outside." Finally, Dr. Sastroamidjojo's Government hoped to benefit politically from an Asian-African conference at Bandung. Indonesia's first general elections are due to be held in 1955, and the Government feels that the prestige to be derived from the conference should ensure the return of sufficient support to establish it in office for a period of years. That may seem to it to be one way of overcoming the strong opposition likely to be put up by the Masjumi party, which hopes to secure enough votes to oust the present Nationalist-Communist combine.

One thing is certain. Democratic Asia's troubles are not going to be solved merely by the holding of an Asian-African conference, and nobody knows that better than Mr. Nehru. The Indian Government strongly supports the fight against colonialism in Africa; its views are broadcast to the African people, sometimes in a form as embarrassing to its own nationals living in the country as it is to the white settlers. India has always been a stout member of the anti-colonial group in the United Nations, taking up the cudgels on behalf of Tunisia and Morocco, for example, as readily as Pakistan. But that is probably as far as Mr. Nehru wants to go. He will gladly encourage and form part of an international organization which has for its main object the freeing of colonial peoples in Africa from Western domination, but he has no desire to promote a group of Asian-African powers on a basis which might eventually involve him in an alignment as distinct as if he belonged to the Western or the Communist camp. In any case Mr. Nehru realizes that, in the face of the world-shaking issues which beset Asia, issues on which hang world peace and the lives and well-being of millions of human beings, an Asian-African *rapprochement* is at present a matter of minor consequence.

Mr. Nehru sees his goal clearly. His tactics may change from time to time, occasionally in a manner puzzling to the West, but the general trend of his policy is unmistakable. He now describes it as "non-alignment" instead of "non-involvement" because, as he explained in 1954, India has already become "involved" by accepting the chairmanship of the international commissions supervising the Indo-China agreement. Mr. Nehru's ultimate aim is fundamentally the same as that not only of the Colombo Powers but of the nations which comprise SEATO; it is to contain Chinese Communism and the Chinese Communist state within the recognized frontiers of China. So far as India is concerned these frontiers embrace Formosa and, for that matter, Hongkong. They do not include North Korea. The Indian Prime Minister is very anxious to see a settlement of the Korea problem on lines which would unite the whole country under an administration of its own choosing; he does not like President Syngman Rhee, but he would oppose either North Korea or all of Korea becoming a Chinese province.

Mr. Nehru wants to secure peace in Asia by coming to a friendly understanding with Communist China on what he considers to be a reasonable basis, provided—and here is the crucial point—Communist China is willing to give him the solid co-operation he needs. His ideal is the creation of a "peace area" by means of bilateral pacts founded on the five principles accepted by himself, U Nu and Mr. Chou En-lai—mutual respect for each other's territorial integrity and sovereignty, non-aggression, non-interference in each other's internal affairs, equality, and peaceful co-existence. Defensive *blocs* of any kind are, he contends, an invitation to war; they should be replaced by agreements between individual countries of a "live and let live" character. All this means, of course, a clear understanding and firm commitments by both sides.

Before Mr. Nehru's visit to Peking in October, 1954, certain points affecting the five principles were worrying both him and his fellow prime ministers in the Colombo Powers group. Was, for example, the representation in China's National People's Congress of Chinese nationals living in their respective countries consistent with the five principles? How could "non-interference in each other's internal affairs" be squared with the presence in Chinese territory of men like Dr. Singh, the active leader of a subversive movement against the Government of Nepal, and Pridi Panomyong, who appealed in Peking for the overthrow of the Government of Siam? In his quest for enlightment on these and kindred subjects connected with peaceful co-existence with the new China Mr. Nehru had not only the warm support of most of the Colombo Powers but was regarded by them as their advocate.

Peace in Asia manifestly depends on Communist China's attitude to three major problems affecting all her non-Communist neighbours. They are: (1) the position of Chinese nationals in other Asian countries; (2) Communist infiltration and the encouragement of subversive movements outside her frontiers; and (3) the alteration of existing national borders.

India has no real Chinese nationals problem of her own, but the presence of these people is a source of great disquiet to some of her Colombo group associates, notably Burma and Indonesia. In the last census, which gave China a population of over 600 millions, about twelve million Chinese nationals resident abroad were enumerated. Over three millions of these are in Siam, about three millions in Malaya, nearly two millions in Indonesia, nearly a million in Indo-China, over 300,000 in Burma and smaller but growing numbers elsewhere. The number in Burma is relatively small, but the country's long frontier with China makes the Rangoon authorities understandably sensitive. These Chinese nationals constitute a potential fifth column of a highly dangerous nature, since many of them send their children to be educated in China, whence they return as fully indoctrinated Communists.

The subject was raised by Mr. Nehru with Mr. Chou En-lai during the Chinese Premier's visit to Delhi, and it was then understood that Mr. Nehru received a promise that Peking would adopt India's policy of advising her nationals in foreign lands to owe undivided loyalty to the countries in which they were settled. But up to the date of Mr. Nehru's return visit to Peking the Chinese régime had not fulfilled that pledge, if indeed it was ever given, despite renewed representations from the Government of India and other interested governments, including that of Indonesia.

On the contrary, the new Chinese constitution adopted in September, 1954, provided membership in the National People's Congress, Communist China's so-called equivalent of Western parliaments, for Chinese nationals in other countries. Thirty seats for Chinese abroad were allotted as follows: Malaya 5, Siam 4, Indonesia 4, Indo-China 2, Burma 1, North Borneo 1, the Philippines 1, Korea and Mongolia 1, Japan 1, India 1, Pakistan 1, Europe 1, Americas 2, Africa 1 and Oceania 1, four places being reserved for future allocation. A representative to the National People's Congress from Malaya was quoted by the Peking radio on June 20 as saying that the draft constitution gave "immense spiritual aid to the unity of Chinese residents abroad".

In a speech on foreign affairs in the Indian legislature at the end of September Mr. Nehru welcomed statements by Mr. Mao Tse-tung and Mr. Chou En-lai asking Chinese abroad to choose their nationality and advising them either to remain Chinese nationals and to refrain from interfering in the affairs of the countries in which they lived, or to become nationals of their adopted countries and cease to think of China. But there seemed little evidence of the Peking Government seeking to persuade its nationals elsewhere to give up Chinese nationality. Mr. Chou En-lai in a speech to the National People's Congress quoted by the *Manchester Guardian*[1] said of Chinese abroad:

> "They love their homeland warmly. Generally they do not take part in the political activities of the country in which they live. For the past few years they have been living under very difficult conditions in the countries which are unfriendly to China. We hope that these countries will not discriminate against the overseas Chinese and will respect their legitimate rights and interests. For our part we are willing to urge the overseas Chinese to respect the laws of the governments and the social customs of all the countries in which they live".

But this is a very different matter from advising them to give up their nationality. On that issue Mr. Chou En-lai said Peking was prepared "to settle this question and to settle it first with the South-East Asia countries which have established diplomatic relations with us".

One of the first issues Mr. Nehru wants settled is the precise kind of status which the Peking authorities propose for the Chinese population of Asian states wishing to live at peace with China. If the five principles are not mere platitudes, as many people outside India maintain, the Colombo Powers will want something much more substantial than Mr. Chou En-lai has conceded so far. Mr. Nehru has his yardstick, the five principles, and by them he will judge the *bona fides* of China's new rulers on their nationals abroad. He himself has no illusions on the subject. In speeches to the Indian parliament before his departure for Peking he was most forthright, declaring that Chinese overseas, in addition to their numbers, held a

[1] *Manchester Guardian*, October 8, 1954.

commanding position in the economic sphere and thereby frightened many countries in South-East Asia.

Even more significant was his reference to Malaya, which is under Mr. Nehru's pet aversion, the colonial system. It was easy, he said, to talk of Malayan independence, but the Malayans themselves were apprehensive of the Chinese community which was in a majority in their country. From a man of Mr. Nehru's anti-colonial views that was a remarkable admission, but it does show where he stands. And in that stand he has the firm backing of Burma and Indonesia, both of which have raised the question of their own Chinese nationals with Peking. Indonesia demands concrete assurances that Chinese who accept Indonesian nationality would be recognized as Indonesians by Peking, and that those who do not should refrain from any kind of subversive activity.

The second issue major on which Communist China will be judged by her uneasy Asian neighbours is Peking's attitude towards subversive Communist movements in other countries. Reference has already been made to the hospitality which China affords to the Nepalese Communist leader, Dr. Singh, who is conducting a campaign against King Mahendra's Government from Tibet, and to Pridi Panomyong, who issued a call from inside China to the Siamese people to overthrow Field Marshal Songgram's régime.

Here again Mr. Nehru's views are clear and unequivocal. He has consistently denounced Communists in India who look elsewhere for political allegiance as traitors to their own country. In September, 1954, he launched a strong attack on international Communism and the Cominform. "One can understand", he said, "the existence of a national Communist party which had no extra-territorial loyalties. But when a group purporting to be national is tied up with a group in other countries there is bound to be fear that the latter might, for its own ends, utilize the services of the former". The activities of organizations like the Cominform, he added, had certainly caused a good deal of apprehension and disturbance in various countries.

Mr. Nehru will certainly want evidence from Peking that Communist infiltration and the encouragement of subversive movements by China are to cease. Once more he will apply the yardstick of the five principles—especially that guaranteeing "non-interference in each other's internal affairs"—to measure Communist China's sincerity. Again he will have the enthusiastic support of his fellow members of the Colombo group, some of which are far more perturbed about Communist infiltration than is India.

Finally, there is the vague but disquieting attitude of Peking towards lands over which the old Chinese empire at one time exercised sway. These include parts of Indo-China, Siam, Burma and India. China's forceful occupation of Tibet roused uneasy feelings in the minds of her neighbours, particularly India, where indignation was vocal. True, Chinese suzerainty over Tibet could not be questioned, but there have been published in Communist China maps showing areas formerly ruled from Peking of much the same kind as those printed in Mussolini's Italy outlining the possessions of the Roman empire. One such map brings the Chinese frontier to the verge of the plains of Assam east of Bhutan, whereas the border negotiated by Sir Henry McMahon with China and Tibet in 1913 —but never ratified by China—lies a hundred miles farther back, running along the main Himalayan chain to the great bend of the Brahmaputra river. As recently as December 1954, Chinese maps were on sale in India and Burma showing as Chinese territory not only parts of Kashmir and Assam but large areas of northern Burma. When the Peking Government's attention was called to these maps by Delhi a suitable apology was received, with an explanation that the maps had been issued originally by the previous Nationalist Government. Mr. Nehru's reactions to this form of irredentism are as unambiguous as his attitude on the other major issues. The press correspondent who showed him a Chinese map with modifications of the McMahon frontier of Assam evoked the angry retort, recorded earlier, that India would defend her frontiers, "map or no map". He would support any other country which, with the same justification, did likewise. In this he is again the mouthpiece of his Colombo Powers colleagues. If the five principles mean anything at all, they must emphatically ensure "mutual respect for each other's territorial integrity". Also of great interest to Mr. Nehru is Peking's attitude towards Hongkong and Formosa—particularly Formosa, since a Chinese attempt to take it from the Nationalists in present circumstances would almost certainly lead to a world conflagration.

To sum up, Mr. Nehru wants to make co-existence with Communist China a workable reality on terms which he can accept. These terms would connote China's respect for her neighbours' frontiers and strict non-interference with their internal affairs. They would not include, in return, membership of a specifically anti-Western *bloc* sponsored by Peking, Jakarta or any other Asian capital; in that way, Mr. Nehru argues, lies war. The only defensive organization of which he approves is the United Nations, which in his view should comprise all free countries, including Communist China.

If his policy succeeds it may well change the whole outlook on world peace. But its success will depend on China, on Peking's interpretation of the five principles as applied to actual conditions. By themselves the five principles are theoretically admirable; what Mr. Nehru and his fellow prime ministers now wish is for Peking to give them practical effect. The Colombo Powers argue that if subversive movements in their own countries are not encouraged or supported from outside, they will die out as internal conditions improve.

When Mr. Nehru visited China in October, 1954, he received a welcome on a grand scale. On his return he emphasized that he had not gone to Peking with the idea of asking for or giving any guarantees; he went "to understand, to be impressed, and to impress in a friendly way". Yet there is no doubt that Mr. Nehru took occasion to explain very fully to Mr. Mao Tse-tung and Mr. Chou En-lai the attitude and outlook of the Colombo Powers on their problems *vis-a-vis* China and the West. The views of the group were summed up at the time by a Ceylon periodical:[1]

"Free Asia . . . has every desire to live at peace with Communist China and to leave her alone to solve her own internal problems. Manila and its aftermath should serve as convincing proof of this fact. But in return, free Asia has a right to expect demonstration on the part of Communist China that she does not intend to interfere in the internal politics and life of the countries of this region.

[1] *Jana*, Colombo, October, 1954.

This is the only genuine basis possible for the ideal of 'peaceful co-existence' embodied in the Nehru-Chou declaration.

It is only natural that large sections of Asian opinion should regard Chinese promises of 'non-interference' with suspicion. For there are in the free Asian countries Communist movements owing allegiances to both China and Russia, which have proved by their past record that they have no independent political existence but are controlled by the changing winds from behind the bamboo and iron curtains.

As long as these movements continue to function in this way, free Asia must inevitably fear that Communist offers of peace are only a camouflage for a programme of internal subversion, and that this fifth column may become a base for future expansion in Asia.

It is in China's power to allay these fears. . . . Communist China has everything to gain by such a policy. A genuine course of non-interference in the affairs of the free Asian countries, not merely in words but in deeds, would win for her the permanent assurance that these countries would not gang up with any hostile power against her. After Manila, Communist China should need no further arguments that it is in her own interests to avoid driving any further Asian powers into the arms of SEATO."

Mr. Nehru has his critics not only in the West but inside his own country. The right wing Hindu Mahasabha accuses him of being little better than a fellow traveller, and even the Praja Socialists are sceptical of his dealings with China. In America he is often accused of being a Communist dupe or stooge. None of these allegations will bear scrutiny. He is an idealist-cum-realist seeking a way out of a world impasse. If he fails, his defeat would automatically end all belief in Communist China's pretensions to peace. It might still leave India determined not to join any power *bloc*, but it would disillusion peoples now outside SEATO and bring a new appreciation of the value of Western help, both economic and military. Whatever Western people may think of Mr. Nehru's foreign policy—and some of them think very poorly of it—they must remember that it is with him a profound conviction, and that it has the support of the vast majority of the people of India, Burma, Indonesia and Ceylon.

The results of the Asian-African conference held at Bandung in April, 1955, do not basically alter these conclusions. Bandung was a remarkable gathering, marked by two outstanding developments. One was the sharp difference in the attitude towards China of countries like India, which breathed goodwill, and of other Colombo Powers like Pakistan and Ceylon which openly denounced Communist "colonialism". But all the nations represented at the conference were in accord in being profoundly impressed—and here comes the second important factor—by Mr. Chou En-lai's earnest professions of peace not only towards his Asian neighbours but towards America as well. What the rest of Asia and the world now wait to see is whether the policy which the Chinese Premier announced with so much effect at Bandung is to be translated into practice.

How can the Western democracies best help those Asian democracies which are fighting a battle against Communism but do not wish to be involved in any Western-sponsored defence organization? Mr. Malcolm MacDonald, British Commissioner-General in South-East Asia, attempted an answer to that question during a recent visit to Washington. Western aid, he said, "must be consistent with the great principles that lie closest to the heart of the peoples of South-East Asia at this period of their history". These principles were the preservation of Asian national liberty and the promotion of economic progress.

Mr. MacDonald likened the struggle against Communism in South-East Asia to a prize fight of which the first two rounds were over, the first political and the second military, the military round having gone satisfactorily except for Viet Nam. The third round, for which the bell had sounded, would (he thought) be political in character and would be "very dangerous". If economic conditions became difficult the Communists could have success; everything must be done to give Asian governments "in ways acceptable to them" the financial and technical assistance necessary to build up strong democracies.

Direct American help in the shape of Point Four, military and other forms of aid is already reaching Asia in massive amounts, but it is sometimes viewed with suspicion and in one or two cases it has been refused. Another form of assistance, which now embraces the whole range of South-East Asian democracies, including the Philippines and Japan—the latest members—is provided by the Colombo Plan. This Plan was started as a challenge by the Commonwealth to the poverty of its Asian members; in some respects it represents the British equivalent of America's foreign aid programme, but in actual operation it differs sharply from the American project.

To begin with, it is typical of the Commonwealth in that it is a joint affair involving a series of countries on a self-help as well as a foreign aid basis. The Commonwealth foreign ministers who designed it in Colombo in 1950 formed the Commonwealth Consultative Committee on Economic Development in South and South-East Asia, comprising at first only the Commonwealth member states in Asia. Today the Plan covers not merely these countries but Burma, Indonesia, the three Associated States of Indo-China, Siam, Nepal, the Philippines and Japan, together with Malaya, Singapore, North Borneo and Sarawak—all of them linked in a mutual co-operative effort to raise living standards. Other members of the Commonwealth taking part in the scheme are Great Britain, Canada, Australia and New Zealand, and since its inauguration it has been joined by the United States and works in conjunction with ECAFE and the International Bank.

The great virtue of the Colombo Plan in the eyes of the nations participating in it is that it has no political strings of any kind and is the joint concern of all the countries involved; this permits a state like Indonesia, which is unduly sensitive about any form of Western influence, to be represented on the Consultative Committee. Each country is free to revise its development programme as it wishes; the Plan is not a master organization but a means of co-operation among all the member states, each helping the other where possible. A notable feature of the Plan is its provision for the training of technicians of all kinds, ranging from those engaged in agriculture to highly skilled industry, both on the spot and in Western member states. It is along these lines, in greater volume, as well as by direct American help, that the answer to South-East Asia's nationalist problems is to be found.

# INDEX

## INDEX

INDEX

# INDEX